Conversations About Religion

Conversations About

RELIGION

Edited by Howard Burton

Ideas Roadshow conversations present a wealth of candid insights from some of the world's leading experts, generated through a focused yet informal setting. They are explicitly designed to give non-specialists a uniquely accessible window into frontline research and scholarship that wouldn't otherwise be encountered through standard lectures and textbooks.

Over 100 Ideas Roadshow conversations have been held since our debut in 2012, covering a wide array of topics across the arts and sciences.

All Ideas Roadshow conversations are available both as part of a collection or as an individual eBook.

See www.ideasroadshow.com for a full listing of all titles.

Copyright ©2021 Open Agenda Publishing. All rights reserved.

ISBN: 978-1-77170-173-0 (pb)
ISBN: 978-1-77170-172-3 (eBook)

Edited, with preface and all introductions written by Howard Burton.

All *Ideas Roadshow Conversations* use Canadian spelling.

Contents

TEXTUAL NOTE 7

PREFACE 9

RABBI WITH A CAUSE
ISRAEL AND IDENTITY
A CONVERSATION WITH DAVID J. GOLDBERG

Introduction 17
I. This Is Not The Way 22
II. Jewish Values 30
III. Who is a Jew? 36
IV. Cultural Judaism 41
V. Ever Striving 46
Continuing the Conversation 50

RELIGIOUS ENTREPRENEURS?
A CONVERSATION WITH NILE GREEN

Introduction 53
I. Origins 58
II. Sufism 63
III. The Model of Religious Economy 68
IV. Global History 81
V. Terrains of Exchange 85
VI. Modern Implications 94
VII. Ever Onwards 104
Continuing the Conversation 109

BATTLING PROTESTANTS
A CONVERSATION WITH DAVID HOLLINGER

Introduction 113
I. Diverging Protestants 118
II. Drifting towards Secularism? 124
III. Often Overlooked 132
IV. The Missionary Position 136
V. Demographic Diversification 144
VI. William James 148
VII. Strident Atheists 153
VIII. An Empty Stage 157
IX. Future Speculations 166
Continuing the Conversation 169

RELIGION AND CULTURE
A HISTORIAN'S TALE
A CONVERSATION WITH MIRI RUBIN

Introduction 173
I. Historical Beginnings 177
II. Life on the Ground 197
III. William of Norwich 208
IV. Mother of God 219
V. Doing History 225
Continuing the Conversation 237

EXPLORING THE SIKH TRADITION
A CONVERSATION WITH ELEANOR NESBITT

Introduction 241
I. Looking To Connect 246
II. Historical Overview 262
III. Identity 272
IV. Towards Deeper Understanding 280
Continuing the Conversation 294

Textual Note

The contents of this book are based upon separate filmed conversations with Howard Burton and each of the five featured experts.

David J. Goldberg (1939-2019) was Senior Rabbi Emeritus of London's Liberal Jewish Synagogue and an author and columnist. This conversation occurred on January 16, 2013.

Nile Green holds the Ibn Khaldun Endowed Chair in World History at UCLA. This conversation occurred on September 15, 2014.

David Hollinger is the Preston Hotchkis Professor of History Emeritus at UC Berkeley. This conversation occurred on September 8, 2014.

Miri Rubin is Professor of Medieval and Early Modern History at Queen Mary University of London. This conversation occurred on September 26, 2016.

Eleanor Nesbitt is Professor Emeritus of Education Studies at University of Warwick and a poet. This conversation occurred on September 27, 2016.

Howard Burton is the creator and host of Ideas Roadshow and was Founding Executive Director of Perimeter Institute for Theoretical Physics.

Preface

The reader who is keen to pick up this collection in the hopes of being indoctrinated in one or more religions is bound to be disappointed. What she will find instead is an array of detailed, scholarly perspectives on particular religious practices and beliefs both inside and outside their own specific context.

Three of the five experts involved in this collection (**Nile Green**, **David Hollinger** and **Miri Rubin**) are historians who are naturally keen to interpret religious traditions within and beyond their own time and place, while a fourth (**Eleanor Nesbitt**) is an ethnologist and education specialist ideally placed to assess how religious and cultural identity impacts our contemporary multicultural world.

None of them claim to be personal representatives of the belief systems they are so carefully examining, thereby simultaneously providing us with a captivating combination of both insider and outsider perspectives to best compare and contrast different religious-inspired orientations and influences.

The fifth participant, **David J. Goldberg**, clearly *is* a representative of his faith (Judaism); but even he, intriguingly, is able to simultaneously balance an insider and outsider's perspective, such as when he passionately argues that the traditional Jewish values of freedom and justice are deeply at odds with current Israeli practices towards the Palestinians:

> *"I would say that in the 'Jewish DNA'—wherever we may be scattered, wherever we've lived in the world—there has been a sense that the Exodus—freedom, therefore, love of freedom—is a core Jewish value. It's like Kant's Categorical Imperative: it's indivisible. We know that freedom is dependent on so many geopolitical and other factors, but*

as a concept it's a whole one, an integral one. So I think you can't be true to Jewish history by saying, 'We proclaim freedom, but not for the Palestinians.' You've got to ask, 'How can we bring about a just solution that gives them freedom as well?'

"A second Jewish value is one I've defended quite strongly in, as it were, the Christian-Jewish polemic over the years. The simplistic contrast is between Judaism, the religion of justice, and Christianity, the religion of love. I have argued in theological pieces that perhaps justice could be deemed superior to love in the sense that love is partial, while justice should be impartial. Hence all the exhortations in the Bible saying, Don't pervert justice by deferring to the poor or being overly obsequious to the mighty, but justice, justice shall you follow.

"That is, try and keep it an impartial principle: justice, tempered with compassion. In other words, be concerned for the widow, the orphan, the fatherless. That has been a Jewish value, a very strong Jewish value, dating back to the Five Books of Moses, back to the Bible; and one that I think, again, allied to freedom should bring about a more balanced assessment of the Israel-Palestine conflict and the just claims of the Palestinians.

"This has, unfortunately, been disregarded. The classical defense used to be: This is a tragic conflict of two rights, and therefore insoluble. The standard line goes: How can we bring about some kind of a compromise between two rights?

"Well, again, I must say quite frankly, getting older and more fearless, I don't view the situation as a tragic, equal conflict between a very tenacious memory of The Promised Land of 3000 years ago and the fact of expelling maybe up to 750,000 people who actually live on the land and have been living there for generations."

UCLA self-described "historical anthropologist" **Nile Green**, meanwhile, capitalizes on his scholarly background by deliberately adopting the unsettling language of the model of religious economy in an effort to force people to rethink established nomenclature that all too often simply reinforces false stereotypes.

"Religion might have come down from the past, but what happens with them and how they're deployed—how tradition, religion, and religion as tradition survives in the world and takes its new shape—is always affected by the conditions of the marketplace, the range of skills of an entrepreneur, and the relationships he can make, or tries to make, with a set of consumers. Religion is thus always made anew at any particular period through the hands of the entrepreneur.

"It's a conscious way of moving beyond this idea that we already know what imams are and we know what it is that they do. It also creates a level playing field for many readers who are trying to go that one step deeper with the study of Islam. Perhaps they now have some familiarity with terms like 'imam', 'Shi'ite', 'Sunni', 'Sufi' or 'sheikh'. I want to say that, in a sense, you can forget all of that. All of these people are religious suppliers. That's what's important.

"Many of them are doing many similar things notwithstanding their sometimes different labels. And one of the reasons why they're doing the same thing is because they're very often competing in the same market terrain for the same consumer base.

"There are two things that a religious supplier can do: he—or more rarely she—can copy the same product and services of his rival suppliers in the marketplace, or he can innovate.

"What I've described is a common set of core principles of practices and processes that are actually going on. And this wider, sometimes confusing, vocabulary of 'imam', 'Sufi', 'sheikh', and so forth, actually hides the common set of principles dictating the moves of all of these players in the marketplace."

UC Berkeley intellectual historian **David Hollinger**, on the other hand, highlights how intercultural exchange initially motivated by a desire to proselytize others, often results in some rather unexpected and decidedly ironic conclusions.

"There's an enormous tension that's built up, where the cosmopolitan missionaries and their children then come back to a society that had sent them abroad for the purpose of making the rest of the world more like them.

"There's the original refrain of, 'We who live in Nashville, we who live in Dayton, Ohio, we who live in St. Paul or Worcester, Massachusetts and so forth—we know what Christianity is. We may embody it imperfectly, but we know what it is, we have it. The Chinese don't have it, the Congolese don't have it, so we need the missionaries to go over there and make them like us.'

"So the missionaries come back and say, 'Well, you know, I'm not sure that what they really need is to be like us. They do need things, naturally. But do you know much about the civilization of China? Let me tell you about Confucian traditions…' And then some guy will stand up in the pew and say, 'We here in Terre Haute did not send you to China to come back and tell us how interesting the Chinese are.'

"The tension between the cosmopolitan missionaries and the provincial churchgoers thus becomes more and more tense, and the missionaries begin arguing that the whole missionary project needs to be reconfigured. It's the missionaries themselves and their children who push this the hardest."

Sometimes, of course, the world of scholarship being what it is, deepening one's religico-cultural appreciation requires a peculiar combination of reflection, hard work and serendipity, a particularly revealing example of which is provided by Queen Mary University of London medievalist **Miri Rubin**'s insights provoked by her bemusement at the seemingly sudden appearance of the Virgin Mary in the medieval European mindset.

"I found that it's so peculiar that Mary, who we take to be absolutely fundamental, particularly in the Catholic tradition, the Christian tradition in the Middle Ages, is that really, there was a moment of utter emergence: you wouldn't find it in the first millennium.

"In fact, if you just read word for word, Mary doesn't turn up that much even in the Gospels. Mary is in some very important locations, like in the creed that arises in the fourth century from Constantinople in these very formative councils of the church. It's actually very important in the world of apocrypha from the second century. There's a total fascination with Mary. Where did she come from? How did this Jewish girl become the mother of God?

"There was this drama of how after this peculiarly nebulous presence, ultimately the European Mary developed. Because even in, let's say, the seventh, eighth, ninth century, I'm not saying that Mary wasn't known. Of course not. But it was a version of Mary that was very much created in the Eastern Mediterranean, particularly in the Byzantine end: it was very much at the level of courtly elites and so on. But from about the 12th century, Mary is everyone's mother: she's Europe's mother. She is omnipresent in so many different forms and media.

"So one of the things that surprised me was indeed this issue of the temporality: that there's actually a story to be told about Mary, that it wasn't all the same. There is dramatic change. And it was important to reflect on it: what does it mean to have this figure of a mother at the heart of the visual, spiritual and emotional worlds of Europeans?"

But lest you conclude that all of these fascinating research insights might not be terribly relevant to our modern, often officially-secular age, University of Warwick ethnologist **Eleanor Nesbitt**, will quickly set the record straight.

"One of the things that has been important to me has been realizing the significance of method, methodology—particular methods in the creation of knowledge—and in my case in ethnographic research.

"I feel that one of the most important things for all of us, is to be sympathetically critical of just about anything we're told or find and to be always asking ourselves: What is the agenda? What is the motivation? What's the agenda of whoever it is who's created a webpage or written a book or declared that such and such is the case?

"And there's also the key notion of reflexivity—that's something which has come to be more and more important to me—recognizing that, certainly in research, we change what we research and we are changed by what we research.

> *"That's actually ongoing in life as a whole. And being an ethnographer it is actually just being a human being: you're using observation, and particularly listening—you're using the faculties that we use in the whole of life. And if in 'the whole of life' we become just a little bit more reflective and reflexive, I believe that's a better way forward than necessarily becoming more committed to a particular philosophy or a particular religious path."*

So perhaps there is some indoctrination going on after all: merely urging us to wilfully adopt a more thoughtful and explicitly open-minded approach to others regarding their beliefs and traditions. Whatever they might be.

Rabbi with a Cause

Israel and Identity

A conversation with David J. Goldberg

Introduction

Chasing Ourselves

What does it mean to have an identity? If I proudly refer to myself as an Australian Muslim, what, in fact, am I doing? Simply resorting to tribalism? Unthinkingly slotting myself into a little box that I happened to have been born into? Establishing my home team?

Or is it somehow much deeper than that, an essential human need to identify with a fixed set of traditions and rituals in order to bring real meaning and perspective to life?

Maybe, somehow, it's both at the same time.

David J. Goldberg, Rabbi Emeritus of London's Liberal Jewish Synagogue has thought long and hard about this issue, particularly when it comes to his own cultural group, the Jews. His 2012 book *This Is Not The Way: Jews, Judaism and Israel* caused the usual storm of controversy resulting from his openly critical comments of some aspects of current Israeli politics.

But the real reason he wrote the book, he told me, was to address these deeper issues of identity head-on—in particular, how a sense of Jewish identity might be somehow disentangled from the religious elements with which it has been awkwardly enmeshed for thousands of years.

> *"I was really bothered by the difference between the theology—that as a Rabbi I was expounding weekly at services in prayer or sermons— and the reality that the overwhelming majority of Jews nowadays are not believing Jews.*

> "They are Jews for any number of reasons—tradition, family, persecution, you name it—but belief in God, certainly the God of the Five Books of Moses, the Old Testament, comes way down the list. And I wanted to explore this; and as honestly as possible, my own ambivalence about it, my own belief."

A prime consequence of this deeply personal exploration is David's conclusion that more credence should be given to the notion of the Cultural Jew, as opposed to its Zionist, Orthodox or Progressive counterparts. The Cultural Jew may be religious in the traditional sense, but certainly isn't necessarily so and sometimes isn't at all.

Moreover, in his customarily forthright style, Rabbi Goldberg admits that he has moved beyond some core elements of traditional Jewish religious dogma himself.

> "I don't believe in an interventionist God, which is really the sine qua non of Jewish theology: that God has a special relationship with his people, Israel, he looks after us come what may and has an ultimate plan of redemption for the world and for the role of his people, Israel. I don't accept that."

So no special divine link, then. No more "chosen people". But what does the Cultural Jew believe? What defines her?

> *"The answer,* says David, *comes down to traditions and values."*

Tradition we largely interpret through rituals. For Cultural Jews, like anyone else, this means adherence to certain rites and ceremonies for birth, marriage, annual holidays and so forth. Encountering old friends, eating particular foods, singing special songs, all of these are signs of the overarching need for the creation and maintenance of rituals that exists in all of us.

But by far our greatest need for ritual, he points out, occurs during a time of mourning.

> *"It's amazing how people who've gone the furthest away from Judaism, as it were—sometimes even quite elaborately disowning any*

involvement in it whatsoever—nevertheless when their parent dies, they want to say the memorial prayer Kaddish over the body. And they will want it in transliterations if they can't read Hebrew, just to be able to say it. So the prevalence of honouring the dead, remembering your parents, is a very deep thing in all cultures."

And because all of this is so obviously personal, so inextricably tied to our own memories, experiences and sense of self, the notion that any third party might somehow feel itself competent to pass judgment on any one person's sense of identity mediated through these very traditions is patently absurd.

This might seem like an obvious statement. But look a bit closer and things get murkier, particularly for the case of the Jews, as for the better part of two thousand years rabbinic teachings have stipulated that, aside from the odd case of official conversion through a strictly delineated formal procedure, only someone of a Jewish mother can be properly considered Jewish.

To Rabbi Goldberg, this way of thinking is another example of inflexible and outmoded dogma that the Cultural Jew would be well to discard.

"I say, basically, 'A Jew is anyone who says he or she is one,' because it would not be for me—it would be arrogance in the extreme—to turn around and say, 'Oh no, you're not, because your mother or your grandmother wasn't Jewish.'

"So if they tell me, 'I regard myself as Jewish,' I would say, 'You are Jewish, because you have voluntarily undergone a form of self-identification, which is the most honest kind of identification.'"

As you might imagine, this type of talk doesn't sit too terribly well with most of Goldberg's more conservative colleagues. But then, he's pretty used to their criticism by now, having long developed a reputation of being a stern and trenchant critic of some of the more controversial policies of Israel, particularly when it comes to the treatment of Palestinians.

Because according to Goldberg, you see, Jewish values matter every bit as much as traditions. Freedom and justice, he's convinced, are the most important aspects of Judaism, the cornerstones on which the entire Jewish identity rests. Which is precisely why he feels so compelled to publicly vocalize his frustration when he sees these very core values being so blatantly compromised through the ongoing Israeli treatment of Palestinians in the occupied territories.

> *"I deliberately caused great, great outrage in 2002 or so when I used the dreaded word 'apartheid' for what goes on. I made the very clear distinction, as I'm making now, between Israel within the green lines (the pre-1967 borders) and Israel in the occupied territories where there is military rule—where for heaven's sake people travel on separate roads so they don't have to meet, where the Jewish settlers are under Israeli law and the Palestinians are under military law.*
>
> *"Now given this patent difference in their status, their rights, their liberties, what else is it but apartheid?"*

A book like *This Is Not The Way* is the natural result of Goldberg's continued sense of outrage, a *cri de coeur* towards a people he's convinced are drifting increasingly further from their long-held moral north:

> *"I want you, my people, my stiff-necked, obdurate people, to please consider what this is doing to our sense of self and to Jewish values."*

For Rabbi Goldberg, it seems, being a Jew is open to virtually anyone. But it should really mean something.

The Conversation

I. This Is Not The Way

Motivations and responses

HB: Why did you write *This Is Not The Way*? What were your motivations? What did you hope to accomplish?

DG: Well, the effect it had was totally different from my intent. Maybe I'm being naive about this, but in fact only three of the eight chapters deal with Israel. My views about Israel, my critical views, have been well known for a long time. But having retired, being at the end of my working career, I was really bothered by the difference between the theology—that as a rabbi I was expounding weekly at services in prayer or sermons—and the reality that the overwhelming majority of Jews nowadays are not believing Jews.

They are Jews for any number of reasons—tradition, family, persecution, you name it—but belief in God, certainly the God of the Five Books of Moses, the Old Testament, comes way down the list. And I wanted to explore this; and address as honestly as possible my own ambivalence about it, my own belief.

Personally, I think the most radical thing I say is about who is a Jew. I basically say that a Jew is anyone who believes that he or she is one, because it would not be for me—it would be arrogance in the extreme—to turn around and say, "Oh no, you're not, because your mother or grandmother wasn't Jewish." That strikes me as a sort of fascist way of doing things. Goebbels would have accepted that sort of thing: "*I decide who is a Jew...*"

But all of that has been ignored in a way.

HB: The comments were all focused on Israel?

DG: Yes. I suppose a critic, a reviewer is looking to give it the right sort of headline.

HB: So I do very much want to explore cultural identity: *How do we decide who is a Jew? What does it mean to be a Jew? What are Jewish values?* and so forth. Then I'd like to talk more generally about the whole idea of religion in society, as well as the matter of interfaith dialogue, something that you've been at the forefront of as well.

But I do also want to talk about something that is specifically linked to Israel. I think there is an important issue to discuss surrounding your concern of how in the public consciousness Israel tends to be regarded as equivalent to Judaism, that this country and its policies are somehow the spokespeople for the Jewish people, and that if one is critical of Israel or if one is critical of Zionism, then one naturally runs a risk of being labeled as anti-Semitic, and so forth and so on.

And if one is a Jewish person who is critical, one gets these labels of being a "self-hating Jew" as you've said yourself. In fact you mentioned in the book's prologue that you were considering calling it *Confessions of a Self-Hating Jew* before being talked out of it by others.

But getting back to the responses: you said that you wanted to explore those particular issues, the broader issues of who is a Jew, religious versus cultural values, but the focus of the response was just on Israel.

Was there anything related to this response—any criticism that was related to this bias on Israel—that you thought was insightful or useful to move things forward in any particular way?

DG: No. Not in terms of a global effect. I mean, the book was quite widely reviewed. *The Telegraph*, *The Jewish Chronicle*, and others did quite a few reviews, which were on the whole very favourable. And interestingly, although they concentrated on my views about Israel, I did detect a change in tone, which obviously reflects the way that the constant apologias for Israel over the years have now worn thin.

But these reviewers are mainly, it has to be said, Jewish ones—which is in a way preferable because the non-Jewish ones are expected to be critical of Israel in the public perception.

The Jewish reviewers are probably more sympathetic than they used to be to my views, actually—maybe the voice crying in the wilderness for a long time now gets more credence than it once did. As I put it sardonically, I've almost become a national treasure now. That happens when you get older. Take somebody like Wedgwood Benn, who was the terrifying figure of Marxism or something, or Dennis Skinner on the back benches of the House of Commons. When you get old enough, you become cuddly and lovable in your eccentricities. So I think, maybe I'm moving into that public persona now.

HB: That doesn't make you toothless, though, does it?

DG: Well, I hope not. But I think that as you get older, you have less hope of changing the world and probably spend more time observing its follies with wry amusement, saying to yourself, "*We've been there before, we've seen this before.*"

Which is why, as I say, when I read the newspapers, I always start with the sports news now. Because that really is new. Everything else on the front pages I've seen before.

HB: I You dedicate *This Is Not the Way: Jews, Judaism and Israel* to Tony Judt, who famously rose to prominence as far as being a public intellectual is concerned—he was of course for a long time very highly regarded as an academic historian—in the United States through the controversial essay he wrote in 2003 in *The New York Review of Books* criticizing Israel.

And you mentioned your affinity with many of the things that he had said, specifically this notion that the Holocaust is often overused to justify Israel's behaviour, come what may. In addition, there is the concern of identifying any critical assessment of Israel or Israeli policy with anti-Semitism, along with the denial of the fact that a "Jewish lobby" actually exists. In fact the acknowledgement, or the attempt to recognize the Jewish lobby as an existing organization, is itself tantamount to anti-Semitism.

DG: Yes. Ipso facto it's anti-Semitism.

HB: It seems to me to be a clear attempt to muzzle popular discourse, an attempt to muzzle rational, reasonable criticism. Is there a sense, then, that that muzzling has finally been overcome, that people are talking more and more openly about these matters? Do you get a sense that it is more and more acceptable to at least publicly engage in this direction?

DG: I think so; and particularly with the young, actually. Peter Beinart wrote a book recently about this issue—I haven't read it yet, it hasn't been published in the UK. He wrote an article in *The New York Review of Books* a couple of years ago that, together with this recent book—as I understand—describes how alienated the American Jewish young are becoming with this constant "Israel good/ Palestinians bad" simplification of a very complex debate.

So hopefully it is having an effect, a willingness to not go through the same tired old arguments of, *We've put forward a peace plan and they rejected it; they don't want peace...* which is indicative of the very simplistic level at which, I'm afraid, the debate in America does take place.

HB: That's certainly true. But to be fair, this is also a global phenomenon. That sort of simplicity is not exclusively American.

DG: Well, I'm always aware, you see, when I go to continental Europe, when I speak to Jewish audiences in France or in Italy, that those 22 miles of "La Manche" saved me from a very different experience of the Holocaust.

And it is still visceral with the French and Italian Jewish communities, as two examples, and therefore one has to modify the way in which one states the argument that we've used the Holocaust for too long as an excuse.

I can feel free to say that quite openly in England or America or South Africa or places like that, but I've got to be much more deferential when addressing people there, because I can really put their hackles up very easily by appearing insensitive to what their grandparents' generation went through; and therefore you lose the argument before it's even begun.

HB: But doesn't that cut both ways? Because it seems to me that this sense of manipulation, this sense of the "utilization" of one of the greatest crimes against humanity ever perpetrated, by bringing it out as a cudgel to deny dispassionate, rational criticism of an existing state is simply opprobrious and deeply offensive.

Perhaps I'm getting carried away, but I really feel quite passionately about this: that out of respect for the enormity of what the Holocaust is, it should not be cheapened, it should not be used as a political tool. So, while I obviously appreciate what you are saying about the need for sensitivity, I personally get indignant when people trot out this horrible crime against humanity and therefore somehow dull its impact by using it every single day as a justification for something that properly has nothing to do with it whatsoever.

DG: Well, you're absolutely right. It started with Menachem Begin, actually. He was obsessed by the Holocaust and had an abiding dislike of Germany as a result. He made that mad comparison during the Lebanon invasion and the siege of Beirut, crowing that he had caught "Arafat Hitler in his lair". To make any comparison of the two was, in my view, a sign of a deranged mind.

Indeed, in Begin's very controversial time as Prime Minister in Israel, there were several occasions when Holocaust groups, groups of survivors, protested publicly at his constant harking on the Holocaust. He cheapened it. And so you are absolutely right: there is far too easy a tendency to invoke it on every occasion and therefore cheapen it.

HB: You talked about the difference in your treatment of the Holocaust that occurs when you go across the English Channel and find yourself in the land where people were deported and killed. When one goes further afield—in the other direction, towards the United States—it seems that these words and concepts are thrown around even more glibly.

Which, of course, is not to say that people aren't sensitive, but in my experience, in addition to the moral cheapening involved that we've just talked about, there is also a state of entrenched paranoia: everybody is out to get us, so anyone who is opposed to some action that Israel is taking is displaying his true anti-Semitic colours that were there all along.

Which leads one to ask, *Is there anything, logically, that this particular state might do that might garner criticism from those who so stridently defend it? Is there anything that they might consider beyond the pale?* If one looks closely at the more militant sectors of the Jewish lobby in the United States, there clearly seems to be this view that anyone who criticizes any policy decisions of Israel whatsoever is something horrible: anti-Semitic, or whatever.

And you, Tony Judt, and others have pointed out this sort of behaviour many times—logically it puts any dispassionate critic of Israeli policy in a very difficult situation.

DG: I think where it leads you, ultimately, in the argument, is to say: *Well, yes, maybe Israel has done certain things that can be criticized, but we are still better than Syria or Saudi Arabia; we are the only democracy in the Middle East.* And that becomes the ultimate rationale and justification, as it were. We make mistakes like any democracy makes mistakes. That is the fail-safe position.

HB: Which is a far cry from the grand, glorious dreams of the founding of the State of Israel—to find that things have become reduced to: *Well, we're better than Hamas.*

DG: Yes, I know. It's a great moral equivalence test, isn't it? I agree that it's fairly threadbare, and one can also unpick it by recognizing that, while Israel is indeed a democracy within the green lines—it's a very robust and critical democracy—but what goes on in the so-called "occupied territories"—I won't call them "Judaea and Samaria" to justify certain orientations, nor will I call them "the disputed territories", which for a while was a favoured gambit of whichever Israeli government was in power—is certainly not democracy.

I deliberately caused great, great outrage, back in 2002 or so, when I used the dreaded word "apartheid" for what goes on there. I made the very clear distinction, as I'm making now, between Israel within the green lines, the pre-1967 borders, and Israel in the occupied territories, which is under military rule—where, for heaven's sake, people travel on separate roads so they don't have to meet, where the Jewish settlers are under Israeli law, while the Palestinians are under military law from the time of the British mandate.

Now given this patent difference in their status, their rights, their liberties, what else is it but apartheid?

It was quite interesting. It was a Yom Kippur sermon on "Kol Nidre Night" which is the holiest night of the year. There was a packed congregation with many visitors, and I was aware while delivering it that this sermon was being listened to with great intensity. And at the end one could hear murmurs of approval, but an American came up to me afterward and had to be restrained from hitting me.

I was quite taken aback, as you might appreciate. The papers picked it up, and naturally focused on this use of the word "apartheid": to dare accuse Israel of employing "apartheid tactics" was the most "self-hating Jewish" thing you could do. Now, the word has come much more into discourse, which again is, I suppose, the black arts of PR: how repeated use of a word numbs its effects.

There are, I suppose, two conclusions to make. If you use a word often enough you make it familiar, and then you have to think of an even bigger insult next time: *Who do you accuse them of being like next time?* And then, on the other hand, it just numbs the effect.

HB: But words matter, of course. Presumably the reason why you chose this particular word was to be provocative.

DG: Yes. Deliberately provocative.

HB: Right. And the reason you were, it seems to me at least, being deliberately provocative is that you believe so passionately in the principles that are being violated here.

DG: Yes, exactly.

HB: I want to transition, as I promised I would, to the question of who is a Jew and the question of Jewish values, which is clearly such a frequent theme of yours, not just *This Is Not the Way*, but in your other books as well.

You've been consistently enunciating this idea of justice as a core Jewish value. And so I'm guessing that when you think that the Jewish people can be in any way justifiably tarred with acting unjustly themselves, you feel naturally behooved to speak out and shout it from the highest possible rooftops, because this strikes you as not simply a violation of justice by one particular state, but a violation of what, in fact, it really means to be properly Jewish.

DG: Yes. Well, thank you for defending me in that way. It's very flattering, but basically I think what you're saying is true. Effectively what I'm saying is, "*I want you, my people, my stiff necked, obdurate people, to please consider what this is doing to our sense of self and to Jewish values.*"

Questions for Discussion:

1. What does it mean, exactly, to be "a self-hating Jew"? To what extent is that a reasonable categorization of a personality type?

2. Do rabbis have a greater moral responsibility than members of their congregation to speak out against perceived injustices?

II. Jewish Values

Freedom and justice

HB: What are Jewish values? What does that even mean, "Jewish values"?

DG: What it means is that over millennia—let's say Moses was circa 1500-1250 BCE, which is where scholars would date the Exodus—so over the three and half thousand years, somewhere, I would say, in the "Jewish DNA", wherever we may be scattered, wherever we've lived in the world, there has been a sense that the Exodus—freedom, therefore, love of freedom—is a core Jewish value.

Heine, the German-Jewish poet, put it very well. He said, "*Ever since, the Exodus freedom is spoken with a Hebrew accent.*"

So I take that to be a very basic Jewish value. It's like Kant's Categorical Imperative: it's indivisible. The great joy and pleasure of moral philosophy is that you get to use your Occam's razor, tackling relativism and so forth, comparing issues. That's very nice and intellectually satisfying, but I think that the basic values are not divisible.

We know that freedom is dependent on so many geopolitical and other factors, but as a concept it's a whole one, an integral one. So I think you can't be true to Jewish history by saying, "*We proclaim freedom, but not for the Palestinians.*" You've got to ask, "*How can we bring about a just solution that gives them freedom as well?*"

A second Jewish value is one I've defended quite strongly in, as it were, the Christian-Jewish polemic over the years. The simplistic contrast is between Judaism, the religion of justice, and Christianity, the religion of love.

I have argued in theological pieces that perhaps justice could be deemed superior to love in the sense that love is partial, while justice should be impartial. Hence all the exhortations in the Bible saying, *Don't pervert justice by deferring to the poor or being overly obsequious to the mighty, but justice, justice shall you follow.*

That is, try and keep it an impartial principle: justice, tempered with compassion. In other words, be concerned for the widow, the orphan, the fatherless. That has been a Jewish value, a very strong Jewish value, dating back to the Five Books of Moses, back to the Bible; and one that I think, again, allied to freedom should bring about a more balanced assessment of the Israel-Palestine conflict and the just claims of the Palestinians.

This has, unfortunately, been disregarded. The classical defense used to be: *This is a tragic conflict of two rights, and therefore insoluble.* The standard line goes: *How can we bring about some kind of a compromise between two rights?*

Well, again, I must say quite frankly, getting older and more fearless, I don't view the situation as a tragic, equal conflict between a very tenacious memory of The Promised Land of 3000 years ago and the fact of expelling maybe up to 750,000 people who actually live on the land and have been living there for generations.

HB: That is, looked at in the cool light of justice, completely objectively, there's a clear difference. This is not an irreconcilable situation. One can actually go forwards towards a just understanding.

DG: One could, if one was dispassionately following one's principles. I had many conversations about this with Afif Safieh, a very great friend of mine who was the PLO representative here.

We always used to say to each other, "Honestly, we could solve the Palestinian-Israel conflict in half an hour if left to ourselves, to sit down."

And I mentioned this in the preface to *This Is Not The Way*. When I retired there was a big farewell service for me, and Afif came and wrote me a beautiful little tribute that I will always treasure. He wrote, "*With enemies like David, I don't need friends.*"

HB: That's quite a tribute, indeed.

DG: Well, I felt so, I felt so. And if that makes me a "self-hating Jew" then so be it, you know. I mean, I can't really intellectually engage with people who can be so ridiculous.

The point is that if there were an adherence to the idea of justice, dispassionate justice, then of course one could solve the situation. It will never satisfy the extremists on either side, because by their very nature compromise is not part of their outlook.

HB: But that's all the more reason why one should, as hastily as possible, try to come to some sort of just solution, rather than to be held hostage to extreme views.

DG: Yes, but one's also got to be aware of, and willing to face, the political implications. Again, maybe I'm incredibly naive. But it seems to me that if 250,000 Israelis want to live beyond the green line on the West Bank, then fine: do so under Palestinian law in the same way that over one million Palestinians live in Israel proper under Israeli law. If you're that attached to the land, then you're going to have to accept that.

HB: I'm not a lawyer, but that does seem to be in keeping with the basic principles of justice that you were enumerating.

DG: I'd have thought so. I'd have thought so. And from the Palestinian side, one's got to be aware that full restoration of the Palestinian refugees since 1948 is not going to happen. And it is a rhetorical flourish to a large extent. As I said in the book, I knew Edward Said slightly. And Edward, with his impeccable Savile Row suits and his position at Columbia University and all the prestige and power that he had...

HB: He is not your typical refugee looking to return.

DG: Exactly—he's not looking to return to Ramallah or Jenin or somewhere. So 750,000 will not be returning. We know that. But surely it's possible, and Israel did offer this—not enough, but originally—to make monetary compensation and reunite families, the way these things sometimes happen after a major conflict elsewhere in the world.

So one would have thought that it is possible to solve this thing, but the goodwill has got to be there. And I think it's patently not there in Israel. I have to say that. The whole settler movement is the tail wagging the dog now, and no Israeli government feels strong enough or principled enough to dare say, "*This is going to involve sacrifices both of land and of citizenship if you want to stay there.*"

HB: I do want to move back away from Israel, but since we're back on it, there was one aspect of your recent book—or rather, the reactions to it—that I found puzzling, so perhaps you can let me know if you were puzzled as well.

When I looked at some of the reviews of *This Is Not The Way*, many highlighted the false equivalence between anti-Zionism and anti-Semitism: this idea that if you say something against Israel you're labeled as anti-Semite.

To me there seems to be another subtlety that is often glossed over. There are three things going on, it seems to me: there is Zionism as a philosophy, there is anti-Semitism as some racial practice—or a racial epithet that is hurled at people, sometimes justifiably and sometimes not—and then there is criticism of Israel.

So for me, the claim that: *The equivalence of anti-Zionism and anti-Semitism is wrong and that's one of Rabbi Goldberg's main arguments*, is not actually the way I read your book. I read it as stating that criticism of Israel should not be equated with anti-Semitism, and criticism of the current policies of the state of Israel is not anti-Zionism at all. That's something actually quite different.

DG: I think you're absolutely right. Zionism as a philosophy or ideology should no more be immune from criticism than communism or socialism, or whatever "-ism" we are talking about. It should take its place in the list of ideologies and creeds that we examine closely.

But I think your point is actually right. I'm a Diasporist, in the sense that I see great value in the Diaspora. I don't believe in putting all your eggs in one basket anyway. And it's a false argument, it's a lamentably stupid argument, to suggest that had Israel existed in 1938 the Holocaust would not have happened, because one wonders what Israel would have done to stop the Wehrmacht in its tracks when it rolled through Belgium and France.

It would have been able to absorb refugees had they got away in time, that is true, but I don't think the existence of Israel simply in itself would have stopped Hitler's mad schemes, or his ability to implement them in Poland and the heartlands of Europe.

So one can be a Diasporist—as for example in his own way Philip Roth is—and proclaim the value of the Diaspora, which I do ideologically and theologically and so forth, but also believe, as I do, in the right of Israelis to have their own sovereign, secure land, as I also believe for France, England, you name it—and, be it said, Palestine as well.

In other words, I believe in the right of a discrete group of people who speak the same language, have a common history and so forth to say: *We are a people, a nation.*

One can believe in that, and yet be intensely critical—as I can be about the Conservative or Labour government in this country.

HB: In terms of how they execute their particular policies, and so forth.

DG: Exactly.

HB: It hardly makes you anti-British to question your government or to take issues with some of its policies.

DG: No, exactly. The excuses are wearing thin now. In the 1950s or the 1960s, there was a sense that, *Well, it's a new country, Israel is a new country. And we've not yet assimilated the horrors of what has happened to us.*

And I would have to say that I don't think we have yet fully absorbed or assimilated the enormity of the Holocaust and what it did to our psyche. Maybe it will take five generations. Have African-Americans "got over" slavery yet? These things do take time, and

I would use the excuse, as I said, in the first 20 or 30 years of the state: *Well, you know, it's a young country, we've got all this to absorb...*

HB: But perhaps the question to be asked is, *Which way are things going?* That is, your book is entitled *This Is Not The Way*. So it's one thing to say: "*Well, it's going to take a long time to get there*," but if you're not going in the right direction, then arguably you're never going to get there.

DG: No, that's true. And I think that it's probably true that purging ourselves of this notion of victimhood will be a very important start actually. I don't know how much we genuinely believe it now because Israel does all these wonderful things in a wide variety of areas, so we're not victims in the real sense of being perennially down, but we like to play the victim: We suffered this, therefore you should give us a certain latitude that you don't allow to other peoples.

Questions for Discussion:

1. Do you agree or disagree with the claim that being critical of Israel is completely distinct from being anti-Semitic? Are there times when the line between the two is blurred?

2. Is there a difference to being "a people", "a nation" or "a country"? In what ways have those terms changed over the last 50 years? 100 years? 500 years?

III. Who is a Jew?

The logic of self-identification

HB: As you alluded to at the very beginning, you make interesting and, I think, what many members of the Jewish community would consider quite provocative claims about who is a Jew, and how one decides whether or not one is a Jew.

Essentially your argument seems to be: *You are a Jew if you think you are a Jew.*

What has the reaction been to that, and what do you actually mean by that?

DG: Well, classically, a Jew was defined by the rabbis as anyone born of a Jewish mother or who converted to Judaism under recognized auspices meaning orthodox auspices, when orthodoxy was the only game in town.

Now, interestingly, in the Bible itself, descent goes through the father not the mother. One finds, "the son of David" or "the son of Isaac" or whatever it might be. It goes through the male line.

At some stage, and scholars don't know exactly when, but they tend to put it in the time of the Maccabean Revolt, when a lot of young men were killed in warfare, it was changed to the maternal line. Hence the expression "*A wise man knows his father*"—men tend to be more irresponsible, and so forth. So it became the maternal line that was paramount and that's codified in the Mishnah and in the Talmud. And that has been the law ever since to determine who is a Jew—that and conversion under recognized auspices, meaning orthodox auspices.

I should just mention that it is interesting that in the Talmud there is a prolonged debate about conversion. In the ancient world there were so many choices and people moved very freely between paganism, monotheism and the new religion of Christianity, which only required baptism: in other words, faith not works. Judaism required circumcision if you were a male, together with study and observance of the dietary laws.

But for those people who have really carefully studied the sources, the consensus is that in ancient times—rabbinic times, meaning around the time of Jesus, the two centuries either way—the usual method was to accept somebody and then to teach them.

This varied, as all social issues do, according to context, demography, and other factors. At times the rabbis are very favourable towards conversion, and it's no surprise that some of the greatest rabbis are of converted origin: Rabbi Akiva and the great Rabbi Hillel, for example, according to the Talmud both had heathen backgrounds.

That would be at a time when life was okay: the Jews weren't being persecuted or under Roman hostility, the boot, whatever. At other times you get critical remarks about converts and conversion, which have to be seen in the sociological context when maybe Jews were being persecuted, or the community was filled with "fifth columnists", informers to Rome.

So one's always got to look at the historical context, but the consensus generally was that you accepted the person and then you taught them. You accepted them after baptism—Mikveh, immersion—together with circumcision for males, acceptance of the dietary laws, and so forth.

Conversion, then, was a much easier process than it became once Christianity became the official religion of the Roman Empire, because then it became a capital offense to convert to Judaism; there were severe punishments if you took a slave, for example, and converted him to Judaism.

So it became much harder to convert people to Judaism. And this remained the norm all through the Middle Ages, when the Jews were frequently under persecution, until the Reform movement which started in Germany in the early 19th century.

Then in the 20th century, the Liberal movement in this country and the American Reform movement declared that they accepted patrilineality as well as matrilineality. In other words, if someone has a Jewish father and he or she is brought up as Jewish, then we accept him as Jewish. More truthfully, it should be called "equalineality", irrespective of mother or father: if they're brought up as Jewish, then they should be accepted as such.

But that has been the minority view, still, in Judaism, because the Orthodox steadfastly refuse such a definition. And likewise on the continent—in France, in Germany where there's a large Jewish population now because a lot of Russian Jews have come in—and in Israel most of all, it's still the traditional definition that holds sway: either through the mother or by conversion under "acceptable authorities".

My response is that nowadays the overwhelming majority of Jews in the world are cultural Jews. In other words, we attach ourselves—irrespective of whether our mother or father or grandmother or grandfather was Jewish—we attach ourselves to the culture, the traditions. Ask a Jew what is it for him to be Jewish although he never goes to synagogue, eats bacon on Yom Kippur, whatever it might be, and he'll say, *"Tradition. Tradition. I like Seder night. I like Passover. It's what my parents did. Jewish history is what I identify with. Therefore I regard myself as Jewish."*

And if they say, *"I feel, I regard myself as Jewish,"* I would say, you **are** Jewish, because you have voluntarily undergone a form of self-identification, which is the most honest kind of identification.

Equally, there are people in this category who would say, *"I've got a Jewish background, but I regard myself as a Christian."* Fine. That is their choice as well: voluntary identification.

And I would say, *What could be truer than the way you define yourself?*

So if someone comes along and says, *"I had a Jewish great-grandparent, and I feel myself Jewish,"* I would say, *"Fine, I welcome you to the Jewish people."* Because anybody who is mad enough to want to join the Jews of his own accord deserves to be given respect for that choice.

HB: Turning things slightly around, there are many people who are Jewish who don't necessarily feel this resonance, although they acknowledge their Jewish lineage. You cite Kafka here specifically, apparently saying something like, "*What have I in common with the Jews? I have hardly anything in common with myself.*"

DG: Yes, absolutely. A very interesting response. And then there's the case of Imre Kertész, who won the Nobel Prize for Literature in 2002. He was not accepted by the Jewish community in Hungary as Jewish, because he had a Jewish father but not a Jewish mother. He wasn't accepted as Jewish by the others even in the camps. His obsession, his main theme, is always self-identity. Not surprisingly: he's not Jewish enough for some, but too Jewish for others, so he gets deported.

And it is a very modern existential dilemma, really, especially in multicultural societies with ever so many mixed marriages across boundaries.

It's very typical in our fluid, modern world to have somebody from England who is sent out to China by her bank meeting someone there and ending up in South Africa or somewhere else entirely. And then if they have children, and what are they?

So I think if people voluntarily say, "*I feel Jewish,*" then it's very shortsighted to say, "*No. You're not acceptable.*" Identity is something we are.

It ought to be like the Mormons or something, you know? The Karaites, the first great schismatic movement in Judaism, they might well have become a very serious sect and early challengers to Rabbinic Judaism, had they not insisted on only marrying within their sect, other Karaites, which does tend to lessen the gene pool.

Questions for Discussion:

1. Do you agree with David that voluntary identification should be the only acceptable way to define one's identity? To what extent could you be considered genuinely a member of a particular cultural group if a significant number of its members deny that you have the same status as they do?

2. To what extent does the Jewish tradition of not proselytizing render corresponding identity issues more acute than other religio-cultural groups?

IV. Cultural Judaism
Beyond religious sentiments

HB: A strong theme that you've raised already today, and one that you raise repeatedly in your book, *This Is Not The Way*, is what I would call "the triumph of Cultural Judaism". You talk about how there are three specific Jewish categories: the Zionist Jew, the Orthodox Jew and the Progressive Jew and you would strongly argue that to those should be added a fourth category: that of the Cultural Jew.

There are a couple of interesting things here. One is that this pares away a large part of the religious aspects of Judaism, putting it simply in the category of tradition.

Related to that, you say a couple of things, which I think are actually quite provocative: you publicly allude to some of the difficulties you have had with religion, you give your views that the Torah is a document written by human beings. You talk about how sometimes when you were preaching in your capacity as Senior Rabbi you were occasionally beset with some feelings of intellectual hypocrisy.

You are sceptical of the idea of an intervening God and the idea of a divinely ordered sense of purpose and history specifically for the Jewish people, which is a cornerstone of faith for many Jews.

Which brings me, finally, to two questions. First, have you faced much flack about these sorts of admissions? And secondly, can this idea of Cultural Judaism really hold in the long term? If you take religion away, in the longer term—maybe 50, 100, 200 years from now—will there still be a coherent meaning to what it means to be a Jew?

DG: The simple answer to your first question is *no*. The response has been much more of the form, "*Gosh, David, thank you for articulating what I feel when I come to synagogue about the prayers, about the liturgy." So no, that wasn't a problem. And the ultra orthodox wouldn't read my book anyway.

But among the non-fundamentalist branch of Judaism—I include in that the United Synagogue, by the way, which is the middle of the road orthodox branch in this country—there were many who'd say, "*It's amazing how much I agreed with David about this particular theological topic.*"

And I think you summarized my position very correctly, very accurately: I don't believe in an interventionist God—which is really the sine qua non of Jewish theology—that God has a special relationship with his people, Israel: he looks after us come what may and has an ultimate plan of redemption for the world and for the role of his people, Israel. I don't accept that.

Moving on now to the interesting question you ask: *What will remain that is distinctively Jewish in a couple of hundred years or whatever if one is simply reliant on Cultural Judaism?*

Well, you see I think Cultural Judaism is a vast category actually, of which religious belief and ritual observance is a part. For some people it's a very important part, indeed a total part, while for others it's just one stone in the mosaic. Ritual is a fairly innate human attribute. We all respond to ritual and need it. Ritual is an important, significant part of us. And Jewish rituals have lasted a long time.

Take circumcision, which more and more Jewish women, incidentally, are questioning nowadays. What I found is that while they question, and many of them might be quite ardent feminists, the force of tradition makes most of them in the end submit to the handing over of their child, even though, while it's one of the signs of being Jewish, it's hardly, as it were, the sine qua non. As it happens many Russian Jews under communism had no opportunity to get circumcised—

HB: "Opportunity" is a strange word to use here, but I take your point.

DG: Well, yes, exactly. And apparently in South America, in Argentina and other places where there is a large Jewish community, it doesn't happen to quite the same extent. So there are differences. But still, the prevalence of this ritual has survived many thousands of years, and ritual will still play a significant part in our lives, I believe, as long as there are people.

We respond to ritual, be it birth, marriage, death. Perhaps the most important ritual is saying Kaddish. Over the years in my ministry, it's amazing how people who've gone the furthest away from Judaism, as it were—sometimes even quite elaborately disowning any involvement in it whatsoever—nevertheless when they die, or when their parent dies, they want to say the memorial prayer Kaddish over the body. And they will want it in transliterations if they can't read Hebrew, just to be able to say it. So the prevalence of honouring the dead, remembering your parents, is a very deep thing in all cultures, is it not? And I think that kind of thing, in however attenuated a form, will last.

Isn't it interesting how the Passover Seder is such a deep, deep ingrained childhood folk memory that, again, the most secular Jew will never refuse an invitation to a Passover Seder.

I think those things will still be there as glue for generations to come, for as long as people do have a need to pay tribute, worship, respect nature, or thank whatever it is that causes the world to go around.

HB: The message that I'm getting from you is that rational, well-motivated individuals with different religious beliefs and traditions can work together to promote the causes of peace and harmony and justice.

On the other side of the fence, however, one hears, or used to hear, from the likes of Richard Dawkins, Christopher Hitchens, Sam Harris and Daniel Dennett. These people say things like, *"These are just silly superstitions that we should get over if we are to mature as a species. We should simply pare all this away, and what you are calling tradition and culture should simply be discarded. We should just be rational agents acting rationally and not superstitiously, and it's about time we moved forwards in this direction."*

How would you respond to those people? If I were Richard Dawkins sitting here and saying those very words to you, how would you respond to me?

DG: Well, the first thing I'd say is, *Would that human beings were rational agents.* I'd love to be totally rational, but emotions will obtrude, won't they? I strongly believe that it is not my place to deride a person's beliefs, whatever they might be. I might not believe that the Earth is square, I might not believe that the moon is made of blue cheese, or whatever. But people do, which hardly betokens complete rationality. So there is, in humans, a sense of the numinous, let's put it that way, which doesn't necessarily have to translate into a belief in the God who made the world.

I would always say that if ancient tradition is shown by modern knowledge and empirical evidence to be wrong, then knowledge must take precedence over tradition, which then becomes just mere superstition.

Likewise, when Dawkins points to all the evil that has been done in the name of religion, I would have to concede a lot of plausibility to it.

I feel it myself. When people murder each other about a wall or a holy temple, it's clear that that is hardly rational behaviour.

And being from the English empirical tradition, I don't so much ask myself whether something is believable or not, but whether or not anybody can actually prove it. Have they seen it happen? That would be my test, ultimately.

Questions for Discussion:

1. Are you shocked at the notion of an influential rabbi admitting that he doesn't believe in an interventionist God who regards the Jews as his chosen people? Do you think that David is particularly unique in his sentiments or simply particularly honest and open about them?

2. Do you agree with David that Cultural Judaism can last for a very long time independent of any link with Religious Judaism?

V. Ever Striving

Multiculturalism, tolerance and losing interfaith

DG: I've discovered through interfaith dialogue that I have more in common with a moderate of another religion than I do with an extremist of my own religion. And every moderate Christian, every moderate Muslim, would agree with that.

Why is that? It's because we're engaged in a universalist discourse.

I'm very proud of being a Jew: I think we are—whisper it softly—a very special, remarkable people, not nation: people. So I'm very proud of that.

But on the other hand I'm constantly nourished by my engagement with a wider culture than merely Judaism. I couldn't imagine living without Shakespeare, without English literature, without cricket, and so forth.

There's always been this tension in Judaism between particularism and universalism: *Is it the God of the Jews? The Hebrews? Or the God of all peoples?*

Personally, I've always been an unabashed universalist. I think I'm a more civilized—that would be the word I'd use—human being having been involved in wider society and wider culture than were I involved only with Judaism or Israel. So that is what I take from mingling with other people and other faiths.

Where I get annoyed with religion is that, as I've been complaining about Judaism, it can tend to parrot platitudes. As I said in the book, ask a Jew what's his core value: justice. Ask a Christian: love. Ask a Muslim: peace—peace is the most frequently used word in the Koran you will frequently hear.

But how many times have the Jews been guilty of injustice? How many times have Christians not shown love? How many times have Islamists gone to war?

We parrot the platitude rather than going deeper, as it were, and say instead, *Okay, how do we really tell our people to try and practice this?* Do we have to get rid of certain key texts in our scriptures that encourage anti-Semitism, hatred of the Jew or whatever it might be? How do we go about this?

A few years ago there was a bomb blast in London and more than fifty people were killed in central London by Muslim terrorists. At my synagogue we held a tri-faith service of reconciliation that I was asked to preach at. I'd started the dialogue with the mosque when it opened in Regent's Park near the synagogue, and it had been a very good close tripartite relationship at first, involving a nearby church. And then it had petered out, largely affected by the Middle East situation.

But suddenly after the bombings it was politic to be involved again, so they came to the service. There was a large attendance and I preached and talked about what I just mentioned now: about the three faiths and their core beliefs, but how often we don't practice them.

And I suggested that it might be an interesting exercise to voluntarily excise use of those passages in the scripture that are provocative. If I'm invited to preach in a church, for example, it would be a very stupid vicar indeed who, at the Gospel reading, took something from the Gospel of John, who is the most polemical and anti-Jewish of all the Gospels. In the same way, if I invited Muslims to the synagogue it would be rather daft to take as a scriptural passage something about annihilating all the inhabitants after having conquered the land. And similarly with Islam, there are bits that are very provocative and inflammatory about Jews.

The former director of the mosque was a very clever leader who was knighted for his leadership of the Muslim community actually. And he was running a Muslim college at which I've taught courses on Judaism.

So I approached him with this, and he said, "*Interesting idea, David. I'll get in touch with you to talk about this.*"

And nothing happened. And the next time we met, because we used to meet quite frequently, I said, "*By the way, anything happening?*" And he said, "*It's not the right time, David, not a politic time.*"

I don't recall what was happening just then, but all he said was "he'd keep it in mind"' Well, he's died since, so it's unlikely anything is going to develop.

For whatever reason, he was not ready to really consider voluntarily dropping, as I said, inflammatory bits of Holy Scripture. Now, I find it equally incredible the way the Church of England is getting into such a twist about women priests or homosexual bishops, coming out with these ridiculous compromises such as saying, *A homosexual bishop is okay if he's in a celibate relationship*.

Yes, believe it or not—you might well look surprised. So if you believe that bishop X is in a chaste relationship with this partner Y and they go to their separate bedrooms…

HB: …then I'm going to listen to him as a spokesperson for the will of God. But otherwise not.

DG: Well, exactly, exactly. Isn't it extraordinary? So I'm quite impatient nowadays with so-called interfaith dialogue, because I don't think it has moved on from platitudes about its own religion or towards another religion, and that's why I've lost patience with it rather the same way that I get irritated by proclaiming Jewish virtues, but not applying them when it comes to the Palestinians.

HB: Well, thank you very much, David. This has been a most stimulating conversation.

DG: My pleasure, Howard.

Questions for Discussions:

1. To what extent is it logically possible to be a universalist while strongly associating with a particular cultural group?

2. How would you respond to the claim, "Any religious leader who abandons his belief in the supremacy of his religion is abandoning his responsibilities to his congregation"?

3. Does recognition of the equivalence of other religions necessarily put one on the "slippery slope" towards secularism?

Continuing the Conversation

Readers who enjoyed this discussion are recommended to read David's books, including: *This Is Not The Way: Jews, Judaism, and the State of Israel* and *The Divided Self: Israel and the Jewish Psyche Today*.

Religious Entrepreneurs?

A conversation with Nile Green

Introduction

The Economic Enabler

Nile Green likes to talk about "religious entrepreneurs", "religious suppliers" and "terrains of exchange", when the rest of us speak of charismatic leaders, emerging sects and clashes of civilizations. What, exactly, is going on? Just some abstract, academic relabelling exercise?

Unlikely. Because Nile is hardly your standard ivory-tower type of historian, wilfully removed from life in the field. Instead, this dynamic UCLA historian of religion is a self-confessed inveterate traveler who consciously adopts the practices of a cultural anthropologist to illuminate his historical understanding.

> "I'm interested in trying to apply the totality of anthropology: that everything is interconnected and can't be taken separately. This is naturally associated with the classical kind of fieldwork model of choosing a small village or some localized area that you can master, in order to see how everything is wrapped up together there: ideology, belief, ritual, daily work, marriage, kinship, and so forth.

> "As my research developed over the years, I've attempted to make use of the real-life intellectual lessons I've gained from interacting with people: staying in a town for months at a time or making repeated visits, forming relationships with people and observing how things work in the present so as to try to understand core principles of social life, human life.

> "Religion in the world, religion in the social world, became my speciality. I've long been focused on trying to flesh out these core principles or processes and evaluate how they change over time, whether they repeat themselves or can be seen to be happening in

different ways over time—this is all linked to my central motivation of trying to apply the lessons of the present to the past."

A different sort of historian, then, surely. But what's all this talk of so-called "religious economy"? Why the off-putting, clinical and somewhat precious-sounding vocabulary?

In the first place, as Nile explained to me, because this language necessarily leads us to regard religion as a dynamic, evolving phenomenon, transcending our naive notions of it being both well-defined and unchanging.

> *"I didn't invent the notion of religious economy, but I think I'm the first person to systematically apply it to the study of Islam. What I'm trying to do with this model of religious economy is to effectively say, 'For me—as a social historian and social scientist—religion belongs, and is developed, and has its life, in this world.'*
>
> *"Religion is developed, exchanged, reshaped and reinvented through interactions between different people. I'm trying to map who creates religion, and who "consumes", or practices religion. There's a dynamic between a production side and a consumption side, to use the analytical vocabulary of the religious economy model.*
>
> *"This model makes us realize that religion isn't as we're often taught to conceive it. Religion isn't something that, in the case of Christianity, was invented by this fellow called Jesus—or some Apostles, or a few significant people later—and then handed down, fully-formed, over the centuries."*

Another thing that invoking the religious economy model naturally achieves, Nile assured me, is to immediately present the user with a richer, more descriptive vocabulary to gauge the diversity of religious experiences that might well elude a non-expert observer. This is, he maintains, particularly relevant when it comes to regarding Islam (his area of specialization) through traditional Western eyes.

> *"In the West, we're more familiar with, and have lived through, Christian history and Jewish history in various degrees. We have*

> that richer vocabulary of description of, say, Orthodox Jews and Reformist Jews. Similarly for Christianity, we all know very well that there are Baptists and Methodists. We understand and appreciate all of that variety.
>
> "The difficulty with Islam is twofold. One difficulty is that there is a lack of familiarity and conceptual clarity. Perhaps we have an idea of Sunnis and Shi'ites, and some people might know that there are these guys called Sufis. But that's a pretty narrow range for upwards of a billion or more people.
>
> "The second problem with that paucity of vocabulary is that, since the 19th century, through the discourse of Islamic reform and Pan-Islamism, Muslims themselves have been invested in saying that 'we are one': one ummah, one global community. In other words, practicing Muslims themselves are invested in obscuring that very plurality.
>
> "But as I foresee it, there will be an increasing pluralization and fragmentation of Islamic authority, which is already going on in the world today."

Nile understands all too well that his religious economy model might be off-putting to many, both in and outside of academe. But in many ways that seems to be very much the point of the exercise.

> "In Terrains of Exchange, one of the things I expressly say is that this whole vocabulary functions as an anti-rhetoric, because I want to shake people out of thinking, 'This is an imam, this is a Sufi, this is a Muslim; and I know what they do.' I want to create this kind of anti-rhetoric that makes people start afresh.
>
> "It's a conscious way of moving beyond this idea that we already know what imams are and we know what it is that they do. It also creates a level playing field for many readers who are trying to go that one step deeper with the study of Islam. Perhaps they now have some familiarity with terms like 'imam', 'Shi'ite', 'Sunni', 'Sufi' or 'sheikh'. I want to say that, in a sense, you can forget all of that. All of these people are religious suppliers: that's what's important."

Important for what, exactly? Well, to go beyond the stereotypes and get a deeper understanding of the past, present and maybe future of what is happening throughout the Islamic world and our own from Sufis to ISIS.

Nile is, after all, not just an expert on Islamic history, but a global historian, a scholar intent on detecting and analyzing processes and principles that apply to many different geographical and cultural regions simultaneously.

And his book, *Terrains of Exchange*, is not simply an account of how the Christian missionary movement affected the development of Islam in the 19th and 20th centuries, it is also about how modified forms of Islam that resulted from interactions with these missionaries were, in turn, repackaged and exported to places like Detroit, Michigan and Kobe, Japan.

To Nile, then, the past, present and future are all deeply intertwined; and if we're going to successfully unpack what is really going on *sur le terrain*, we'd best start off by changing our vocabulary.

The Conversation

I. Origins

How teenage travel can change your life

HB: I'd like to start off talking about your intellectual beginnings, and how you became interested in the Muslim world. I heard a story about you being desperate to leave the UK as a teenager and hopping aboard the first train anywhere, but perhaps that was an overly romanticized version. Is there anything to that story?

NG: Yes. I grew up in the English Midlands during the 1970s and 1980s, where there was a large Indian and Pakistani migrant population. My original idea was to get as far as India. In my mind India was just a vague idea of how far one could go: the end of the road, the end of the rail lines.

I didn't go to India when I was 17, though. I went with a friend, and we got as far as Istanbul. Actually, we got a bit further than that, but the primary destination was Istanbul. And even though it wasn't India—I had this great interest in my mid-teens in Hinduism, perhaps as a result of the legacy of the 1960s and listening to the Beatles, and so forth—there's no doubt that those couple of weeks in Turkey when I was 17, particularly in Istanbul, really changed my life. I was lucky that I'd studied Ottoman history in high school—I had great history teachers in school—and being in Istanbul really brought that history to life.

A year later, the day after I finished my A-levels, I got a flight back to Istanbul and spent the whole summer before college traveling around Turkey by myself. I went to the eastern edges of the country. I wandered across the border into Iran—illegally, as it happens—I'd been meeting all of these smugglers who were doing that every night. This was in 1990, at a point when the war with the PKK was very much on, and helicopter gunships were going out of town every night. At that age, at 18, that was certainly romantic.

And, of course, just the experience of meeting all of these peoples was transformative. I'd heard about the Turks, and I knew about the Ottomans, but those couple of months, really, of immersion into Kurdish matters and the Kurdish struggle, wandering along those border towns with Iraq, left a lasting impression on me. That region is so central to the religious history of the Middle East. Turkey is such a palimpsest of every major religion, minor religion and cult that the Old World has seen.

That really was a life-transforming experience. So much so that, when I went to college, I actually changed what I'd originally planned to do, and went on to study the Islamic world instead.

HB: OK, let me just back up a bit. The first time you go, you're 17. You haven't graduated from high school. You have a summer off and decide to go with a friend. You don't go to India, despite whatever romantic ideal you might have had about it, and instead end up in Istanbul, where you could feel your high-school Ottoman history coming alive.

But why did you decide to go to Istanbul in the first place? Had you really wanted to go to India, and then ran out of money?

NG: Yes, it was pretty much that. I hadn't saved up enough pocket money. There was also a practical element: Istanbul was on the European rail network, and I could get there on a rail pass. There were definitely practical constraints on my travel, but Istanbul also certainly resonated enough with me to make it a desirable destination in its own right.

HB: How long did you stay there the first time?

NG: That first trip was only a taster. I only stayed in Turkey for about two weeks and then worked my way back across Europe. It was the second trip, when I was 18, which really captured my imagination. I spent two months traveling alone, which was a significant turning point in my life. I look back to that point as setting me on the path that I've continued on.

To this day, I still travel to different places every year. This year I was in Myanmar. Last year I was in Chinese Central Asia. A year or two before that I traveled around Afghanistan. But certainly, why I travel through the Muslim world links back to the coincidences that brought me to Istanbul that first time.

HB: And presumably it was during that lengthier second trip that you were first struck by the variety of experiences that the Muslim world is composed of.

NG: That's right. At that age, when I was immature at so many levels, that experience pressed home the importance of one-to-one contact, the importance of being there, being in the field. Indeed, when I began my formal studies of Islamic history as an undergraduate in college, I discovered this tension that has lasted throughout my intellectual life, between the way things are described in books and what my own experiences have been.

Often there was an intellectual disjuncture; and for quite a few years I lacked the confidence to ask if those books and conceptions could possibly be wrong. In particular, as you hinted at, the idea that there is one thing called Islam. There are many layers, or pluralities, as I'd seen on the road: all of the complications and nitty-gritty of real life. I had observed the plurality and diversity of Muslim experiences, in addition to the tensions and the conflicts.

During my undergraduate studies I developed an interest in Sufism, in part due to an inspiring teacher. I read books on the wonderful poetry of Rumi, but it became clear to me while living among these communities as a participant-observer in India, Pakistan, Iran and elsewhere, that there are many tensions. These were very real-world issues, not just about doctrinal things, but about matters like landholdings, income, stipends for Sufi masters, and so on.

It was that kind of travel that still, to this day, forms my empirical base for clarifying what is real, in order to prevent myself from drifting too far into abstractions—theologically, conceptually, methodologically, or whatever else.

HB: That seems to be a common theme throughout your work: *What is happening on the ground?* In *Terrains of Exchange*, you explicitly invoke this idea of *sur le terrain*, looking at the reality of situations on the ground: real people, real circumstances and the real varieties of experiences. On the ground, as it were, these circumstances can't be neatly compartmentalized into religious orientation, economic interests, and political structure the way we often do in abstract language. At the same time, as a historian, you're naturally looking for broader-based categorizations so as to form general explanations of historical events. It seems to me that there is a tension between the two perspectives that is constantly in play.

NG: That's right. During my *Wanderjahre*, as it were, my traveling years between the ages of 18 and 30, I'd be on the road between five and nine months per year. Throughout my PhD I spent one year linked to my home institution, and for the rest of it I was abroad. During those years it wasn't clear to me that I would even become a historian. I always had interests in history, but I thought of myself as being an anthropologist with an interest in the past, trying to see the long imprint of the past on the present.

I still think of myself in many ways as being a historical anthropologist, or something like that. I'm interested in trying to apply the totality of anthropology that you've just hinted at: the idea that everything is interconnected and can't be taken separately. This is naturally associated with the classical kind of fieldwork model of choosing a small village or some localized area that you can master, in order to see how everything is wrapped up together there: ideology, belief, ritual, daily work, marriage, kinship, and so forth.

As my research developed over the years, I've attempted to make use of the real-life intellectual lessons I've gained from interacting with people: staying in a town for months at a time or making repeated visits, forming relationships with people and observing how things work in the present so as to try to understand core principles of social life, human life.

Religion in the world, religion in the social world, became my speciality. I've long been focused on trying to flesh out these core principles or processes and evaluate how they change over time, whether they repeat themselves or can be seen to be happening in different ways over time—this is all linked to my central motivation of trying to apply the lessons of the present to the past.

Questions for Discussion:

1. Should historians also make a conscious effort to be aware of the present? Additional expert perspectives on this issue can be found in numerous Ideas Roadshow conversations with historians, such as Chapter 3 of **The Passionate Historian** *with University of Oxford historian John Elliott and Chapters 2 and 4 of* **Eating One's Own: Examining Civil War** *with Harvard University historian David Armitage.*

2. Have you personally been in situations where what you've experienced does not gibe with "official accounts" that you've read about?

II. Sufism
Beyond the stereotype

HB: I'd like to talk a little bit about Sufism, because it seems to me that in your book, *Sufism: A Global History*, a central theme that arises right from the very beginning is the notion of correcting the false impression that one might have about Sufism. Once again, you approach Sufism from this perspective of being "on the ground": you look at what people who were later called Sufis actually considered themselves, and then more broadly at how Islam may or may not have changed deeply according to their influence, which was often later relegated to a sort of mystical fringe. You discuss this historical reinterpretation by people who came along in the 19th and the 20th centuries and had their own particular universal and historical framework.

In short, then, it seems to me that you are looking at Sufism as a window, or concrete example, of measuring the potential disconnect between what actually happened and our later, more abstract assessment of things, which might well be coloured by various different additional motivations. Is that a fair judgment?

NG: Yes, I think so. Let's take a standard definition of Sufism that people will perhaps be familiar with. Usually, Sufism is defined as Islamic mysticism. Certainly that was my experience as an undergraduate being taught by Julian Baldick, a major scholar of Sufism who wrote a book called *Mystical Islam*. It's a very fine book, but it is in line with that standard notion that Sufism is mysticism and thus a disembodied set of experiences. How do we touch those experiences? How do we grab hold of these theological or abstract ideas?

HB: It's almost like people would look at it as the Kabbalah version of Islam. That was the sense that I had before I looked at your book.

NG: That's right. Going back to those empirical lessons from the road, when I first went to India at the age of 20, I went to see a Sufi shrine, thinking to myself, *This is where the Sufis will be.*

From that first of what would be many shrines that I visited, I realized that what was happening there was an entirely different thing than what my own teacher or the majority of other scholars had written about. There was hardly any abstraction here; no one seemed to know these key concepts and terms that apparently the whole shebang was about. Instead, what Sufism looked to be all about, at the bluntest level, was transactions of money in exchange for ritual blessings. It was about landholdings. It was clearly a business.

And it was also a means of expression of devotion for people who were illiterate, or certainly not intellectual elites. There didn't seem to be much mystical religion going on here, particularly not mysticism as it was developed by the Edwardians, who seemed to see mysticism as this very separate religion from ritualism made of very high-order concepts. The Sufism I observed being practiced in India was ritualistic religion in perhaps its most extreme.

And that experience in Delhi at the age of 20 pushed me to say, *"I want to understand these shrines, these rituals, these practices of saints."*

The way I've come to explain it nowadays in my simpler, encapsulated description of Sufism, is that this is Catholic Islam, in just the same way as there was a Catholic Christianity before the Reformation.

In the Muslim world, before the reformation that began in the 19th century and is still ongoing, there was an Islam of saints and holy men, of great monasteries with their landholdings, of miracles attached to the pilgrimages and the saints associated with these shrines and monasteries. These monasteries and their holy men, their leaders or abbots if you like, were often closely connected with rulers through relationships of patronage and mutual transactions of miraculous capital for material capital.

Those relationships are attacked and undermined with the reformation of the 19th century onwards in the Muslim world, similarly to what happened during the Christian Reformation.

HB: But this was mainstream before that?

NG: Right, this was mainstream. Well, in many parts of the world today it is still mainstream. It is mainstream for much of Africa and India and Pakistan, much of Southeast Asia; and also in surprising amounts in places where I did a lot of travel, like Egypt, Yemen, Syria and Morocco. These are still places where the Sufi orders and—if you like, "Catholic Islam": saints and shrines and pilgrimages—are still very much alive today.

There are very good reasons why the reformists would have attacked it, just as there were very good intellectual, political, and economic reasons why Luther posted his *Theses*. It's not as if I am a proponent of this reformation, nor do I want to say that it's a bad thing.

HB: Right. That's not the point. You're looking at the evolution of these things, how they change.

NG: That's right. In the earlier period one can see that it's the sheer power and influence of Sufism—or as I prefer to call it, Catholic or Sufi Islam (which was, as you say, just normative Islam before the great reformers came)—that actually triggers the reformation process that starts in the latter part of the 19th century.

Sufis had real power. They were hardly these guys who retreated into a corner as renouncers of the world. They weren't at all. These were, in many cases, the *éminences grises*, the powers behind the throne.

HB: The Richelieu type.

NG: Yes, the Richelieu of their day. And there were many of them, right into the 20th century. When Libya becomes independent from

Italian rule in the mid-20th century, it's a Sufi brotherhood and a Sufi family, the Senussi Sufi order, that gains power and becomes the ruler of independent Libya. Still today, many of the MPs of independent Pakistan are from Sufi landholding families.

We can see similar sorts of things in many parts of the world to this day. Sufi influence has been pushed back by the reformers, but it's still very much there as part of the political and economic fabric, together with what might be called the spiritual or "purely religious"—whatever that might mean, exactly.

I don't want to undermine those elements, but again, as we've already mentioned, the goal is to get a *histoire totale*, a complete history: one needs an integrated picture to gain true understanding. Often, with students, I use the analogy that we know the paintings of Michelangelo in the Sistine Chapel, but we also need to understand the strength and the power of the Catholic Church, the Borgia popes and other factors, because that's all part of one package.

HB: He didn't create his works in a vacuum.

NG: That's right. It doesn't reduce the beauty of those paintings any more than what we're talking about now reduces the beauty of Sufi poetry. For me this is the tension: the reality of the world and the human condition. One needs to grapple with the two together.

HB: Moreover, it might give you a much clearer sense of why Michelangelo might have painted or sculpted one work, as opposed to another.

NG: Absolutely.

Questions for Discussion:

1. How do you think most Muslims would respond to Nile's characterization of a "Muslim reformation" analogous to the Reformation in Christianity? Might it depend on where in the world those Muslims were and which community they associated themselves with?

2. Do you think that some people might have an "emotional investment" in portraying Sufis in a particular way?

III. The Model of Religious Economy
A use for economics, finally

HB: There are two themes that I'd like to highlight concerning religion as a topic of sociological and historical study. I should emphasize that we're not looking at particular doctrines here, beliefs about right or wrong interpretations, or any of that.

The first theme is this idea of religion as a dynamical force in society: an essential, evolving force, not only through larger-scale reformations, but also smaller incremental periods of adaptation and movement.

The second theme is a notion that we've already referred to: that there is no one Islam, just as there is no one Christianity, Judaism, or Hinduism. If one looks closely, one notices an increasing variety of doctrines, of experience, of practicality, and so on.

It seems to me that these two themes are incorporated in this notion of religious economy that you invoke at length. I must admit, though, that when I first read this I thought to myself, *What is this whole "religious economy" business, anyway? What is he talking about here?*

So let's turn to that. Is it fair to say that this model of "religious economy" is deliberately designed to account for these points I've mentioned, and perhaps a good deal more besides? Moreover, what are we talking about here, exactly? What do you mean, precisely, when you speak of "religious economy"?

NG: To answer your first question first: certainly, what I've tried to do is develop the idea of religious economy for such purposes. I didn't invent the notion of religious economy, but I think I'm the first person to systematically apply it to the study of Islam. What I'm trying to do with this model of religious economy is to effectively say, "*For me—as a social historian and social scientist—religion belongs, and is developed, and has its life, in this world.*"

Religion is developed, exchanged, reshaped and reinvented through interactions between different people. I'm trying to map who creates religion, and who "consumes", or practices, religion. There's a dynamic between a production side and a consumption side, to use the analytical vocabulary of the religious economy model.

This model highlights two things that are really useful and important.

First of all, it makes us realize that religion isn't as we're often taught to conceive it. Religion isn't something that, in the case of Christianity, was invented by this fellow called Jesus—or some Apostles, or a few significant people later—and then handed down, fully-formed, over the centuries.

HB: A static, monolithic thing.

NG: Right. Of course this is how religious practitioners always present it: religion consists of that core truth that was revealed and then handed down in the language of tradition.

The model of religious economy takes us away from that view by demonstrating that religion is being constantly recreated and invented. The model looks at tradition as a resource, a social resource in the world that can be deployed by what I would call "religious entrepreneurs". It's not that there's no room for tradition, but in the model of religious economy, religion is always deployed, reinvented, reshaped, and suppressed.

So that's one of the very useful things about religious economy: it breaks us away from the idea that religion just gets passively handed down a continuum. It's constantly remade at any point in history. Sometimes that change happens more dynamically at some points than others, as we've seen in a period like the Reformation. But it's important to bear in mind that change is happening at any point in time. History is always being remade in the present.

The second very important thing that religious economy does, which is particularly needed with regard to Islam, is that it gives us an analytical vocabulary for understanding plurality and diversity—and, moreover, what I see as the process of diversification and pluralization.

In the West, we're more familiar with, and have lived through, Christian history and Jewish history in various degrees. We have that richer vocabulary of description of, say, Orthodox Jews and Reformist Jews. Similarly for Christianity, we all know very well that there are Baptists and Methodists. We understand and appreciate all of that variety.

The difficulty with Islam is twofold. One difficulty is there is a lack of familiarity and conceptual clarity. Perhaps we have an idea of Sunnis and Shi'ites, and some people might know that there are these guys called Sufis. But that's a pretty narrow range for upwards of a billion or more people.

The second problem with that paucity of vocabulary is that, since the 19th century, through the discourse of Islamic reform and Pan-Islamism, Muslims themselves have been invested in saying that "we are one": one ummah, one global community. In other words, practicing Muslims themselves are invested in obscuring that very plurality.

But as I foresee it, there will be an increasing pluralization and fragmentation of Islamic authority, which is already going on in the world today.

HB: Perhaps another aspect is a lack of rigorous hierarchy, as it were. You don't see such a hierarchical structure with all religions, but you certainly see it with the Catholic Church, say, where you have a sense of who, exactly, is the boss. At different points in time, there was the caliphate, but my understanding is that there were repeated struggles over which one was the true caliphate and which one wasn't.

I would guess, then, that there wasn't nearly as much of a systematic organizational structure in Islam as you have in some other religions, which I think allows for perhaps even greater diversity, but at the same time makes it harder for an outsider to say exactly what's going on.

NG: Yes. And this might be a way that we can start unpacking this idea of religious economy. The kind of thing you've described is what I would call a monopolistic religious economy, where there's one dominant player in the marketplace, like the Catholic Church in the golden era of Spanish history: a very dominant player in the religious economy linked to the state, supporting it.

But there are many different types of religious economies, as there are different types of commercial economies. So, what do I mean by "religious economy" here?

First of all, I think it's important to recognize that the language of the religious economy model is an application of the core concepts of economics in order to understand religious transactions. Now, through two hundred or three hundred years of the use of economic theory and models to explain commercial transactions, we've gotten used to that idea, as if they're somehow real.

But of course, "capital" is an abstraction, and "entrepreneur" is an abstraction. So what I'm trying to do is apply a very clear and consistent analytical vocabulary and model. I've borrowed the language of economics to apply to the study of religion. But I should stress that what that language is not doing is reducing religion purely to economics.

HB: Of course. It's a metaphor, as it were; a high-level metaphor that you're able to map onto religion.

NG: Well, I'd say it's more than a metaphor. I'd say it's actually more of a model and an analytic vocabulary. I believe in it more than a metaphor, if you like.

But let's return to this most basic point: that religious economy is the idea of trying to map the holistic pattern of exchanges and interactions in the social world of religion, which I call "the marketplace", or "a terrain of exchange", in the language of my book, *Terrains of Exchange*. Those marketplaces can exist under many different conditions. One extreme of that condition is a monopolistic marketplace, when the state puts all of its resources and power into enforcing a following so that people subscribe to only one particular player in the religious marketplace—for example, the Catholic Church at the height of Spain, as we said earlier.

The other extreme is, if you like, the most "liberal" type of religious marketplace, when the state completely moves away from being a player: it doesn't sponsor anybody in particular and allows, and perhaps even enables, a kind of pluralization of players, and thereby competition, in the marketplace. Of course, these are theoretical poles: at no point in history is any one of these two extremes actually lived through.

HB: Just as in economics: you almost never have an iron-clad 100% state monopoly on the one hand—black markets always exist—or complete libertarianism on the other.

NG: Absolutely, yes.

We have, then, this model of the state being regarded as a player, or not a player, or perhaps some kind of median participant when there may be an occasion to regulate the market in the middle. Maybe the state is more like a manager of religious economy. One finds that sort of role particularly in the pluralistic societies, where the state might only intervene for, say, a religious riot. Or in our modern-day sense, in terms of terrorism, where the state may step in and say, "*Oh, this is not religion; this is politics.*"

So, there is this broad range between the state having complete control of the marketplace, the state being completely absent from the marketplace, or the state being in some regulatory-type role somewhere in the middle, with various degrees of distinction.

Now, what's going on within the marketplace? I think the core insight of the model of religious economy is that religion is shaped through the interactions and the mutual transactions between the forces of supply and demand. To make that more concrete, those are real people: religious suppliers and religious demanders.

Looking at that kind of interaction between suppliers and demanders takes us away from the language of tradition and the way we normally think about religion as being handed down, or maybe simply given to us, by the priest or the prophet. Now we're looking at a dynamic relationship between consumers and providers.

Let's look at the consumption side, the demand side of the marketplace, and how that might change the actual thing itself: the products and services that the religious supplier provides.

First of all, let's think of medicine. For much of human history, religious suppliers, religious figures, and religion itself have been in the business of supplying things that we would now think of as being medicine. Religious suppliers would heal the sick, cure blindness, give prophylactic medicines, talismans or whatever to prevent people from getting ill.

But as time passed, medicine developed. In parts of the world where doctors and advanced medical supplies aren't available, many people will still go to a religious figure. But by and large nowadays we don't think of religion as being in the business of diagnosing and treating cancer, of preventing the spread of malaria, or any of those things.

The outcome of that is that the demands of what people want their religious supplier—their priest, their Sufi master or whatever—to provide have changed. Which means that the actual thing itself, religion, has changed. Religious suppliers, in Christianity nor Islam, don't provide much of that service anymore. As a result, religion as a concrete thing has changed—that is just one of many examples of the demand side of the marketplace in action.

Meanwhile, looking at the supply side in the language of religious economy is very interesting, because it gives religion more of a dynamic social life. We can look at different kinds of religious suppliers. Some might be more conservative suppliers, perhaps from a family business of suppliers who have been supplying the same product, the same religious services, for centuries in some cases. A Sufi order might be an example.

Then there's another case, the figure of the religious entrepreneur, whom I talk a good deal about in *Terrains of Exchange*. They want to enter the market, but maybe they don't come from a religious family, or don't have the credentials of coming from a famous college or madrassa. The question is, *How do they get followers in the marketplace if they're not already born into it, or certified as having a position of authority there?*

Well, just like what we say when using the language of economics, they will innovate: they will provide something new for potential consumers. Or they might undermine their competitors.

What we start seeing going on—especially in religious economies where the state has a smaller role, where the state isn't favouring one player, one religious firm or institution as I would call it— we start to find the potential for competition between different religious providers supplying to the demand side of the marketplace, which reciprocates with establishing a following, together with transactions of money, donations and so forth. There is a flow of social power from the followers to the providers, from the demand side to the supply side.

And this flow of social power, in turn, provides strong motivations for people to opt for becoming religious entrepreneurs. Religion becomes a very attractive career path, particularly in parts of the world where there are limited avenues of social mobility, as is the case in much of the Muslim world today.

So there are clear incentives for people to become religious suppliers or religious entrepreneurs, but this also creates the preconditions for religious competition.

HB: Sure. The status quo wants to be squashing these guys, presumably.

NG: Absolutely. There are two kinds of conflict.

There might be theological conflicts, which could even boil over into sectarian violence that we see increasingly in more and more competitive and unregulated marketplaces where the state will not— or even, in some circumstances, cannot—intervene.

But one also sees typical patterns of innovation: doing something new, or reaching a new group in the marketplace, a new set of religious consumers that have never been reached before, such as women, the poor, the illiterate and so on.

As in any economy, communication technologies and means of distribution of the product are absolutely crucial to the functioning of religious economies. That's why my work, particularly in *Terrains of Exchange*, looks at this period from 1800 to 1940. This is the period my colleague and I, James Gelvin, have called "The Age of Steam and Print" in a book we did together (*Global Muslims in the Age of Steam and Print*).

It's during this period that steam travel and printing is first accessed by Muslims (Muslims don't begin to print until about 1820). And these new technologies—which enable one to travel, to distribute one's product, to print in the vernacular languages of the Muslim world—become great additional tools for religious entrepreneurs.

HB: Here again, one sees the explicit parallels between the economic entrepreneurs who harness technology to do innovative things and break into their marketplace, and the religious entrepreneurs who do exactly the same thing.

NG: That's right; and that's why I think that the model is useful. We don't often think of technology and religion together. Technology is typically in the domain of science and engineering, while we think of religion being studied by those in the humanities, or theologians.

But the two come together fundamentally. We see that happening explicitly in the book I just mentioned, *Global Muslims in the Age of Steam and Print*. We see it in printing, in steam travel, in the telegraph to some degree. The photograph becomes a very powerful religious technology, particularly for charismatic masters who want to spread their personal brand. And, of course, now we see that very much with the rise of new technologies and new media, particularly social media.

Again, the point is that religion is produced through interactions in the social world between religious consumers and religious suppliers, involving the spread and the giving over of power from the mass consumer base to the much more narrow supply side. We have a kind of triangulation of power and access to power. Social media of any kind, whether that's a printing press or an iPhone, are absolutely crucial to the production of religion and the consequent production of social power through religion.

HB: One of the points you had alluded to before, but I think is perhaps worth mentioning explicitly as it certainly struck a chord with me, is that this model of religious economy is quite a different and unexpected way of looking at things. It knocks you out of your preconceived mindset, and as a result you're forced to reimagine the world in a way that you might not have ordinarily.

More specifically, instead of falling back on the attitude that you know what Islam or Christianity is—because you've studied them, by extrapolating on your own personal experiences, or mediated through popular culture or *CNN*, or what have you—all of a sudden you're forced to grapple with a different vocabulary and a different perspective. You're forced to look at the issues and develop your understanding in a different way, a way in which your previous vocabulary might not have suggested. I think that's a wonderful aspect of this model.

NG: Well, thank you. When I wrote the book *Bombay Islam*, which was my first foray into using the language of religious economy in a big way, a lot of people told me, *"There was so much I loved about the book, but calling people 'religious entrepreneurs' put me off."*

In some ways I was actually quite pleased with that, and I've also taken that on with this latest book, where I've written that this whole language of thinking about religious entrepreneurs—supply, demand, the religious firm, and so forth—is highly significant, because as the great sociologist Michael Mann has explained, organizations and institutions are key to the production of social power. So the transition from the single entrepreneur to the firm is absolutely key.

But, of course, this vocabulary, as you say, puts people off. In *Terrains of Exchange*, one of the things I expressly say is that this whole vocabulary functions as an anti-rhetoric, because I want to shake people out of thinking, *This is an imam, this is a Sufi, this is a Muslim; and I know what they do.* I want to create this kind of anti-rhetoric that makes people start afresh.

That's really what I see happening in these sets of social transactions. Religion might have come down from the past, but what happens with them and how they're deployed—how tradition, religion, and religion as tradition survives in the world and takes its new shape—is always affected by the conditions of the marketplace, the range of skills of an entrepreneur, and the relationships he can make, or tries to make, with a set of consumers. Religion is thus always made anew at any particular period through the hands of the entrepreneur.

So again, it's a conscious way of moving beyond this idea that we already know what imams are and we know what it is that they do. It also creates a level playing field for many readers who are trying to go that one step deeper with the study of Islam. Perhaps they now have some familiarity with terms like "imam", "Shi'ite", "Sunni", "Sufi" or "sheikh". I want to say that, in a sense, you can forget all of that. All of these people are religious suppliers. That's what's important.

Many of them are doing many similar things notwithstanding their sometimes different labels. And one of the reasons why they're doing the same thing is because they're very often competing in the same market terrain for the same consumer base.

There are two things that a religious supplier can do: he—or more rarely she—can copy the same product and services of his rival suppliers in the marketplace, or he can innovate.

What I've described is a common set of core principles of practices and processes that are actually going on. And this wider, sometimes confusing, vocabulary of "imam", "Sufi", "sheikh", and so forth, actually hides the common set of principles dictating the moves of all of these players in the marketplace.

HB: And not only does it bring some commonality within that particular marketplace, my sense is that it has a broader humanizing effect in terms of commonality between people in different marketplaces.

Which is to say that, instead of saying, "We Christians", "We Jews", "We Hindus", or whatever, "We understand our structures and beliefs, but those guys over there—they're crazy," we might naturally begin to see similarities between our own approaches and those of others.

It seems to me that there are natural aspects of a resonance with the human condition that I'd like to get back to later when we look at the implications of all of this for our present-day attitudes, but the point I want to make now is that invoking this language of religious economy might well naturally diminish this sense of "otherness" that so often comes to the fore.

NG: I think so, absolutely. What I am trying to find here are core principles of the life of religion in the human world, the social world. These same principles would apply to Muslim, Christian, Jewish, Hindu, neo-Pharaonic religious entrepreneurs—whatever it might be.

HB: Do you see many neo-Pharaonic religious types around these days?

NG: I think one of my neighbours in Los Angeles is one of those, actually.

But yes, you're right: this isn't a model that is exclusive to Islam. It can be Jewish religious economies, or it can be Christian. What I'm most interested in throughout *Terrains of Exchange*, which is a work of global history, is the beginnings of the types of religious interactions that shape our world today, and looking into how the interactions came about.

In the marketplaces I look at, one might have a Christian entrepreneur wander into what has traditionally for many years been a mostly Muslim religious marketplace, where most of the consumers and the suppliers are Muslim. Or you might have a situation like some of the case studies I look at in India, where you have Muslim or Hindu religious entrepreneurs with a corresponding marketplace that is largely Hindu or Muslim.

What that means is that there's no particular reason, all other things being equal, why religious entrepreneurs should only draw upon the tradition of Islam when they innovate. For religious innovators in a broader, more cosmopolitan consumer base, they might well want to mix in elements of Hinduism and Islam.

In many of the cases I'm looking at, there is an enormous impact of predominantly 19th-century Christian missionaries from Britain and the US entering the Muslim world, the religious markets where Muslim suppliers and consumers traditionally dominated. Christian missionaries had such a huge impact because they were very highly organized and efficient religious firms.

The great missionary enterprise had very efficient means of collecting revenues. They appeared as friendly societies with well-structured mechanisms for donations of money and pledges, very effective financial techniques.

Missionaries also had very effective means of distributing themselves and their product, and they were thereby great entrepreneurs. They did this not only through vernacular printing—they were great investors in printing in Persian, in Urdu, in Malay, in many languages of Muslim societies—but also by reaching out to formerly under-served communities in the marketplace: women and the poor, particularly the urban poor in cities like Bombay.

They transferred techniques from the marketplaces in places like Birmingham or Manchester. In one of the cases I look at in the book, we see a religious entrepreneur, a British missionary, who learned his techniques among the religiously under-served working classes of industrial Birmingham and then transferred those techniques to the religiously under-served working migrants who came to Bombay.

One starts to see, then, in these more pluralistic economies in the global age from the 19th century to the present, Christian and Muslim religious entrepreneurs competing against one another. And what starts to happen then is adaptation. Competition between them is, of course, going on, but the different religious entrepreneurs adapt and adopt each other's techniques; they try to out-innovate their competitors.

An example of this is given in one of the case studies I look at in the second chapter of the book, "The Christian Origins of Muslim

Printing". Innovation comes about when these new Christian religious firms, the missionaries, entered terrains of exchange in various Muslim marketplaces, from the Caucuses through to India, the Malay world, Persia and many other places. The missionaries brought with them vernacular printing in the local languages of different peoples. Muslim religious entrepreneurs very quickly caught on to that and adapted what had been Christian religious technology for their own ends.

Questions for Discussion:

1. What do you think Nile means, exactly, when he says, "I'd say it's more than a metaphor. I'd say it's actually more of a model and an analytic vocabulary. I believe in it more than a metaphor"?

2. To what extent is being "put off" or made to feel uncomfortable an essential part of the learning process?

IV. Global History

A new way of looking at historical processes

HB: I want to get into specific examples and the structure of *Terrains of Exchange* in just a moment, but before I do, I'd like to reflect a bit more upon the notion of global history.

First, my understanding of your approach to global history is not to look so much at the evolution of a particular political structure or social structure in one place over a certain period of time, or even, in the broader intellectual historical tradition, examine a particular concept over an even longer period of time and see how it evolves. Rather, as I understand it, the idea here is to look more broadly at the world and try to assess key practices happening in different places during a specific time period—in your case, mid to late 19th century up until before the Second World War.

Examining what is happening over a fairly wide geographical area in a fairly limited period of time strikes me as a different and interesting approach from that of a more standard historical perspective. Would that be a fair characterization of it?

NG: Yes, I'd say so. I think one of the aims of global history is to detect processes that happen on larger stages through exchange or interaction, not necessarily encompassing the whole globe, but certainly moving beyond, let's say, nation states and particular regions as units of analysis. I think you're right, too, that the spatial dynamic is key.

With regard to the study of religion, and religion studied globally—to link up to our conversation about religious economy—I think one of the benefits of this approach is to give a different perspective. When we look at the ways that the trajectories of Islamic religious history have been understood, either on a local or global level, it's often been through this paradigm of Weberian sociology: that there has been a kind of Sufi Islam that has moved towards a more rational Islam.

HB: As we "progress", as it were, and become more secular.

NG: That's right. There is this narrative of Weberian sociology, of increasing levels of disenchantment that has culminated in a more modernist Islam, for the reformist Islam of the latter 19th and 20th century.

One of the useful things that the model of religious economy does is to explicitly declare that we're not looking at a fixed trajectory, and still less a teleology, that takes us from Sufism to disenchanted reformists, or "Protestant Islam" as it's sometimes called. What we're focusing on are many different terrains of exchange and many different marketplaces.

The interaction of supply and demand—the choices and preferences of the consumers combined with the intellectual and other strategic abilities of suppliers—may be such that one might get that Weberian movement towards a disenchanted, rationalist, Protestant Islam.

HB: But one might not.

NG: That's right. One might not. Or one might go in very much the opposite direction. One might move from a Weberian Protestant Islam "backwards"—in Weberian terms—towards a more "enchanted" Islam. That's what I talked about in my book *Bombay Islam*.

There seems to be this paradox. Bombay had the first railroad in Asia, the first gas lamps and so forth. How could it be that what seemed to be the most industrialized—and in those terms, modern—city in Asia in that period became a production and distribution centre of the "enchanted religiosity" of Sufis, holy men, miracles and pilgrimages?

Bombay was thus quite the opposite from what Weberian sociology describes, together with what most of the study of Islam has told us is what Islam is in the modern period. There is this disjuncture.

But the way to look at this is simply as a consequence of a demand in the marketplace, the nature of the religious consumers in and around Bombay and the Indian Ocean who had their preferences. They wanted more personalized, miraculous religious supplies that could actually serve them in their lives and needs.

HB: So this brings me to my second point with respect to the notion of global history, in addition to the one mentioned before about looking at what is happening across a wide geographical area during a relatively brief time period.

As you said just now, there is also a focus on individual communities, this vital idea of, as we said at the beginning of this discussion, being on the ground, taking into account the particular attitudes of the people who are right there—what they have to eat, how they interact, what their particular needs are—rather than simply imposing some larger theoretical framework.

So on the one hand there is this global interplay with the broader-based world by comparing and contrasting disparate geographical regions at the same time, but there are also these important exchanges on the personal micro-level. So you get this intriguing combination of micro and macro that are both actually very important to getting an understanding of the full picture. Is that a fair characterization, you think?

NG: Yes, absolutely. It certainly goes back to the earlier part of our conversation when I was talking about learning my craft and assessing my own input as a historian, in terms of my personal sense of the importance of those on-the-ground, empirical data.

That's a problem I had, actually, as I became, bit by bit, a global historian. I'd written a book on microhistory and employed a historical-anthropological take on how history should be written. But much of the way the practice of global history has developed over the last 20 years since it emerged has been a kind of top-down approach:

really large-scale processes, models, or "world systems", as they're sometimes called, that leave little role for not just individual life, but more significantly the vital aspect of choice and decision-making—human agency, humans shaping the world.

My motivation here is not simply to construct "history with a human face", but rather driven by a belief that these factors of choice and decision-making are actually key to understanding how historical change—the occurrence of different trajectories of history—actually happens.

As I've written in *Terrains of Exchange*, I think all global history is microhistory writ large. It's a kind of summing up of many of these individual encounters at a kind of composite level. What I'm trying to grapple with are those two ends of the spectrum.

We need to have that larger picture of interactions and processes that I describe with the model of religious economy—transactions and religious exchanges, in my case. But for it to be genuine history, to have the empirical basis of history as a social science, we also need to grapple with the nitty-gritty of individuals interacting, together with the core cumulative outcomes of those real, human interactions.

Questions for Discussion:

1. Do you think that if Max Weber were alive today he would still believe in the "Weberian secularization thesis"?

2. If all global history is, as Nile says, "microhistory writ large", are there times when it is simply impossible to do, or do sufficiently well, for practical reasons?

V. Terrains of Exchange
Motivations and responses

HB: In *Terrains of Exchange* you break things up, as I understand it, into three basic categories.

The first category is that of the response by the indigenous community when first confronted with a foreign presence. Missionaries come to a particular place, say, and engender a meeting of cultures. How do the locals react? How do they respond to new messages and potentially new technologies?

The second part describes the internal developments and adaptations of the religion that result from, or are at least related to, these exchanges to various aspects of the religion, such as the development of a Hindu Sufism.

Lastly, you talk about how these exchanges might, in turn, spur these religious groups on to export their own ideas further afield. A moment ago, you referred to Bombay as a source of sending Islamic ideas to other parts of the world; and in your book you talk about the exportation of Islam to places like Detroit and Japan.

One of the things which is perhaps obvious in retrospect, but certainly something I hadn't expected, is how, in the first category, the responses can be—and presumably often are—in two places simultaneously. That is to say that there is a response where the exchange directly occurs, but there is also, inevitably, a response back in the "home country" as well.

Take the case of missionaries. It's not just that the missionaries go to various places and affect, in one way or another, the views and attitudes of those whom they encounter. There's also the story of what happens to them personally, and how they subsequently affect the cultures that they return to, be it Oxbridge colleges or what have you.

There is a certain sense of mutual intellectual and religious development that is occurring. It may not be perfectly balanced and equitable—and in many cases it certainly wasn't—but that doesn't deny the fact that it's a two-way street.

NG: Certainly what is at the heart of the method of religious economy, thinking about global history's patterns of exchange and outcomes of exchange, is that old, social scientific method of a dialectic: something happens, the opposite happens, then a third thing comes out—the model of a thesis, antithesis and synthesis.

What I see happening over the roughly 150 years I deal with in the book, around 1800 to 1950 is, as you've said, these three stages. I call one set of chapters "Evangelicals", the next is "Innovators" and the third is "Exporters". These feature the interactions, and adaptations between different Muslim, Christian, and Hindu religious entrepreneurs, which lead to new syntheses, such as Hindu Sufism.

What I see happening is a large-scale global process of Christian missionaries under the influence, and with the ability, of imperial outreach through the British Empire. But the British Empire is a particular kind of empire, distinct from the Spanish and Portuguese Empires. For very strategic and political reasons, it allows freedom of religion and the state's withdrawal as a religious player from any of its domains, any of the markets, which it governs. This enables a plurality of religious players to enter the marketplace, including Christian missionaries from the United States as well as from Britain. They're the ones I focus on. I also look at German missionaries in the Caucuses in the Russian Empire.

What these Christian religious entrepreneurs bring to many of these Muslim societies, these formerly Muslim-dominated marketplaces, are—as I've already mentioned—these new techniques of vernacular printing, new techniques of organizing, and the religious firm as a "mission", the very idea of the mission and its outreach to new or under-served participants in the marketplace: women, the urban poor, and so forth.

We see a process of adaptation as local religious entrepreneurs, or new religious entrepreneurs, start to innovate and adapt these same techniques. They start to found their own missions, their own new religious firms based on the mission model, as well as adopting printing and other technologies like photography.

It's very interesting when we look at many of the most influential religious firms in the world today that actually emerge in this period. Many of them have adopted key words from the Christian vocabulary, words like "preaching".

Tablighi Jamaat, one of the world's largest and most influential Muslim religious firms, means "a preaching society". We have words like "mission" adopted into Urdu straight from the English. There are other words, like Da'wah, or "inviting", that demonstrate a particularly Muslim spin, or take, on the practice of outreach and missionary propagation.

So one has a picture in which first there's the impact of new Christian players in these marketplaces. Then there's the second stage, where Muslims start to innovate and adapt, reacting to the new Christian players in the marketplace. This is followed by the third stage of export.

It's here when I think the book becomes global history, highlighting what I see as the core moment when Islam truly becomes a global religion through these many different entrepreneurs with their different religious products—indeed it might be more helpful to talk about the "Islamic religions" here. That's when the religious entrepreneurs, who have adapted to the new market conditions with the new Christian players, start to export their versions of Islam.

They export their products and services to entirely new terrains where there was no Muslim presence before. The last two chapters of the book examine Muslim religious entrepreneurs from India who move to Japan and to the United States, establishing the first mosques in Japan and the United States.

What I think is particularly interesting about that is tied to another observation that one can see throughout much of our contemporary world, in the United States, Britain, Hong Kong, Japan and elsewhere.

What I'm referring to is the role of very effective Indian Muslim religious firms and entrepreneurs in positions of leadership, even where the religious communities forming the demand side of the market they supply—their followers, if you like—are not necessarily of Indian background.

And one of the reasons for that, I think, is that India is the one place in the British Empire that has been most subjected to a strong missionary presence; and thus, in turn, the most subjected-to of this entanglement of global history, religious history, and imperial history.

The missionary entry into the marketplace in India is certainly much deeper than any other region of the world. Those interactions are so much more intense, and Indian religious innovations and adaptations are therefore so much more honed and skilled, as a result of the competition with these missionaries. Consequently, when they move elsewhere overseas they are extremely skilled in successfully navigating through this wider global world—not least because of their mastery of the English language—which makes them very effective religious entrepreneurs in the Anglosphere to this day.

HB: It's all rather ironic, isn't it? Not quite what the British imperialists had in mind, I'm sure.

NG: Absolutely. It is a form of blowback.

HB: Indeed. It also makes me think of another conversation I had not too long ago with UC Berkeley historian David Hollinger, who is writing a book on the missionary movement from a different perspective (*Protestants Abroad: How Missionaries Tried to Change the World but Changed America*). David, as you probably know, specializes in the split between what he calls Ecumenical and Evangelical Protestants within the United States as described in his book, *After Cloven Tongues of Fire*. His work concerns the battles between them, and the sense of how the missionary movement became increasingly dominated by those of an Evangelical orientation during the latter part of the 20th century. In his view, many Ecumenical Protestants came to believe that the missionary movement was too closely related to colonialism, which they gradually came to look upon as inappropriate, if not actually immoral.

But that's not all. My understanding is that these missionaries begin to appreciate aspects of other ways of thinking that they encountered in different places. To use your language, they come to appreciate that sometimes these foreign firms are more attuned, better suited, to the needs of their market. And presumably it starts to dawn on them that there may be aspects of such practices that would help them in their local communities back home.

The results of these exchanges, then, are seen in many different ways. David is looking at it from one particular filter— not through the filter of Islam per se—but it seems to me the core arguments are equally meritorious and that there are clear links here.

NG: Thank you. I do think the value of any kind of explanatory model comes down to how many additional insights it can supply about different phenomena. In terms of these kinds of exchanges you mentioned just now, one of the useful aspects of religious economy is that it shows that the different outcomes might be cosmopolitanism or competition, they might be sectarianism or social harmony. It depends, among other things, on the particular agenda of the religious entrepreneur together with the preferences of a given market terrain, those core exchanges between supply and demand.

For example, one of the things I look at in the book is the evolution of Hindu Sufism. That is predicated on a particular socio-political environment, a particular market terrain. This is, I think, important to appreciate for today's political strategists who are examining places like Pakistan and Afghanistan and asking themselves, "*If Sufism is so attractive, and has these claims to being a real Islam, why don't more people follow it? Why doesn't a particular type of Islam spread in a particular environment?*"

That's why I think the holistic model is important, because you might insert a particular religious entrepreneur somewhere, but you also have to ask if he matches with the demands of the marketplace, and the other competitors within that marketplace who might apply means that are violent or otherwise non-pluralistic. All of these factors lead to very different outcomes.

HB: Perhaps I'm being a little too agreeable, so let me not try to be disagreeable, but instead ask you some questions about people who might be disagreeable.

First of all, I can imagine that you might have received criticism from some of your academic colleagues who reject your whole approach of religious economies, saying words to the effect of, *"Well, Nile seems to have all sorts of things to say, and he appears to be a well-travelled and knowledgeable fellow, but all this talk about religious economies within a context of a global history of Islam is going a bit far. He thinks he can rewrite what it is we've been doing for a very long time."*

Have you had those sorts of reactions? I know that *Terrains of Exchange* hasn't come out yet, but presumably you've already done a fair number of talks about it. Moreover, as you've already mentioned, *Bombay Islam* uses a lot of the same concepts and vocabulary.

NG: There have certainly been people who've objected to what they feel is a reductive vocabulary: one shouldn't talk about religion, Islam or otherwise, in this kind of economic language that reduces, or fails to capture, what religion essentially is. I think that's a fair criticism, except that I never claimed to be capturing the "is-ness" of religion.

As I say very clearly, if we want to know what it is to be religious, or to know the spiritual dimensions of religion, there are methodologies, particularly phenomenology, that capture the quiddity, the "is-ness" of what religion is—what it's like to be a Muslim or a Sufi or whatever else.

HB: And you're not talking about the truth-value of any of this, nor do you pretend to.

NG: That's right. I'm really concerned with the level of social interactions, understanding the social world. That is, I'm not concerned with either the hereafter or any kind of value judgement. One critic wrote a lengthy article about *Bombay Islam* and said that what I'm doing there is applying the language of neoliberalism to Islam.

HB: Like you're from the Chicago school somehow.

NG: Right. I think the central point of this line of criticism was with the idea of choice, individual choice. But again, when one takes the larger view of what I'm saying, the important point is that choice has its constraints. Choice—here, the individual consumer's choice in the religious marketplace—is only one factor in the larger outcome of what a religious firm or entrepreneur needs to succeed in the marketplace.

So I think there's a problem with that critique as well. Rational choice theory, as it were, is only one part of the larger set of factors within a marketplace, one set of variables in a marketplace that determines this very wide spectrum of possible outcomes.

With regard to *Bombay Islam*, I suspect that another criticism was that I was somehow invested in trying to push this idea that Sufism, or some type of "enchanted religiosity", wins out, based upon my earlier work on Sufism. But that was something that was very particular to a specific marketplace, the Indian Ocean marketplace in the latter part of the 19th century, where Bombay as a production centre managed to dominate. One doesn't see that in other market terrains.

That's something I hope can be seen more clearly in *Terrains of Exchange*: in some cases Sufis do quite well, in some cases it's very different and the result is a more stripped-down, reformist organization based around mosques, with no room for Sufis whatsoever. Again, it's a question of looking at different terrains and the very different outcomes that arise from each one.

At its core, *Terrains of Exchange* is trying to grapple with the question, *What is this thing called global Islam? Is there such a thing?*

I'm trying to bring together two things: Islam and globalization. How do the two come together?

In the past, the dominant theories have typically supported an idea towards religious uniformity and standardization, a more Weberian trajectory that tends to result in a form of single global Islam that will have such and such characteristics depending on the particular characterization of the commentator.

What I'm trying to show is quite the opposite—which is, I think, the core message of *Terrains of Exchange* and the model of religious economy as applied to Islam in the modern period. Through all of these many interactions and many different, more competitive, marketplaces, what has happened has been an increasing pluralization of Islam. Many more religious entrepreneurs, and many new religious firms, have been able to emerge quite successfully in these under-regulated religious markets—partly through imperialism, and partly with the appearance of failed states in many regions of the world that signify a lack of state dominance or regulation of the religious terrain.

I believe that at this point in the 21st century, we actually have, concretely, more religion—more religious firms, more religious services, more religious entrepreneurs, and more religious suppliers—than at any point in history. We don't have, then, a modernization theory that religion gets left out of the world as the world progresses toward modernity, nor do we have a monolithic Islam, a globalized Islam.

We have, instead, the opposite: a fragmentation and a pluralization of Islam worldwide. There are many more Islams, because there are many more firms, entrepreneurs, innovators—newcomers into the market—than ever before.

I think those insights are really important politically as well. When we turn to places like Syria and Iraq, with the rise of the Islamic State, we see a classic example of a new, very innovative, religious firm that is using the resources of tradition, but is crucially using many new religious technologies as well—we know they've been using Twitter and other social media. Of course, the third element is that they're serving an under-served religious demand base of young men from various countries of the world who feel their other religious suppliers, their traditional leaders, aren't reaching out to them.

Questions for Discussion:

1. To what extent does adopting a "market vocabulary" to account for the historical activities of religious groups diminish the uniqueness and impact of the religious experience? In what ways, if at all, is this different from any other attempt at interpreting the sociology of religion?

2. Is it possible to write a history of religious movements without explicitly addressing the "is-ness" of religion?

VI. Modern Implications
Lessons from history?

HB: This is all very well and good as a descriptive way of understanding what has gone on in the past and what is going on now. But the obvious question is, *Well, so what? How does this affect my understanding of why one historical process happened instead of another, or might help me to better conclude what might happen in the future?*

My sense of reading your work is that you do a wonderful service in using this new language and breaking down old, often trite categorizations that were far more monolithic than they should have been, and might not even have applied at all. By combining this overarching view with these micro-levels of exchange—this idea that all global history is microhistory writ large, as you said earlier—I think you do a great service in pointing the way towards a much deeper understanding of what happened before and what is happening now.

For example, I think it's highly significant that, when looking at the situation from your perspective through the model of religious economy, one discovers that there are many different types of Islam extant today and that understanding this proliferation is tied to understanding the entrepreneurial mentality, the law of supply and demand, and appreciating, as an anthropologist would, what is happening on the ground.

But the problem is—at least to me—that this natural reliance on appreciating local factors makes things terribly messy. Since every situation is locally different, this seems to make it very difficult for the model to have any general predictive power at all. Do you get that kind of criticism?

NG: I haven't, but I think it's probably the people I'm dealing with. Historians are more used to looking backwards, and I think many historians are very reluctant to even talk about predictions. But I see myself as a historian within the tradition of the social sciences, and there is clearly a tradition within the social sciences of creating models with an element of predictability.

I do think the religious economy model does that. I don't think that the core examples in the book necessarily do that, because they are investigations of particular times and places. But in the introductory chapter I try to lay out the model so that people might extrapolate from that.

I think that if one understands even those core basics in a given terrain—who the religious suppliers are, what the demands are, what the overarching conditions of the marketplace are, such as whether the state is a player or if there is no control as in a failed state—one can see that there's an element of predictability.

This extends to being able to predict what kind of religious services—what kind of suppliers and firms—will flourish in a particular market condition and in what way. I think if one adds up the elements of what's there, one can recreate the marketplace and see. I found the same in observing world events with my own model in recent years. I don't think many of my predictions have been far wrong, to be honest. That's not my job, technically, as a historian…

HB: But it's useful to check.

NG: It is; it's reassuring. I do believe in this empirical element of the present world, which I try to develop my models to apply to. After all, history is ongoing. It's the present as much as the past.

But the other helpful thing that the religious economy model does is offer a way of understanding religion for ordinary people who are simply living their lives. Let's take two examples.

One could be a non-Muslim college student, perhaps a Jewish or Christian student, who has Muslim friends. Confusion can naturally arise because one friend says Islam is this, and the other says Islam is that, and another one says it should be this or that. The news media are saying other things, perhaps some rather dreadful things—especially if one is watching Fox News—about jihad or terrorism, but these still have some empirical basis. How does that young person understand what Islam is? Which is the real one? Is it a good thing or a bad thing? Is it a threat to the world or not? Those are very pressing questions for young people around the world today.

HB: And older people as well.

NG: And older people, that's right.
    In that way, I think that thinking about different religious entrepreneurs, different firms, different services, gives a much easier way of moving beyond what this college student hears all around her from every direction. All of them are saying, *"This is the real Islam."* The Islamic State is saying that via Fox News. Her friends who are veiled are saying that. Her friends who aren't veiled are saying that. Everyone is telling her, *"This is the one true Islam."*
    But being able to step back and analytically say, *"These are different religious firms, suppliers and consumers, with their different individual needs, different group needs,"* actually manages to offer explanations, so that the student can now say, *"Okay, that's why."* Now she can counteract the poverty of the descriptive vocabulary that she was faced with earlier.
    Another example would be young Muslims themselves. Maybe they're not college students. I grew up in a town that not many of us got out of, a town called Tipton. It's a very depressed, working-class, post-Industrial town that has been in great decline since the 1970s. I only know of a few people who left there: one is me, and the others were the Tipton Taliban who ended up in Guantanamo Bay—young Muslim students of Pakistani heritage, if I remember correctly.
    I think young people like that, young Muslims who might not have had the privilege of a college degree in the humanities or in Islamic studies and might fall prey to religious entrepreneurs bent on producing social power from followers, might find some use in the model.

I think it actually empowers the consumer, empowers the young individual Muslim, to say, "*Okay, the power lies with me here as the follower, not with the imam, not with the preacher who is saying you must follow me or you'll go to hell or whatever it is*." They can say, "*I have a choice here. There are a range of Muslim religious suppliers, a range of Muslim religious firms. The power lies with me to choose between them, to choose the Islamic services I want, the Islam that actually has a better, more useful role in my life as a human being in society.*"

So I think the model does something to empower young Muslims like the kind of guys I grew up with in a heavily immigrant area in England.

HB: Are there some people who are concerned that this sort of language and dialogue and approach will naturally and irrevocably lead to a secularization of their beliefs? I know that's not what you're saying. I know you're staying away from that, and I know you're not promulgating anything with respect to what is true and what people may or may not believe.

However, one can imagine that if one is a fervent Christian or fervent Hindu or a fervent Muslim or what have you, the notion of regarding the spread of my faith and the varieties of my faith within this framework of economic structures might well seem one more step towards abstracting things in a way that will inevitably lead to a secular perspective. Whether or not that's true I don't want to argue about. What I'm asking is, Have you received that sort of commentary from other people? Are there people who actually fear that it would be inappropriate to look at the history of their religion or the orientation of what's actually happening on the ground within this framework for that very reason?

NG: I've no doubt that that would be the case. That would be the case among many believers.

I think I see myself as someone not on a secularizing mission, but rather as a humanist, albeit working with methods of the social sciences. I would like to think that I'm not undermining people's faith,

I think faith can be a blessing and a great help for many elements and points in life. I would hope that there are empowering tools in this methodology, as I've said, for the faithful as well as the faithless.

As a humanist, I think those empowering tools would help people choose and select a form of religiosity—a set of obligations and a leader—that would actually serve them better in their human lives and serve their wider societies better as well. I would say that even for the faithful, the possibilities might include a more reflective type of faith, one that is more mindful of the broader ramifications and implications of faith commitments.

HB: I know this isn't your area, but I'd also like talk a little bit about contemporary policy implications of looking at the world with this model, this framework.

As you were saying, compensating for the poverty of the descriptive vocabulary is important, so that one can go beyond thinking, *This is what Islam is*, any more than, *This is what Christianity is* or *This is what Judaism is* or *This is what Hinduism is*.

But one doesn't just hear that sort of rhetoric on Fox News; it's heard all over the place. Without going into the details of the whole "clash of civilizations" idea, it's worth emphasizing that what we're talking about here is hardly just a rhetorical device, it's a whole framework that many use to interpret how they think that the world actually is. And this, I think, in turn has obvious policy implications.

So here's the question, finally. Notwithstanding the fact that you're on the history faculty at UCLA, if all of a sudden you were the Secretary of State, or if you were Foreign Minister, what sorts of things might you do differently so that, on a societal level, we could all be more aware of the sophisticated nuances that lie behind your approach?

NG: Well, I think one of the first things to recognize, on the Fox News side of things as it were, is that there are certain religious entrepreneurs and organizations on the Muslim side that really are promoting a clash of civilizations. I'm not trying to pretend that there is no one doing this.

But I think what is important to realize is that the Muslim world and the Christian—or sometimes secular—world of the West have been integrated for at least the past 200 years. There are Muslim communists and Muslim secularists. To talk about a clash of civilizations, as if there are two such distinct, coherent things, is simply a rhetorical device from the right—Muslim, Christian, Western, what have you.

In fact, there are no two worlds or civilizations. They've been deeply integrated even in religious terms, and that's what I'm trying to show here. We know about imperialism, we know about economic globalization, but I'm trying to say that, even in religious terms, the very vocabulary of religious organization is often borrowed or adapted or reused from the organization of Christian missions and other Western Christian religious firms.

HB: Or Hindu Sufism.

NG: Or Hindu Sufism, that's right. There's a kind of integration; there isn't a pure and pristine Islam, even though many religious entrepreneurs strategically and rhetorically will try to say, *"That's what I've got, that's why you've got to follow me."*

At the level of policy, it becomes very difficult and varies according to different terrains. Let's take two examples. I'm not going to go into judging which one is the better, but I think it can help to compare the constraints of even a Secretary of State within his own religious marketplace, the country he lives in. Let's compare the United States, Russia, and France.

In the United States, one has a core constitutional commitment to the idea that the state is not a player in the religious economy. It has a very limited role to even ask the religious faith of its citizens, let alone modulate or constrain them in any way, constitutionally as well as morally. My sense of the American religious political psyche is that it's much more difficult to regulate the marketplace in this country.

There are a great many religious players, particularly in an unregulated religious marketplace. In the case of colonial India, the British have their same kind of political traditions of freedom of religious practice, coming out of John Locke and a growing tolerance throughout the 17th century, which they take to India. America inherits that too.

It's very difficult to regulate a marketplace, particularly in the US case, with that core constitutional commitment that the state doesn't play a role. So there are real constraints to legally and openly regulating the religious marketplace and the number of firms in this environment.

Now, let's look at France and Russia. These are two states with a much stronger history of the state's role in regulating every element of social life, cultural life, and indeed religious life. One example of this is the ban on various forms of hijab in France. The French Minister of the Interior has a much freer hand, politically and morally, to regulate the religious marketplace than his American counterpart. Which is what has happened.

The Russian case is much more closed altogether. One has a very dominant state that has always controlled its religious economy, apart from that little window that I look at in the book when Russia's religious economy really did become more pluralized. In the Russian case, the Russian state, Putin or his friends, have a much easier political and social job of clamping down or controlling religious organizations of any kind, whether terroristic or the most liberal. And that's exactly what they've done.

In Britain, meanwhile, there has been that shared Anglo-Saxon model of commitments to religious freedom. I think this is one of the real dilemmas for people like myself who really cherish those traditions of religious freedom and openness and plurality, people who've grown up in a neighbourhood that was as much Hindu and Sikh and Muslim as it was Christian. But I think there are real problems there.

What we have seen across Europe is that many vocal, right-wing and terroristic Muslim religious entrepreneurs have, in the last 20 years, relocated to Britain because it was possibly the most under-policed, or under-regulated religious economy in the Western world. That's something I feel strongly about.

Not least because in the early years of my PhD, I was very close to being kidnapped and killed by a group of terrorists who ultimately traced their leadership back to within a few miles of where I was living at the time in North London. So I naturally feel very strongly about all of this.

HB: Back up a moment. I wasn't expecting this. Do you want to talk about that incident at all?

NG: The events I'm talking about were in 1998, when a number of British tourists were kidnapped, and ultimately killed, in Yemen. This was traced back to the figure Abu Hamza, who was recently deported to the United States and convicted of a series of charges related to terrorism and kidnapping.

This is my closest experience with those dilemmas between religious freedom of expression and entrepreneurship to the level of terrorism, such as Abu Hamza.

HB: But there's also foreign policy, which is significant in terms of how the United States should react to this particular threat, and whether or not it is actually a threat. Put another way, it's very easy to see a direct application of these matters when it comes to foreign policy. If you believe that there is one fundamentalist Islam that's out there and must somehow be eradicated, that leads you to one path.

However if you start looking at Islam as a plurality—yes, there are some extreme versions of it that are advocated by particular people, but by and large it is a plurality—if you start looking at Islam in much broader terms, it seems to me that this has natural implications not only for foreign policy, but also more generally in how you might interact with your own citizens.

Do you see where I'm going with this? Again, I'm trying to put you on the spot. You're the Secretary of State. Granted that, with respect to American domestic policy, there is this matter of the Constitution and precedent that needs respecting. But then there's the question, How should you frame the debate with your colleagues, with the media? How would you more broadly like to frame the discussion of the United States' role in the world, what its goals are or should be, and what it is promoting, vis-à-vis this broader understanding of religious economies?

NG: One issue that I think the language and analytical vocabulary of religious economy helps us with is that real bugbear that comes up between the liberals and those on the right. A concrete example of this occurred during one of President Obama's speeches, when he said words to the effect that Islamic State (IS) is not real Islam, because all real and true religions promote peace.

The problem is, of course, that right-wing commentators pick up on that and say, *"Look, these Islamic State leaders are saying, 'This is Islam.' Surely, these guys **are** Muslims. They look like Muslims, they pray like Muslims, they say they're Muslims. Isn't this Islam?"*

Thinking through that language of religious economy helps us to say instead, *"Well, these are Muslim religious entrepreneurs. These are Muslim providers of Islam, and that's a different thing."* Now we have a more explicit and useful vocabulary to talk about what is going on, which I think is helpful.

Now one sees that, while some religious entrepreneurs use violence, many don't. What we're talking about here is a particular sub-group of religious entrepreneurs, the violent religious entrepreneur. There's a certain subgroup of the religious firm, the terroristic religious firm. Those characteristics belong to a particular firm that has particular modes of organization and services that it provides to its consumers, its followers.

This vocabulary helps us see Islamic State (IS), Al Qaeda, or whomever, as religious entrepreneurs who supply a certain demand base. The vocabulary shows that they are in a larger marketplace in which they are just one particular segment.

I think knowing that might well lead to deliberate policies of isolating them within a given marketplace. Now whether or not it's the role of the US or Britain or any other outsider to administer religious economies in other domains of the world is a separate question entirely.

One way forward has been to use counter-cultural diplomacy and techniques of cultural diplomacy. These policies are to some degree underway in various places, and the British Council has been doing this for many years.

That can be very important to countering the propaganda of Islamist organizations that are very anti-Western, providing a different type of information, a different type of image of American society and of the West. In the 19th and the 20th century, and moreover in the 21st century, the core tool of the religious firm and entrepreneur, the core tool within the marketplace, is communication and communication tools. As Secretary of State, one might spend a bit more time thinking carefully about a communicational diplomacy, a communicational foreign policy, rather than something based more primarily on violence and war.

Questions for Discussion:

1. *To what extent is the Western media responsible for increased levels of societal intolerance towards Islam?*

2. *Do you agree with Nile's view that "the American religious political psyche is that it's much more difficult to regulate the marketplace" in the United States? If so, why do you think that is?*

VII. Ever Onwards
Much to do

HB: I'd like to talk just a little bit about the impact that these ideas have had in your view within the community of scholars. By "these ideas" I mean not only religious economy per se, but that model more generally—whether or not it applies to religion or some other sociological phenomenon—together with your more globalized approach. In other words, this combination of looking at issues in a broader geographical context at simultaneous intervals of time matched with a more specific sense of what is happening on the ground. Is this combination of approaches something that people are becoming more receptive to, in your view?

NG: I'll start with the question of religious economy. The interesting thing there is that this isn't only a way of understanding Islam, and still less not a way of undermining Islam. It can be applied to all religions; and indeed it's actually the history of Christianity and the sociology of Christianity where that model was first developed by the American sociologist Rodney Stark, particularly in his book co-written with Roger Finke, *The Churching of America* (2005). It explained how America comes to have so many different churches and such a vibrant and dynamic and competitive religious economy.

Across the sociology of religion, the model of religious economy has been around for a while. I think it's here to stay, and I would like to think that my work will help it be further applied to the study of other Muslim phenomena further back in the past as into the future.

HB: Which types of other phenomena?

NG: I think one can understand early Islamic history in this way as well. After all, Rodney Stark re-wrote the early history of Christianity as he sees it, the development of Christianity and the path it took in the first couple of centuries, through the model of religious economy. I think that could equally be done for understanding the history of Islam, even the figure of Muhammad himself as a figure in what was already a pluralistic religious marketplace, together with the strategies and choices made by early Muslim religious leaders in terms of borrowing and adaptation.

We know the Islamic laws are an adaptation partly of Roman provincial law and of elements of Jewish law. Those elements of borrowing in a marketplace, of adaptation as well as innovation, are actually key techniques in a pluralistic religious marketplace. So I think the early religious history of Islam can be re-written in this way.

One can similarly see that there are periods of Islamic history when one has, for example, the Safavid revolution in early modern Iran, when the Safavid state over a period of around a century manages effectively to "Shi'ize" Iran, to turn Shi'ism into a state religion of Iran, which has continued to the present day, with Iran becoming a persecuting, state-dominated, religious economy. That has a trajectory going back to around 1500. One can see quite long-term trajectories here of the state's domination of a religious marketplace.

There is a parallel here with Russia, where one has a relatively monopolistic, non-pluralized, religious economy. Again that's not to say that all Christian economies are like that. This is a distinctive Russian case.

I think that helps us today to better understand Iran, where the state dominates religious exchanges and religious entrepreneurship, compared to the case in neighbouring Iraq, where the collapse of the state structure has led to a kind of anarchistic religious economy where anybody can become an entrepreneur and there is less state regulation than even in the US. As a result, religious leadership crosses into the level of violence and crime, which is not regulated in failing states.

These kinds of insights can be applied to very different places and very different times.

HB: Right. Future projects? I know you just finished your book, but you probably have some other ideas in mind as to what you would like to do in the future. What would those be?

NG: I'm finishing up writing a book on the history of the first group of Muslim students ever who came to study in the West (*The Love of Strangers: What Six Muslim Students Learned in Jane Austen's London*). They were six Iranians, probably aged about 21 or so, who came to study in England in 1815. Their chaperone was an Englishman called Captain D'Arcy, who is the archetypical D'Arcy-figure, really at the heart of Jane Austen's world.

One of them, Mirza Saleh, left a Persian diary of around 300 pages of the five years they spent in London, which allowed me to recreate that world, what it was like to be a Muslim student from Iran in London in the 1810s, in the Regency period.

That's another kind of micro-historical project, to try to help create a longer history for the cosmopolitan London in which I studied, a place that's very sacred to me. I wanted to bring together my own student years in London and a historical project there. I hope *Terrains of Exchange* is a page-turner of sorts, but this new one has certainly been written as more of a page-turner.

HB: You've used the past tense now twice, I've noticed. So you've finished this book already?

NG: Yes, the book's pretty well finished. I'll have to look for a publisher now, I guess.

HB: Wow, you're quite a prolific fellow. Okay, so you've finished that. ***Now*** what's on the horizon?

NG: I was trying to avoid that question. For a number of years now I've been trying to genuinely clear my desk, which is one of those

Sisyphean tasks, but I think I'm approaching it. I really just want to literally clear the desk and I'm deliberately making no plans.

HB: That's not an answer. And I don't believe it. You've got to have something that's rattling around in your mind, something you'd like to do. It could be conjecture; it could be half-formed. But there has to be something.

NG: All right. A book on al-Andalus.

I used to live in Spain: I had a house there opposite a medieval Almoravid Moorish castle. Al-Andalus is a celebrated example of where the Islamic and European Christian world met. It had an afterlife through literature—through Washington Irving, through Byron, through Urdu poets from India who came in the 19th and early 20th century and wrote poems in Urdu about the mosque of Córdoba.

I'm fascinated by the whole legacy of al-Andalus, so I might well write about that. I've been collecting notes for years. That's a pet project I've been promising myself to do one of these days.

HB: Very good. Anything else? Anything you'd like to add?

NG: Not really. I don't think we talked about the Kobe mosque, though. If you ever go to Japan and want to see the wonderful surviving relic of Islam's great age of globalization in the long 19th century through the 20th, go visit the Kobe mosque in Kobe, Japan. It's one of the most beautiful, most unexpected sites in the whole of East Asia.

HB: Thanks, Nile. That was great.

NG: Thank you—you've really been the Melvin Bragg I've been looking for: a well-prepared and kind of judicious but very fleet-footed interviewer. Every question was very apt and keeping up with the direction of things. That was very satisfying for me.

Questions for Discussion:

1. Are there certain modern political and economic environments where religious forces are more likely to thrive than others?

2. Is it more acceptable in Western nations to subject Christianity to socio-historical analysis than other religions? If so, does this represent a double standard?

3. Do you think that the world will become, on the whole, much more secular 50 years from now? Less secular?

Continuing the Conversation

Much of this conversation was based upon Nile's book, *Terrains of Exchange: Religious Economies of Global Islam*. Those interested in deeper perspectives on many of the issues discussed here are referred to some of Nile's other books: *Bombay Islam: The Religious Economy of the West Indian Ocean, 1840–1915*; *Global Islam: A Very Short Introduction* and *Sufism: A Global History*.

Battling Protestants

A conversation with David Hollinger

Introduction

The Exception That Proves the Rule?

I am not an American, but I sound like one. Which means that I often get asked, by bemused Brits or French or Germans, why is it that, in this increasingly secular age, organized religion seems to play such a disproportionately strong role in contemporary American life.

I don't know the answer to that question, but I thought that David Hollinger might. Hollinger, after all, is a highly regarded intellectual historian at UC Berkeley who has spent many years of his life carefully documenting the unique role that different strands of religion have played in 20th-century American culture. In particular, his book, *After Cloven Tongues of Fire: Protestant Liberalism in Modern American History*, describes in considerable detail the evolving fault lines between two different branches of American-style Christianity.

Liberal or Ecumenical Protestants, such as the famed American public intellectual Reinhold Niebuhr, not only represented a very different sort of cosmopolitan, intellectual Christianity than their Evangelical Protestant rivals, but for many years were widely considered little less than an essential part of the modern American project.

> "When you've got a society that is as heavily invested in Protestant Christianity as the United States is in the 1930s, where there are all these modern ideas that somehow need to be absorbed, the notion of using the Christian Protestant inheritance as a means for engaging with all of this modernity, rather than just throwing yourself out into what was often perceived to be a chaos of secularism, has a very important function.

"That's why I wrote this book, actually: to make clear that Ecumenical Protestantism was a hugely important aspect of 20th-century American history—and that it is usually ignored because we just talk about the rise of Evangelical Protestantism.

"We forget the role of Ecumenical Protestantism, which enabled millions and millions of Americans to engage in questions and aspects of modern life that they would not have felt comfortable engaging in had they not been provided, by people like Reinhold Niebuhr, within a suitable Protestant framework."

What's more, these Ecumenical Protestants didn't just provide the intellectual scaffolding of modernity for millions of Americans. They also, by and large, ran the entire country.

"If we want to understand the history of the United States in the 20th century, we've got to confront Ecumenical Protestantism because it is the foundation for so many of the things that happened.

"It's important to remember how thoroughly Protestant, at least nominally, the American establishment used to be. In the year 1960, if you were in a position of authority in something big—in foundations, in universities, in museums, in the courts, in the congress, in the White House, in federal agencies, in corporations—you were almost certainly raised in an Ecumenical Protestant milieu, in the milieu of the Presbyterians and the Episcopalians and so forth.

Well, that was then. But what about now?

One broader theme behind this discussion is the notion of "secularization theory"—the idea, put forward by the likes of Max Weber, Émile Durkheim, Sigmund Freud and Karl Marx, that as cultures become increasingly modern and scientifically advanced, the role of organized religion will steadily lose its influence. By the 21st century, the evidence for this claim is nigh on overwhelming throughout virtually all of the developed world, from Normandy to New Zealand.

Except, that is, in the United States.

"Often, we talk about American exceptionalism, but I'm not sure that term helps us that much. The big issue is secularization. We've been saying for many years that the industrialized societies of Northwestern Europe have become very secularized. But the United States is also a highly industrial society, and there are many things about it that are very much like England, Denmark, Germany, Sweden and the Netherlands, but yet there are all these people in America who are still religious.

"Now, it is often asserted to say that American history disproves secularization theory: that once you have greater physical safety, more income distribution, greater technology and greater political participation—all the aspects of classical modernization—then religion would naturally become less important.

"It is said that the United States disproves this, but I don't think that's so. I believe it's possible to see how the same mechanisms that have advanced secularization in the industrialized societies of Western Europe have done the same in the United States but at a slower pace. I think that the chief differences between the two are linked to two important aspects: constitutional and demographic."

And so David develops his argument: that when properly considering the historical impacts of an immigrant culture driven by incoming religious dissidents combined with a uniquely secular Constitution that encouraged the establishment of a wide variety of religious communities outside of the ambit of any one state-sponsored sect, America doesn't, in fact, represent a counterexample to the secularization thesis after all, but merely a special case of a vastly more diverse society that starts off with "more religion to be overcome", as it were, in the first place, requiring correspondingly more time to "become secular" than other industrialized societies.

Well, perhaps.

Listening to David's well-measured phrases and carefully constructed line of argumentation has unquestionable appeal, particularly when the alternative appears to be the seemingly impossible conclusion that the one country that is home to the lion's share of the world's top research institutions has somehow uniquely resisted the call to enter the modern world.

Just don't turn on American TV.

The Conversation

I. Diverging Protestants
Ecumenical vs. Evangelical

HB: I'm going to start off with a candid admission: when I picked up your book, *After Cloven Tongues of Fire: Protestant Liberalism in Modern American History*, and read the blurb on the cover that describes how it penetratingly investigates the distinction between Ecumenical and Evangelical Protestantism in the United States, I thought to myself, "*I don't even know what we're talking about here.*"

So, for other people out there who are starting off from a similar position, who may not be at all familiar with these distinctions, let's just start with a rough background on what "Ecumenical Protestantism" is all about and how it can be distinguished from "Evangelical Protestantism", together with a brief summary of its large historical impact on American society.

DH: Generally speaking, we talk about the history of Protestantism in the United States as operating on a two-party system. The two parties constitute themselves somewhat differently from century to century and generation to generation, but by and large the fundamental difference is one between what we can call "conservative" and "liberal" dispositions. In the 18th century, there is both a more rationalistic, enlightened style of Protestantism that moves in a Unitarian direction, and a more evangelical, revivalist strand. There are thus two parties, and through the 19th century there are various versions of this.

In the 20th century, we have two distinct episodes that highlight these distinctions. The first is the famous "Modernist-Fundamentalist Dispute" of the 1920s.

The Modernists took modern science very seriously. They accepted the Bible as a historical artifact written by many people at many different times, and they wanted to accommodate religion with modern standards of cognitive plausibility.

On the other hand, the Fundamentalists resisted all of this and took the Bible literally. They would say something like, "*This is the foundation on which we want to live.*"

Now, the Modernist-Fundamentalist Dispute—which for many was highlighted explicitly by public quarrels about Darwinian evolution in The Scopes Trial and so forth—solidifies in the 1940s into the version of the two-party system, which continues to this day, of the Ecumenical Party and the Evangelical Party.

Now, "Ecumenical" is a term that comes into vogue partly because, from the 1940s onward, the liberals—the people who were the most interested in modernity and who want religion to be up-to-date and to respond to modern challenges—are impatient with the sectarian divisions that divide different Protestant groups from one another. They're eager to minimize those distinctions and be "Ecumenical," applying a sense of unity. They began establishing more and more trans-denominational organizations, such as The Federal Council of Churches, The National Council of Churches, The World Council of Churches and Church World Service, as well as a variety of agencies that will enable Presbyterians, Methodists and so forth to work together.

In the meantime, while this Ecumenical Protestantism is taking form—and I'll comment a little bit more about that in a moment—it is defined partly against what comes to be called "Evangelical Protestantism". Now, Evangelical Protestantism is a direct inheritor of Fundamentalism, but it includes other things that are not quite as text-driven.

When we talk about Evangelical Protestantism, we're talking about a 1940s merger of Fundamentalism with "Pentecostalism," especially, and other kinds of emotionally-centred Protestantism.

The Pentecostals are organized around the second chapter of *Acts* (from which, incidentally, I took the title for *After Cloven Tongues of Fire*: the time when all of the saints are able to speak to one another as if in their own languages because of the intervention of the Holy Spirit).

Pentecostals are not driven so much by a rigid interpretation of the entire Bible, but rather focus on authorized emotions from just a couple of texts, especially that one I just mentioned from the second chapter of *Acts*. The Fundamentalists believe in the Bible as a whole, so their challenge is to show how even the book of *Leviticus*, which has all these wacky rules for how you're supposed to live, can be reconciled with the Sermon on the Mount and Matthew's gospel in the New Testament, because they want the whole thing together.

Evangelical Protestantism thus draws from Fundamentalism, and gets most of its leadership from it, but yet liberalizes in a fashion.

The great figure for Evangelical Protestantism would be somebody like Billy Graham. You have, then, a kind of, basic gospel. It's not elaborate, it's not intellectually ambitious, but it's certainly Bible-centred; you affirm the authority of the Bible and match the emotionalism of the Pentecostals with the text-loyalty of the Fundamentalists.

Now, the reason I talk about Evangelicals in that way is that the best way to understand Ecumenical Protestantism is in terms of its rivalry with the Evangelicals. By the early 1940s, the two movements start defining themselves in relation to one another.

I talked earlier about the Modernist-Fundamentalist Dispute of the 1920s, which highlighted the distinction between the two camps. Another clear signpost occurred in 1942, when those who are moving in an Ecumenical direction are preoccupied with what the world is going to look like after World War II.

A group of Ecumenical Protestants who had been pacifists, together with another group who had been so-called "realists" (more concerned with the standard exercise of power in the world), had been quarrelling in the 1930s about peace and war. But by the 1940s, they bury the hatchet and come together to hold a big conference in 1942, in which Ecumenical Protestants outline what is quite a radical program for what the world should look like after the war.

They're very critical of the British Empire, they're critical of colonialism, they're critical of racism, they're critical of nationalism, and so forth. This conference becomes a big push towards what becomes the United Nations; and they all pronounce themselves in favour of Presbyterians, Episcopalians, Methodists and Baptists and so forth working together.

HB: Seeking common ground for these ideals, these human ideals.

DH: That's right, precisely.

Meanwhile, the Evangelicals are very suspicious of the social engagements of the Ecumenicals—all this stuff about emphasizing what's going on in the world. They think that we should instead be focusing on human hearts.

"The trouble with the Ecumenicals," say the Evangelicals, *"is that they're too interested in worldly institutions."*

They believe that the gospel, as we're told by Jesus himself to preach it, requires that we go out and get people to accept Christ, so that their priority should be preaching, not all this institutional development. *"What is all this United Nations stuff and human rights?"* they'd say. *"What really matters is Jesus and bringing people to Christ."*

So, while the Ecumenicals become more and more broad-minded, more and more worldly, more and more eager to engage in projects like the United Nations and disarmament—ways in which to make the world better institutionally—the Evangelicals hold back from that and say, *"Look, what matters is changing human hearts, instead of all this institutional business."* The Ecumenical Protestants and the Evangelical Protestants then divide on a number of issues on precisely those lines.

The great example, which is of the most interest to most historians, is the American Civil Rights Movement, where many Ecumenical Protestants were in the forefront in 1946.

Their organization comes out against Jim Crow and says, *"We need legal changes for this."* Meanwhile, the Evangelicals are saying, *"What we need to do is to change human hearts. Racism is a sin of the heart, so we don't need laws on this, we need to change things first."*

As we proceed through the late 1950s and 1960s, these Ecumenical Protestants are shoulder to shoulder with Martin Luther King—and he's one of them, he's a classic Ecumenical Protestant—and many of them participate in his demonstrations and are thrown in jail.

Whereas the Evangelicals think this is pushing too hard. The Evangelicals are also grounded more in a Southern demography, which has something to do with this. There's a significant educational gap between the two, and a regional gap as well.

If you look at the constituency that Billy Graham builds for the Evangelicals from about 1947–48, onwards (his career only begins to decline in the 1990s when he was very old), it is primarily—not exclusively, but primarily—white people from the small towns and small cities of the South and mid-West of moderate education who have been born into families that are at least nominally Protestant and usually in this fundamentalist, evangelical tradition, rather than these liberal traditions.

The Evangelicals generally do not appeal—again, this is very general, but as an overall sociological fact, it's irrefutable—to big-city dwellers. They also do not draw from the really impoverished rural poor, from academics, from secularists, from industrial workers or ethno-racial minorities. The constituency for the Evangelicals, even though there are urban dimensions to it, is very much small-town, small-city and suburban.

The Ecumenical constituency, meanwhile, has been, from the beginning, a much more highly-educated one with a fairly strong class position. If you look at the United States in 1950, the Ecumenicals are the strongest among the Episcopalians, the Unitarians, the Northern Presbyterians, the Northern Baptists, the Methodists and, to some extent, the Disciples of Christ.

Whereas the Fundamentalists are stronger among the Assembly of God, Christian Missionary Alliance, a variety of "steeped-in-the-blood-of-the-lamb Baptists" and so forth.

So there's a class difference and an educational difference between the two, while there are, of course, exceptions.

But to sum up, Ecumenical Protestantism comes out of a long, liberal tradition in American religious history, which is given point by the issues over which they disagreed with the Evangelicals beginning in the 1940s.

And this book of mine, *After Cloven Tongues of Fire*, is organized especially around what happens to Ecumenical Protestants during this period since World War II, and the role that they played in American life.

Questions for Discussion:

1. Did you have an awareness of the distinction between Ecumenical and Evangelical Protestants before reading this chapter?

2. To what extent do you think that an "ecumenical mindset", or "big tent philosophy" inevitably leads to a divergence of views that make it more susceptible to attack from more focused rivals?

II. Drifting towards Secularism?

American religious exceptionalism

HB: Well, what surprised me when I read *After Cloven Tongues of Fire*, I think, can be categorized in two different ways.

From the outsider's perspective (bear in mind that I'm not an American), one tends to regard America as this religious-crazed country. If you look at things more globally, from Europe or Canada or Australia or New Zealand or what have you, there's a sense that the United States is a country where organized religion plays a disproportionately large role in both government and in the hearts and minds of the people in this increasingly secular age. That's the sense that, I think, many people have around the world.

So, one interesting aspect that your book raises is that you actually have to look more carefully at what is meant by "organized religion". What most people have in mind by this, and what I certainly had in mind, was effectively evangelical Christianity. In other words, there was a real lack of appreciation on my part for these two parties and the battles that happened, as you've described. So, that's point number one.

The second point is a lack of appreciation of how strongly influential members of this Ecumenical Protestant group actually were when it came to affecting American policy as public intellectuals: as advisers to government, and, more generally, as people who made a tremendous impact on the growing culture of the United States, not only from the post-World War II era onwards but also even before then. That, too, I think, is lost on a lot of people—it was certainly lost on me.

You mentioned the Civil Rights Movement, which is presumably the most flagrant example of this. But another one that I thought was very illustrative had to do with the role of missionaries: how, as I understand it, after the Second World War, Ecumenical Protestants pulled back from the missionary movement because they regarded it as fostering imperialism and infringing on universal rights.

So my understanding is that this created a gap where the Evangelicals, in a way, rushed in, and increasing numbers of missionaries were of an evangelical disposition.

And I thought, *Well, that's really very interesting, because now I'm getting a much clearer sense of who were the influential proponents of these modern beliefs and ideas that resonate so much with my own*—imperialism is a bad thing, racism is a bad thing, oppression of women is a bad thing—these Ecumenical Protestant leaders reflected the opinions and values and ideals which were triumphant in the secular world, globally.

DH: Yes. First, regarding the missionaries. Indeed, quarrels about what missions should be undertaken is one of the major factors that animated both the Evangelicals and the Ecumenists, because the Ecumenical Protestants, very early on, begin to be worried about cultural imperialism. They increasingly move their missionary endeavours away from preaching and conversion towards social services and education, building all these hospitals and so forth.

Zhou Enlai used to talk about the magnificent contribution that the missionaries had made to China because of all these colleges and medical schools. There were a number of examples like that throughout the world.

The Evangelicals, in the meantime, got very fed up with these Ecumenists for giving up on preaching. There were a number of quite fierce battles about that all the way from the 1920s down through the 1960s, by which time the Ecumenists are largely out of the business of missions. There are more American missionaries abroad in the world right now than at any time in American history, but they are Evangelicals—graduates of Biola and Wheaton —instead of Princeton and Yale, the way they used to be.

I'll come back to missionaries in a moment, but first I'd like to pick up on a couple of other things that you said. I think your image of the United States as a much more religiously-engaged society than any of the societies of Northwestern Europe is correct, and I was struck by that fact when I gave some lectures in Denmark this last year.

I mentioned, in passing, that one of the great figures in American history in the 1930s through the 1960s, Reinhold Niebuhr, believed that Christianity was the only viable foundation for democracy: that there were more Enlightenment-oriented versions of democracy, but they would all ultimately fail unless they became Christian. I was alluding to this, not to endorse it, but to explain that this was an important part of American history.

And here I am at the University of Southern Denmark in Odense, surrounded by all these young Danes who are thinking, "*Well now, wait a minute, we've got a democracy here, but I don't know any Christians.*"

So, my description of this played about as well with the Danish undergraduates as if I had said, "*Well, on my way here to give this lecture, there was a delay in Copenhagen because a spaceship landed and there were Martians all over town and the cops couldn't get me through.*"

The level of incongruity was comparable, which is to say that your image is right. Now, this leads to what I think is a really fascinating question about how different the United States is from Western Europe.

Often, we talk about American exceptionalism, but I'm not sure that term helps us that much. The big issue is secularization. We've been saying for many years that the industrialized societies of Northwestern Europe have become very secularized. But the United States is also a highly industrial society, and there are many things about it that are very much like England, Denmark, Germany, Sweden and the Netherlands, but yet there are all these people in America who are still religious.

Now, it is often asserted—I think wrongly, but it's very common nowadays—to say that American history disproves secularization theory: the old idea promoted by people like Max Weber, that once you have greater physical safety, once you have more income distribution, once you have greater technology and greater political participation—all the aspects of classical modernization—then religion would naturally become less important.

It is said that the United States disproves this, but I don't think that's so. I believe it's possible to see how the same mechanisms that have advanced secularization in the industrialized societies of Western Europe have done the same in the United States but at a slower pace. The chief differences are two things really: a constitutional and a demographic consideration.

The constitutional consideration is that you've got church-state separation from the time that the Constitution is adopted in the late 18th century onward. The significance of that is that the need that people have for intimacy and belonging, for communities and voluntary societies, is more easily met in the United States by religiously-defined communities and affiliations than it is in Europe, because in Europe religion is traditionally part of the state through these established churches.

HB: And you point out that the American Constitution was the only such written declaration in the 18th century that didn't refer to God.

DH: That's right, yes. So, what happens is that the US Constitution doesn't have God in it, and there's no established church, and the various States that did have established churches do away with them by the beginning of the 1830s.

What happens as a result of that is that religiously-affiliated communities become more available to the public than in Europe, because you can become part of these without associating them with any civic powers. Tocqueville was right in the 1830s to talk about this, to talk about religion and voluntary society in the United States.

There is, then, a constitutional factor that makes religion more important in the United States through voluntary societies, paradoxically, since we don't have an established church.

Now, the second thing that makes the United States different is demographic: the United States, as a "settler society", is dominated from the beginning by dissenting Protestants—which is to say, Protestants who dissent from the Church of England, Protestants who dissent from the Lutheran Church in Sweden or in Germany and so forth.

In the United States, then, you have Episcopalians and Lutherans, but you have vast numbers of these Presbyterians and Methodists and Congregationalists and Baptists and Quakers. Right from the get-go, then, in the late 18th century, these are the people in the settler society that are mostly in charge: they have social power, they have the class position.

In other words, the folks who are running the society from the beginning, come from a "more religious than thou" point of view, you might say. They begin as really involved in religion, as dissenting Protestants, even though they're doing all of this in a place that has adopted an effectively secular Constitution.

As time goes on, then, there is "more religion to be overcome", you might say, and it's crucial to understand that the United States is radically different from any of the societies of Northwestern Europe in that it is overwhelmingly an immigrant-receiving society. There is a steady flow of immigrants that comes in from all of these countries, and they are more in need of communities to provide intimacy and belonging than is the case with those American inhabitants who inherit a proprietary relation to the land.

All these immigrants come in, and since religion is available to them as a way of establishing their voluntary societies, the constitutional and demographic aspects of this work together. Large numbers of immigrants come in from Ireland, and they become very Catholic in the United States because it is a way for them to establish their community.

Meanwhile, the Irish don't have any trouble figuring out that the institutions of the society are biased against Catholics: they're run by all these Congregationalists and Presbyterians who don't like Catholics.

In that way, religion becomes very important to the Catholic population, together with all these different kinds of Protestants who come in from Europe. They establish their own little communities. Religion, then, has an additional power in the United States due to the fact that it's an immigrant-receiving society. This combination of things, I argue, enables people to continue in their religious affiliations for a longer period, even while experiencing all of the classic syndromes of modernization that apply to England, Germany and the Netherlands.

Now, all that said, there's an interesting postscript recently, which is that the statistics are finally catching up. If you look at American poll data of the last 15 or 20 years, religious affiliation and religious identity is declining precipitously. The last set of polls show that something like 20% of the population of the United States assert no religious affiliation whatsoever. That's a long way from what it is in the Netherlands or Belgium, but it's statistically significant. If you argue, as I do, that the history of the United States does not refute classic secularization theory but actually vindicates it, these recent events are consistent with that.

But part of the story as well, to allude to something that you mentioned a while ago, is that religion in the United States includes all these liberals, all these Ecumenical Protestants and Liberal Catholics.

The popular image of religion that you get from Europe is that it's not really religion unless it's kind of "wacky," and so you have this notion of these "Bible-thumping" characters and people who are ignoramuses. Well, Reinhold Niebuhr was not an ignoramus; and a lot of the people who led Ecumenical Protestantism were well-educated and really tried to come up with versions of Christianity that would be consistent with modern science and social science. So, you have this liberalization.

HB: But that was then.

DH: That's right. And I think that Liberal Protestantism as we're talking about it, Ecumenical Protestantism, is, among other things, a "halfway house" to secularism. It's a place where a lot of people can be, in the United States under the circumstances that I've described, for a couple of generations, maybe. But gradually the need for the religious part of it drops out.

That's why, since the 1960s, the Ecumenical churches have declined so much—much more than the Evangelical churches. The Ecumenical churches and their numbers have declined, in part, because they're already so far towards secularization that they can move easily into that, whereas the Evangelicals are still fighting this.

It's also the case that the Evangelicals resisted modern, liberal views of gender. According to them, women were supposed to be in the home; and the result of this was huge differences in birth rates. If you take the whole baby boom era from about 1947 down through the 1970s, Ecumenical women would often have far fewer children than Evangelical women.

This also, then, accounts for the decline in numbers and for the robustness of the Evangelical Protestants in the United States. In addition, the Evangelicals had the idea that people should stick with "home truths" and avoid the acids of modernity, that the old verities are really right. Whereas the Ecumenists were more inclined to urge their children to experience modernity, telling them, "*Make up your own mind.*"

This, too, has a lot to do with how it is that religion in the United States has become more and more Evangelical, because the Evangelicals are deliberately remaining constant, whereas the Ecumenicals are naturally declining. So, you might say that, if there is such a thing as the "spiritual capital of Christianity", that spiritual capital is increasingly in the control of the Evangelicals.

Now, that doesn't necessarily mean that the Ecumenicals are losing out, it just means that they're gaining other things, so that the "post-Protestants", as I like to call them, are all these folks who were raised in an Ecumenical environment and now are increasingly secular, but it's not as though that background doesn't mean anything to them. There is a kind of continuity there.

In summary, then, the Ecumenical Protestants move very strongly in an Enlightenment, rationalist, scientific, liberal direction and adapt all these modern ideas, and the Evangelicals resist that for a very long time. So you get this two-party system, right down to the present.

Questions for Discussion:

1. To what extent do the experiences of other "immigrant-receiving" countries, such as Canada or Australia, support or contradict David's views?

2. How do you think most Ecumenical Protestants would respond to the characterization that David presents in this chapter?

III. Often Overlooked
Reinhold Niebuhr's legacy

HB: There's this dynamic it seems, between withdrawing from the world and engaging in the world; having "home truths" and literal interpretation of the Bible and going out and engaging with the world.

And my understanding is that the title of your book, *After Cloven Tongues of Fire* is an explicit reference to this distinction. You mentioned earlier this scene from *Acts* when people can suddenly understand each other across the language divide by speaking in the word of Christ, and the question is, *Well, what happens after that? What do you do next? Do you take this knowledge of Christian values and apply it to, and engage with, the world?* And my sense is that is a core aspect of what the Ecumenical project, as you describe it, was really all about.

DH: Absolutely.

HB: I'd like to return for a moment to Reinhold Niebuhr and the bewilderment of those Danes that was equivalent to spaceships suddenly landing, because, to me, this is a really important point to emphasize.

Nowadays, one says, "*Well, of course, these values that we hold true as secular values and principles—that colonialism, racism, misogyny are terrible scourges which must be eliminated, that helping people who are less fortunate is an unequivocal moral good, that there are universal rights of mankind—have no need to be necessarily associated with Christianity, as Niebuhr steadfastly maintained.*"

But on reflection, it's clearly a necessary position for him to have maintained, because otherwise, the argument is, "*Well, look, if you're just picking these values that might have been (or might not have been) mentioned in the Bible, then what do we need Christianity for at all?"*

That is, it seems to me essential for him to adopt such a position so that he could both envelop a spirit of tolerance while maintaining the preeminence of his particular beliefs.

This way he could say, *"Yes, all roads lead to this position: we'll have productive and meaningful conversations with Buddhists and Confucians and animists and everyone else, we're not going to put up barriers and walls and we'd like to move forwards to explore human institutions and human values, but at the end of the day, of course, it only really makes sense from a Christian context."* It seems that he had to have said that in order to avoid devolving into rampant and unequivocal secularism.

DH: Well, when you've got a society that is as heavily invested in Protestant Christianity as the United States is in the 1930s, where there are all these modern ideas that somehow need to be absorbed, the notion of using the Christian Protestant inheritance as a means for engaging with all of this modernity, rather than just throwing yourself out into what was often perceived to be a chaos of secularism, has a very important function.

That's why I wrote this book, actually: to make clear that Ecumenical Protestantism was a hugely important aspect of 20th-century American history; and that it is usually ignored because we just talk about the rise of Evangelical Protestantism.

We forget the role of Ecumenical Protestantism, which enabled millions and millions of Americans to engage with questions and aspects of modern life that they would not have felt comfortable engaging with had they not been provided, by people like Reinhold Niebuhr, with a Protestant framework for doing so.

Now, that's not to say that there's a teleological aspect to this, that's not to say that everybody who enters Ecumenical Protestantism is going to reject the faith and become a full secularist eventually, but it is to say that a lot of people will do that. And that's okay if it enables them to continue to function psychologically and be socially productive in society.

However, there will be others who will stay with Protestant Liberalism. I don't think that Protestant Liberalism is going to die in the foreseeable future. There are proponents today in England, in the Netherlands, less so in Denmark—Denmark is one of the most secular societies in the world—but even in Denmark there are a handful of these liberal clerics around.

So, an advantage of Liberal Protestantism, in all its varieties, is that it's there for people who want that particular kind of combination. But the big point that I want to make—and I'm so glad that you've picked this up from my book—is that, if we want to understand the history of the United States in the 20th century, we've got to confront Ecumenical Protestantism because it is the foundation for so many of the things that happened.

Nowadays, it's easy to forget this. On the Supreme Court today there are six Catholics and nobody who was born into a Protestant family. Now, this would have been inconceivable years ago. When Kennedy ran for president in 1960 there was all this flap about *"What are we going to do about the Catholics taking over the country?"*

I can't quote anybody specific who said this, but I can well imagine that some would have exclaimed, *"Sooner or later we'll have **six** Catholics on the Supreme Court."* And then everybody would call those people bigots and say that all that is just outrageous paranoia.

So, this transition has now happened, but I use that as a dramatic example to remind us how thoroughly Protestant, at least nominally, the American establishment used to be.

In the year 1960, if you were in charge of something big—in the foundations, in universities, in museums, in the courts, in the congress, in the White House, in federal agencies, in corporations—you were almost certainly to have been raised in a liberal, Protestant milieu, in the milieu of the Presbyterians and the Episcopalians and so forth.

There are obviously exceptions to this, of course. There were Jews on the Supreme Court going back to Brandeis and Frankfurter, as well as prominent Jewish industrialists. There were important Catholics too, eventually (Catholics come into higher class positions much later). So there are exceptions to this, but these are exceptions to a rule.

One of the reasons, I think, that people are a little bit slow to pick up on this today—and maybe to confront it as frontally as I try to do in my work—is that we're a little bit afraid that this will happen again. I mean, we're so glad to have a pluralistic society that is free of the old Protestant hegemony, that if you talk too much about all of these Protestant contributions to American history, maybe you will devalue all of the non-Protestant contributions.

HB: Oh, I don't think so. I think most people just don't remember things.

DH: Maybe they don't. Well, if that's the case then I feel better about it. But it is an empirical fact that America was a deeply Protestant civilization for a very long time and understanding its liberal part as well as its reactionary part is important.

Questions for Discussion:

1. Is American society generally more tolerant, more intolerant or just intolerant in different ways compared to what it was 50 years ago?

2. Do you think that the lack of recognition that Americans generally give to their Ecumenical Protestant heritage is related to a concern of devaluing the contributions of others by comparison as David fears, or is simply a case of not being aware of the past?

IV. The Missionary Position

Encounters with The Other

DH: I was eager to pick up on something you mentioned a moment ago when you were talking about the missionary experience. I'm actually writing a book about that now (*Protestants Abroad: How Missionaries Tried to Change the World but Changed America*), and one of the things that's so important about Protestant missionaries is that they're the Americans who learn the most, the earliest, about the world outside the North-Atlantic West.

Nowadays, when we're so preoccupied with globalization and species-wide questions like climate change and the need to recognize the integrity of cultures around the world to overcome provincial biases, it's interesting to trace back American society's interaction with this world outside the North-Atlantic West.

If you go back to, say, the period before World War II, you had some diplomats and business connections abroad, a little bit of military and some journalists and travel writers, but, overwhelmingly, the majority of what the average American knew about Asia or Africa or Brazil came from missionaries. These were the "point people", you might say, in the American involvement with the rest of the world.

And when they came back from abroad, they would bring into their church communities and trans-denominational organizations a different set of concerns and perspectives. They would say things like, "*Well, you know, we're very worried about the difference between Congregationalists and Presbyterians, or about the difference between Northern Baptists and Southern Baptists, but let me tell you, when you're in China trying to explain Christianity to the Chinese, that doesn't make sense to them.*"

We had a lot of Dutch Reformed missionaries in Japan as well as many German Reformed missionaries—two very prominent, American organizations. But try to explain to potential Japanese converts why they should become Dutch Reformed Christians rather than German Reformed Christians.

So there's enormous tension that's built up, where the cosmopolitan missionaries and their children—who are a very important part of this story, I'll give some examples in a moment—then come back to a society that had sent them abroad for the purpose of making the rest of the world more like them.

There's the original refrain of, "*We who live in Nashville, we who live in Dayton, Ohio, we who live in St. Paul or Worchester, Massachusetts and so forth—**we** know what Christianity is. We may embody it imperfectly, but we **know** what it is, we **have** it. The Chinese don't have it, the Congolese don't have it, so we need the missionaries to go over there and make them like us.*"

So the missionaries come back and say, "*Well, you know, I'm not sure that what they really need is to be like us. They do need things, naturally. But do you know much about the civilization of China? Let me tell you about Confucian traditions...*"

And then some guy will stand up in the pew and say, "*We here in Terre Haute did **not** send you to China to come back and tell us how interesting the Chinese are.*"

The tension between the cosmopolitan missionaries and the provincial churchgoers thus becomes more and more tense, and the missionaries begin arguing that the whole missionary project needs to be reconfigured. It's the missionaries themselves and their children who push this the hardest.

Take someone like Pearl Buck, the Nobel Laureate and author of—among many other works—*The Good Earth*, who was perhaps the most famous of the missionary children. She's going around in the 1930s declaring, "*The whole missionary project has got to be reformed.*"

Now, she was pretty much pushed out of the Presbyterian Church for this but she's not alone, there are a lot of people like her. The rule of thumb—and as with all rules of thumb, there are important exceptions—is that the more missionary experience you have, the more deeply embedded you are in Chinese, Japanese, African culture, the more critical you are of the missionary project itself and the more sceptical you are about the sectarianism of American Protestant Christianity.

These are the leaders of the Ecumenical movement. These are the people who push the Presbyterians and the Northern Baptists and Methodists further in the Ecumenical direction.

Is it really so important that baptism occurs in a certain way? The Baptists do it one way, and the Episcopalians do it in another. "*Of course it's important!*" exclaim people in the pew. "*We've been doing this for centuries: our preacher has told us how important this is, we've educated our children in our Sunday school to do it this way.*" And the missionaries respond, "*Well, okay, but maybe we need to change that a little bit. Maybe that's wrong.*"

This tension is very important, and directly leads to a globalization and internationalization of the Ecumenical Protestants, which is not participated in by the Evangelical Protestants until the 1970s and '80s. By the 1970s and '80s, they begin to copy the Ecumenical Protestants, but it's still a struggle.

HB: How do they copy them? I would have thought that they would be quite different.

DH: Well, there's a big conference of Evangelical missionary leaders in Switzerland in 1974 at Lausanne. By this time Evangelical missionaries have been increasingly subjected to criticism for not having strong enough social service programs and for being so exclusively into conversion. It's partly the Ecumenical Protestants who have been making this complaint, along with a number of the younger Evangelical missionaries and their supporters.

Billy Graham and others set up this conference specifically to make a compromise. And they do. They come out with around 18 or 19 principles, one of which is that the diminution of inequality and poverty in the world is an important Christian mission.

Now, had they said that in 1935, the Fundamentalists would have hit the ceiling because that's precisely the sort of thing the Ecumenicals were being attacked for. But by the 1970s, even the Evangelicals begin to move gradually in that direction.

The Evangelical missionary projects that have been in place from the 1970s down to the present day are actually increasingly modelled on the old Ecumenical missionary projects, but they are heavily in denial.

I've interviewed a number of people involved in this, and they will say, "*Oh, yes, we still believe in conversion, we still believe in the Bible as before.*" They will cover themselves on this, but from the view at 30,000 feet, which is what we historians are supposed to be good at, I see all sorts of de facto continuities. The Evangelicals are always afraid to admit that they're following the Ecumenicals, just as the Ecumenicals are usually afraid to admit how secular they're becoming. There are thus existential reasons, you might say, vested-interest reasons, for these self-representations.

HB: Well, that must give you a feeling of optimism, because it means that these people are becoming more open-minded, more sensitive to the people on the ground, more aware of the key issues at stake, and so forth.

DH: Absolutely; and they definitely are that. I mean, it's a struggle but they are definitely moving that way—and that's, again, consistent with my argument that classic secularization theory is correct.

To return again to this theme of classic secularization theory, the people who want to say that it's dead will say, "*Look at the enormous growth of Christianity all over the global South. Look at the Christians in the Congo, look at the Christians in Sri Lanka.*"

Well, okay, but what kinds of Christians are they? These are impoverished people. These are people without physical security. These are people with very little education. These are people with only spotty technology. In other words, they are consistent with all of the classic, Weberian secularization theory criteria.

There's also a question as to how broad our definitions are. What purchase do we get on the average congregation in South India or in Zimbabwe? What purchase do we get by calling these people "Christians"? Well, they invoke Christian symbols, they declare themselves to be followers of Christ, but how similar is their culture to the culture of Christianity in the North-Atlantic West? There's a question there.

Many of the people who maintain that Christianity is triumphing rather than declining count everybody: you count everybody who makes a declaration of Christianity and you don't distinguish between, on the one hand, say, the American Unitarians and others in very different environments.

I heard a great paper given at the American Historical Association a few years ago (this is an extreme case) where this guy was talking about the church in South India that he had been studying.

One of the most famous evangelists in South India—a South Indian himself, an indigenous person—was explaining how he'd just gotten back from Heaven and had just a terrific conversation with the Apostle Paul. People would ask him questions like, "*Oh, did you see St. Peter?*" to which he'd reply "*Yes, I saw St. Peter too.*" And this guy would go on about how he'd been to Heaven and seen these people, and tell them about how Paul had some very good ideas about Church organization, and so forth.

Now, do we really get any help by calling this guy part of the same religious formation as even Billy Graham, to say nothing of Reinhold Niebuhr or the people who run the World Council of Churches?

There are, then, under the symbolic rubric of Christianity, even of Protestantism, a great variety of approaches.

Now, many religiously-committed scholars study these differences conscientiously and effectively just as secular scholars do—and this is a great boon—but I find that the religiously-committed will be very eager to affirm the unity of the Christian faith community as a whole, whereas I usually argue that the salient solidarity today is not the community of faith per se, but the epistemic and political community.

This gets me involved in some very interesting discussions at workshops. Even though I'm a flaming atheist, I'm often invited to Ecumenical Protestant gatherings, and I will often suggest to these people that their real enemy is the Evangelicals and those who advance obscurantist ideas about the faith, while their real allies are the secular liberals, that there's a great continuity between what goes on in Union Theological Seminary, The Pacific School of Religion, The Chicago Divinity School and the secular intelligentsia. I basically tell them, "*This is really your home, guys.*"

Now, they resist this. They are very reluctant to give up on the community of faith as the relevant solidarity. They are terrified of the "slippery slope to secularism"—and you can understand, keeping with what we've been saying, why this is a problem. If you're a clergyman, if you're a seminary president, if you're the professor of a seminary, you've really got to stick with the program.

And then, this guy Hollinger comes along who says, "*Well, you can stick with the program, but you can still hang out with all us atheists and free-thinkers and people who aren't terribly interested in religious issues, but we have a lot more continuity and we're all against misogyny and colonialism and so forth.*"

They're naturally very reluctant, because to give up on their solidarity with the Evangelicals presents a terrible problem for them leadership-wise, and I'm very sympathetic to this.

HB: And the Evangelicals are, of course, very keen to paint them this way: "***You're** crypto-secularists and **we're** the **real** Christians.*"

DH: Precisely. They say, "*If you hang out with too many of these secularists, just think what's going to happen to you.*" There are so many variations on this in the history of Protestantism.

I like to joke about my own family. I had an aunt in the Church of the Brethren, German Baptist Brethren, my ancestral denomination—this was in Gettysburg, Pennsylvania. In 1913, when she was fifteen years old, she refused to wear the bonnet. In those days, women of the Pennsylvania Dutch—the Amish and the Brethren and the Mennonites—all had to wear these bonnets.

Her attitude was, *"The Lutheran girls don't have to wear bonnets, the Presbyterian girls don't have to wear them, why do I have to wear one?"* Well, that was just the way it was.

So she's kicked out of the church at the age of 15, and it was said that only terrible things could befall her. And, indeed, they did: she married a Presbyterian. This was bad enough, but then—just to show you that the old church ladies were right—she had a daughter and the daughter married an Episcopalian!

And, even worse still, the woman who married the Episcopalian had a daughter who married…a Mormon! Now, at this point, the deity intervened and made the woman who married the Mormon barren, as they say in the Bible, because, if she'd have had a daughter, she might have married…a **Ca-Ca-Catholic!**

And there was a similar Catholic thing in my own upbringing when I was a child in Idaho. There was a kid who lived across the street who was from a Catholic family. And my mother, who was a very proud Ecumenical Liberal, was very pleased that she had a son who was willing to play with this kid.

My mother said that it was all right for me to play with him because he was from a very nice Catholic family, and she would brag about this. She thought it was just great that she was liberal enough to have her son play with a Catholic. Now, the church ladies were dubious about this, as she explained to me later, and they told her, *"If your son spends too much time hanging out with Catholics, bad things are going to happen: you should stay with your own kind."*

HB: Well, they were right. Look where you are: at Berkeley.

DH: That's right. And I became an atheist, my daughter is gay, and my son married an Episcopalian. So, it just shows that, once you deviate from the natal community, anything can happen.

But this tension that I write so much about between cosmopolitanism and provincialism is a very big thing in American history; and it's especially big in religious history, because religion is a context in which people have such strong loyalties.

Questions for Discussion:

1. To what extent are contemporary worldwide secular movements, such as combating climate change, "missionary projects"?

2. Does widespread tolerance of religious and cultural differences necessarily lead to an increasingly homogeneous world?

V. Demographic Diversification
Cosmopolitan spies and other issues

HB: It's not just religious history, though, but really a more general phenomenon, which is something that I wanted to get to. You introduce this term "demographic diversification": that if you have a set of beliefs for which you claim sort of universality, but then you go out and talk to people outside of your neighbourhood, country, or even continent and you find that, in fact, people have wildly different beliefs, attitudes, customs, that might well cause you to doubt the universality of your belief system.

Religion is an obvious domain in which this happens, but it happens all over the place in all sorts of different areas. This notion of coming to terms with the fact that your provincial values might not well apply as universally as you had naively believed applies not only to religious history, but also to economics, ethics, and all sorts of other areas.

In particular, you talk about how you were influenced by somebody of Jewish descent—Joseph Levenson—who was studying China while applying this integral metric, this filter, of cosmopolitanism versus provincialism.

DH: Yes. Sometimes it is called the "Water Theory of Liberalism," referring back to the times when people travelled mostly by water. Seaports were traditionally the scenes of greater liberalization than mountainous or inland environments. There are still remnants of this today, where you can see San Francisco and New York as rather different from, say, Topeka, Kansas.

HB: Or Switzerland, for that matter.

DH: Yes, that's right. Again, with all of these generalizations there are lots of interesting exceptions, but there clearly is a sense that a broadened experience will challenge a presumption of what's right and will require some sort of readjustment.

And, again, that's why Ecumenical Protestantism is so important, because it is a frame of reference within which people can explore more and more of the world and find ways to bridge where they've been to where they might want to go. This way they have at least a working set of priorities for what they want to select from out there in the world, because there might be a lot they see that they don't subscribe to and want to be against it.

It's not, therefore, that everything out there is of equal value—the cosmopolitan side of the cosmopolitan-provincial distinction doesn't, of course, entail that at all—but it is a matter of reassessing things, taking more things into account. So, a cosmopolitan will adopt views that are based on a wider range of options having encountered many more things, whereas the provincial is more likely to take as valid whatever is inherited: the inherited culture is the be-all and the end-all.

Once more, that's why these missionaries are so important. By the time you get to World War II, when the American government and the foundations and universities are interested in dealing more with the rest of the world—which they haven't done much up to that point—it's the missionaries and the missionaries' children who come to the fore.

When the universities develop the Foreign Area Studies programs during the twenty years after World War II, it's overwhelmingly missionary sons, like Edwin Reischauer or W. Norman Brown, who play integral roles.

There are many examples of this. When the OSS, the predecessor to the CIA, gets going, they need people who really know about these different parts of the world. They need spies who are good in Arabic, for example. Well, missionary sons are typically the ones who really know it.

There's a great case that I came across recently: a guy who had been born and raised in Beirut, Lebanon and came from a Presbyterian missionary family. He was a Marine veteran of World War I, and he comes back into the Marines in 1941 when the US enters World War II. And instantly, the head of the OSS, "Wild Bill" Donovan, who desperately needs spies who know Arabic, latches onto this guy.

He gets him from the Marine Corps and says, "*You're going to be my guy in North Africa—all of it.*" So, here's this missionary's son who goes off to North Africa; he's fluent in Arabic and can recite long passages of the Koran in three Arabic dialects. He's the guy that you want to go out and "deal with the Moors," as he called them.

Later on, he does the same thing in Saudi Arabia and Yemen. He's somebody who can actually organize against the Nazis in Vichy-controlled Algeria and Tunisia and Morocco at that time because he's fluent in these languages.

There are a number of examples like that, where it's the missionary children who will be brought in to perform these services. They also tended to be very sympathetic to local causes, like Arab nationalism, such as this fellow Bill Eddy I was just mentioning.

After the war he goes into the CIA (he's one of the designers of the CIA, in fact) and he keeps telling Truman, "*You know, we've got to be tuned in with the Arab nationalists. We have big interests over there, so the future of that part of the world should be important to us, and they rather like us. They don't like the British Empire, they like us.*"

Well, what happens in the dynamic of the Cold War, of course, is that the United States adopts more and more of a British-Empire perspective. We orchestrate the coup in Iran in 1953—throwing out Mosaddegh, putting in the Shah—and we support Israel against the Arab States. So there are a lot of things that change, but what's interesting about the missionary sons is that they were the ones who were most pro-Arab at a time when there was very deep anti-Arab prejudice in the United States.

HB: I suppose it's rather like Lawrence of Arabia.

DH: Yes.

HB: I mean, if you're out there and you get to know the people, you speak their language and you sympathize with their needs and desires and so forth, your perspective naturally changes.

There's a tactical aspect to this, clearly. If I want to run the American Intelligence Service, I need to have people who speak all sorts of different languages and who can sympathize with the locals on the ground.

DH: And very few people did. It was tough.

HB: Right. But on a larger level, this is a question of tolerance.

DH: That's right.

HB: It is a broader moral issue, an understanding of what makes us human. And this is, as I understand it, what the Ecumenical Protestants really reflected and put front and center as part of their agenda. This is what Reinhold Niebuhr was enunciating—albeit with some synoptic Christian context—the importance of these fundamental values of looking outside, of being a universalist.

DH: Yes.

Questions for Discussion:

1. How frequently do you think the notion that "everything is of equal value" is levelled at cosmopolitans by their critics as a natural consequence of their views?

2. How important is a genuine understanding of local sentiment for a successful implementation of foreign policy initiatives? Are there times when such an understanding might prove to be detrimental?

VI. William James

Interpretations and misinterpretations

HB: I'd like to switch gears for a little bit, now, to talk more about religion and science.

It seems to me that there's a strong Ecumenical Protestant link here too through William James that I'd like to get to, but first I'd like to back up and speak more generally about these processes that you specifically highlight for how Ecumenical Protestant values converge to those of the Enlightenment.

We've spoken about one already, this so-called "demographic diversification", where widespread interaction with people from a variety of different backgrounds naturally and inevitably leads to a broader, cosmopolitan perspective, and we've talked about the active role of missionaries in bringing this about.

Another process is something that you refer to as "cognitive demystification": how our sense of the truth changes as a result of our growing scientific awareness—that as our knowledge of science progresses, we have less and less recourse to regard the world around us in a mystical, spiritual, religious way.

This notion of science being the great slayer of religious superstition clearly had its roots in the Enlightenment and was significantly extended into the 19th century and beyond.

So now we come to William James, who strikes me as a fascinating fellow, not least because he appears to be claimed as a standard-bearer by just about everybody for just about every possible cause: science, religion, spirituality, psychology, empiricism, pragmatism, what have you.

You write about James in some detail in *After Cloven Tongues of Fire*. You talk about how he deliberately (and somewhat viciously) misrepresented W.K. Clifford's largely unread argument in *The Ethics of Belief* in James' much more famous lecture, *The Will to Believe*.

This was interesting to me for two reasons: first, because it's always fun to see public intellectuals duke it out, but also because I naively thought that all Clifford was spending his time on was mathematical stuff, like inventing Clifford Algebras, while it turned out that he was also preoccupied with making strong public pronouncements of his agnosticism.

But rather more substantially, it seems that James' principal agenda was to somehow find a way to marry scientific understanding with religion. More specifically, in *The Varieties Of Religious Experience*, he seemed to be trying to allow for some sort of well-founded presence of religion within a scientifically-dominated world. Is that a fair assessment?

DH: It is certainly the case that he is preoccupied with the religion-science issue, and he is afraid that science will eliminate religion altogether. He doesn't want this; and his "genius," you might say, is turning his anxiety about the situation into terms that were so creative that a great many people found them helpful in dealing with this.

Now, even though I think Clifford was a much clearer thinker than James was, James has been much more influential—hardly anybody reads Clifford any more. In fact, that paper of mine where I go back and analyze what Clifford actually said, is unusual in the literature because normally people just assume that James was correct about Clifford. But that's not really so important as what James did.

What James did was to denounce secularism with such vitriol that the very halting affirmations that he simultaneously made for religion were taken much more seriously than they would have been had they been examined in a vacuum that did not include his polemical anti-secularism, particularly his attacks on Clifford.

If you read his great works, *The Varieties of Religious Experience*, *Pragmatism*, and *The Will to Believe*, you see that he's surrounded by this Protestant culture, all these New England, Liberal Protestants that he's close to.

William James was unable to affirm a single, Christian doctrine—the religion that he affirms is so general that it reduces to a very abstract theism. Even there he vacillates: at times he even says he's not really a theist, while at other times he is. Yet *The Varieties of Religious Experience* provides four hundred pages of these religious experiences, and he encourages his readers to achieve intimate, empathic identification with all of these people who are experiencing this religious experience.

So it comes across as being very sympathetic with many aspects of religion, especially the Protestant examples. It's an anti-Catholic book in ways that a lot of people haven't figured out, because the religious experiences that he cites negatively are almost always related to these Catholic saints. It's a very Protestant book, a book which can be seen as an effort to vindicate an enlightened Liberal Protestant culture in an age of science by denuding the religious tradition of anything that might possibly conflict with science, but yet covering one's religious ground by being adamantly angry against all secularists.

That's the combination that really works for William James for a very long time. I would say that James is a great secularizer, in that he provides a lot of Protestants with the bridges of the sort that I was talking about earlier, bridges that the Ecumenical Protestants invoke in the '40s, '50s and '60s.

Many of the theologians who follow him, who try to be Jamesian Christians, find themselves going around and around in circles. There are a number of these books that came out in the early part of the 20th century that I've read and found fascinating, because they will say, "*We're going to affirm William James' view of Christianity,*" but then it turns out that they don't have that much to affirm.

They're very much trapped; and then the Fundamentalists go after them and say, "*Well, you're not really Christian at all, are you?*" which forces them to respond in often unusual ways.

For example, there's one guy—Ames, I think, at the University of Chicago Divinity School—who says, "*Well, you know, the trouble with the Bible is that it's an outrageously overrated book.*"

I mean, you're really on the edge of leaving the community of faith if that's your view of the Bible, and this is basically how James' followers think. The people who follow James and who actually read him, then, are entrapped.

There's another group of followers of James who don't read him with the depth that I think is appropriate—the philosopher Charles Taylor, for example—and there's a long tradition of using James' *The Will to Believe* and *The Varieties of Religious Experience* as a validator, as a way of saying that religion is okay.

Taylor is among the people who should know better, because he's such a bright guy and such a terrific philosopher, but I use him as an example just to show that there is this tradition of not really understanding James historically, but cherry-picking the quotes and his anti-secularism. One of the reasons that I wrote the two essays that you're talking about in *After Cloven Tongues of Fire* was to get out there both the historical James and what the historic function of William James is.

His historic function, I would argue, is in providing a series of bridges out of Protestantism towards post-Protestant secularism of the sort that he himself stood on the edge of. You can see this in James from 1882 all the way through his death in 1910. It's quite dramatic, actually, to see his writing: he will come right up to it and stop. There's something to be said for, as we said in the '60s, "*Breaking on through to the other side.*" He didn't.

Questions for Discussion:

1. To what extent could it be argued that the "bridges" that David refers to are really a glorified form of hypocrisy?

2. Does this chapter make you more, or less, inclined to read William James?

VII. Strident Atheists
Evangelism 2.0

HB: I'd like to pick up on the criticism that the Evangelicals directed towards William James and his followers, saying, in effect, *"Well, you're just a secularist,"* by investigating the line between "believers of the true faith" and "science" or "secular views".

Nowadays, there are often very heated arguments in the public sphere, at least in the US, about how religion is toxic and childish and how we must be able to move forwards into a secular world-view that organized religion is holding us back from.

There are two things related to this issue that occurred to me as I was reading your book.

The first is that, once again, I think one has to make a distinction between religion as evangelical metaphysical dogma and religion in this Ecumenical Protestant tradition that you've been talking about. In fact, I found it quite interesting that some of the spokespeople of Ecumenical Protestantism in the past, such as Reinhold Niebuhr, actually accused people like Billy Graham of having a child-like faith and being scientifically irresponsible in their belief and modern understanding.

This is, therefore, neither new nor something unheard of from those of a religious persuasion, so just portraying it as a battle between those of a completely atheistic or irreligious perspective against religious believers is actually misrepresenting not only what could be the case, but what has actually been the case historically.

The second point is that—again, as a non-American—I look at this and can't help but think of it all as rather weird, because there aren't too many other places in the developed world (perhaps with the exception of the UK with Richard Dawkins, although I'm not even sure about that) where the whole issue is that big of a deal.

Most people don't really care that much about this throughout the rest of the world. It's pretty well accepted that we live in an increasingly secular modern world, and people can believe what they want to believe.

You have written about the so-called New Atheists, Sam Harris in particular, and said that he would do well to recognize the historical fact that many Ecumenical Protestants had a very forward-thinking, scientifically responsible view, that he should be aware of history and not misrepresent, not only the present of the United States, but also its great traditions from the past.

DH: Well, yes, I am saying things like that. I think that there are several dimensions of this that invite a little bit more public scrutiny than has been applied so far.

One is that these New Atheists have a series of objections to what they call "religion" in general that are actually quite specific to conservative, orthodox, evangelical, fundamentalist religious movements.

The difficulty with the attacks on the New Atheists is that too many of their critics say, "*You guys don't understand. There's all this sophisticated religion, there's all us Ecumenical Protestants and all us Post-Vatican II Catholics, and you're not paying any attention to us.*" And that's the end of it.

Now, I think that's true, as far as it goes. I think that's a valid criticism of the New Atheists. The problem is that the New Atheists are calling attention to a set of ideas that are still very widespread in the United States, and that the Ecumenical Protestants and the Liberal Catholics would be better off attacking those *ideas*, which the New Atheists are on to.

This goes back to the point that the liberal religious people are too afraid of coming out strongly against the conservatives, too afraid of fracturing the community of faith.

So they dismiss the New Atheists for not understanding how sophisticated their religion is, but they fail to acknowledge that the New Atheists are really right about a lot of American religion. So, that's the spot that a lot of the conversation is in.

I'm actually more sympathetic with the New Atheists than a lot of others are because I think that they continue to call attention to a lot of obscurantist ideas that are still very widespread. And in that way they are performing a valuable function.

However, I think that their successor will do a much better job; and that's Philip Kitcher. He's a philosopher at Columbia whom I would recommend that you talk to. He's written a book on secular humanism, *Life After Faith: The Case for Secular Humanism*, and he has a critique of religion that is much better than anything that comes out of the New Atheists. So I'm hoping that Phil's work will supplant the New Atheists and be harder to dismiss.

HB: I'm sceptical, because I suspect that his press agent isn't as good as these other guys.

DH: Well, yes, there's that. That's certainly true.

But the conversation about the New Atheists is, I'm saying, more important than a lot of the press has granted, but it's important on different kinds of grounds. I also think that the New Atheists are a sign of the resurgence of a style of religious affirmation that many people had assumed was dead, and that's why your earlier comment is correct: that most people aren't worried about this anymore.

But in the United States it's suddenly come up, so that's one thing that's caused it. Another thing is that the rise of Islamic Fundamentalism as a world reality has also generated some of this.

Much of Sam Harris' writing is against Islamic Fundamentalism as well as American Evangelicalism, so that's one of the reasons that it's really come about. But your earlier point is right, that a lot of people have given up on this. It used to be said that Bertrand Russell was the "last Victorian" because he still thought it was an act of great courage not to believe in God.

Well, you've got all these people now raising it again, but that feeling about Russell's angst in his writings of the 1910s to the 1920s was a sign of the passing of that set of preoccupations on the part of a lot of European intellectuals.

Questions for Discussion:

1. What role do you think the spectre of Islamic Fundamentalism played in the success of the New Atheist movement?

2. How would you define "secular humanism" exactly?

VIII. An Empty Stage
America's intellectual exchange deficit

HB: Let's focus on the United States, though, and let's talk about the importance—which is something that you've also written quite a lot about and believe quite fervently in—of exchange of religious ideas in the public domain, particularly when people are using those religious ideas as a way of justifying or supporting public policy decisions.

Again, this seems to me to be something which is, if not uniquely American, not terribly widespread throughout the world outside of the United States and certainly not in many other modern liberal democracies: that people will stand up and resort to their affirmations of faith to justify a number of public-policy decisions and thereby attempt to end conversation, prevent debate, avoid a more detailed examination of the issues.

This is something that I know you feel quite passionately about. And I'm guessing that you're hoping, again, that people of the Ecumenical Protestant persuasion, who have a long history of open exchange, justifying beliefs, distinguishing between matters of personal faith and public policy, can step forwards into that vacuum.

DH: Well, I hope more of them do. I think that you're right, that that's an ongoing problem in American life and it's very hard for politicians to escape this. I mean, I just don't think that any avowed atheist has any chance of higher office in the United States.

There was a series of polls a few years ago—polls are important in this context, not so much because they tell you the truth, but because they tell you what people feel comfortable declaring—that said something like 95% of the people would have no trouble voting for an African-American or a woman for a president, but only 49%

would vote for an atheist. Now, that's a sign of the stigma that is still attached to atheism, and no politician can possibly go against that.

That naturally has a strong impact on the prevailing political landscape. Obama plays to this too. He's a fairly generic Ecumenical Protestant, I would say, and, he will bring in evangelists like Rick Warren in the interests of pluralism from time to time. He continues to play this game, as the politicians do.

What's particularly annoying to me is that there are a whole lot of these Republican politicians who will tell the public, "*You should vote for me because I'm a person of faith*," explicitly implying that this is somehow relevant to the performance of their public duties. But you can't ask them a question about their faith, because if you do that, you're "biased against religion", and you're one of these "arrogant intellectuals that's trying to tell the rest of the world what to think." Instead, you should, "Respect the man's faith!"

So there's *that* kind of reaction, and it's very pernicious. And you have, then, a whole domain of political justification that is ruled out of public discussion.

On the other hand, if we were to decide that religion is *not* relevant to public policy, then you could get away with perhaps not discussing it. Then you could say, "*Well, this is a private matter*," and a lot of Democrats have done that; although they're getting smoked out now, and feel compelled to sometimes wax eloquent on religious matters and get a picture of themselves coming out of a church holding their Bible.

This is an ongoing reality that maybe will be the last thing to change in terms of the secularization of the United States. One thing that could advance it, I think, would be a robust discussion of religious ideas, and the way to do this is to not start with the politicians—they're hopeless—but to get the rest of the society to be talking about this more forthrightly.

Once more I come back to these Liberal Protestants, to these Ecumenical Protestants. If they would come out and say what they *really* think about the ideas that are current at Fuller Theological Seminary in Pasadena, say, if they would come out and say what they really thought and risk losing some of their constituency, I think it would advance the civic health of the society, raise the intellectual level of the society and render what religion shall continue to exist more defensible.

But they're caught in this. And an example of their travail is that all of these traditional Liberal seminaries—Pacific School of Religion, University of Chicago Divinity School, Union Theological, Harvard Divinity School, Yale Divinity School—are in flux, they're in free fall. There are not that many smart, young people who want to become ministers anymore. What's to happen to these institutions?

The places that you might find leadership on this, then, are not coming out as leaders; instead, they're struggling to find what their institutional role would be. I don't want to pretend to know more about that than I do—I'm not on the inside of those conversations—but I'm mentioning it because I think the apparent collapse from within of the Ecumenical Protestant divinity schools is a sign of the continued decline of courage on the part of the Ecumenical Protestant leadership. They're in retreat. They're accepting more Evangelicals into their own schools than they used to, they're making all of these compromises. In some of the meetings that I've gone to, I've heard them say that, "*It's necessary to meet these people halfway.*"

Well, for the last couple hundred years, they'd been meeting secularists halfway too—and a good thing it was—but now they're afraid of this.

I had a particularly interesting exchange with the guy who was the former president of the Unitarian Universalist Association. I suggested that we need a robust public discussion of religious ideas and that they should lead it because this is very much in the Unitarian tradition of Theodore Parker and William Ellery Channing. The Unitarians are the people who did more than any other denominational community to liberalize American Christianity.

"*Do it now,*" I urged him.

"*No, if we do that, we will lose,*" he told me, "*Because the whole culture and the educational style of the United States is such that if you are too aggressive in attacking the Evangelicals, you'll diminish your standing even more."*

He, then, like a lot of the others, wants to make common cause on specific projects. For example, some of the Evangelicals are now interested in environmentalism, while others are interested in poverty-reduction programs. The idea is to join in, pragmatically, with what is basically a secular program—

HB: So that you can achieve some good in some domains.

DH: That's right. Now, I understand that. I can see why they do that, but since I believe that many of the things that are problematic about the culture of the United States today have to do with the continued currency of a lot of obscurantist ideas that cannot meet modern standards of cognitive plausibility, then I'm very eager for us to have a national conversation about those things.

When you look at where the most conservative of the political voices come from, they very often come from these evangelical sites, so that there is a connection between obscurantist, theological ideas and these reactionary, political ideas. I think we'd be better off if there was a more open debate about it. I don't see very many signs of it. In fact, I think that the press is afraid of this.

HB: Why? Why do you think that the press afraid of this?

DH: Well, these are big businesses; and so, without knowing an awful lot about it, I would think that the big media businesses are reluctant to take those kinds of chances.

HB: Right, but it seems that what you're saying needs to be carefully examined because, from my perspective, it seems that there are several, distinct points that you're making. You're not saying that everybody should be secular in the United States, you're not saying that we should do away with religion or religion is silly or anything like that.

It seems to me that what you're saying is that, in the first place, religion and religious views should be a private matter. If people believe in X or believe in Y or whatever it is, that's in their particular, private domain and that's fine and we should respect that.

You're probably even willing, I would submit, to recognize the cold political reality that, yes, it is likely advantageous for people running for political office to have pictures taken of themselves going into or out of church or carrying around a Bible or what have you, because we live in a democracy and people feel comfortable with people of their faith and so forth.

I don't think that particularly bothers you. But I think there is a line that is crossed when people start invoking sectarian religious principles to justify public policy in a country that is supposed to apply these things universally to all people.

In other words, it's completely inappropriate in a democracy to say, "*I believe in public policy A, B, C or D, and the reason that I do is because it necessarily resonates with my sectarian beliefs,*" and then impose that on a body politic which may or may not subscribe to those particular beliefs. That goes against fundamental, democratic principles.

Therefore, if you're saying, "*These are my public policy positions,*" be it because you're inspired by the word of the Bible or because you were visiting aliens last night or because you watched a television program or what have you, then, in fairness, in a non-sectarian, democratic plurality, you have to justify them on their own grounds without appealing to your particular, sectarian beliefs. Otherwise, it's just bullying basically. Otherwise you're just forcing people to absorb it somehow.

Isn't that what we're talking about here?

DH: Well, I would put it this way: I think the root distinction that we're looking for is between motivation and justification. One might have motives—you believe, say, that Israel is right because of the way that you read the Bible—but when you're talking about what American policy should be towards the Middle East, it should not be biblically-based, it should be because of an analysis of something which could be potentially accepted by somebody who did not operate on a biblical basis.

Policies might be appealing to an individual citizen of the United States—a politician—because of her own, personal orientation and religion, but when it comes to defending the policy prescription, defending the legislation, defending whatever is at issue, then the justification should be one that welcomes everybody into it. In other words, it should be a justification that is particular to the polity, rather than particular to the religion that might inform it.

The significance of the distinction is not to say that people shouldn't be religious, but that they should recognize that when they're operating as citizens of a polity, they have an obligation that is specific to that—to carry out those arguments—and much of life isn't political. Much of life is private. Much of life has to do with other kinds of activities.

So this is not an argument against churches, but it is an argument for a division of labour and for recognizing the value of a secular, pluralist, polity that—when you look at the history of the historically Christian West—has taken quite a lot of time and effort to achieve.

I always like to remind people that, with regard to the issue of church-state separation, the Confederate States of America put God in their Confederate Constitution because they knew it was significant that it wasn't in the US Constitution. They got the message and they acted on it. So there are these differences, and I think you're entirely correct in your reading of me on that.

HB: OK, but here's my question: what's wrong with CNN—or whomever—trying to bring this into the public consciousness? This isn't anti-religion, it's not impinging on people's right to believe, or even the power of the evangelical movement—they have the right to do whatever they want to win the hearts and minds of believers across the world and no one is suggesting anything to the contrary—but merely saying that there is the private sphere and there is the public sphere, and if we believe in these particular principles of our body-politic, than we should have a public discussion about that. Why would the media shy away from engaging in that particular effort?

DH: Well, I don't have a good answer to that. I was speculating a while ago that it had something to do with corporate interests, relations to advertisers and the necessity of maintaining connections. But I don't have a good answer to that. I would prefer, of course, that they do exactly what you've described, that they convene such a conversation, but I have seen very little signs of anybody wanting to do that.

The closest I've seen to that is that the Center for American Progress, a big Washington-based left-liberal think tank run by John Podesta, has convened several of these consultations.

I've done a couple things with them. E.J. Dionne and I did a debate there a few years ago in which they brought in about 50 or 60 heads of religious service organizations and we talked about this matter of how religion can play a more progressive role in the society.

But the thing broke apart on the lines that I indicated earlier: that there was a group of people who felt that our early task should be to recognize the importance that Catholic hospitals should not have to provide abortion services or even distribute contraceptives, and this was what was really important if we wanted to establish a rapport with religious groups.

Well, you can imagine how that went over with some of the rest of us. I'm struggling for another example. I would say that the Center for American Progress is the space where I have heard the most interest in pushing in this direction, but I haven't been in touch with them in the last couple years. I haven't seen any of the commentators show much interest in this. One of the *New York Times* op-ed columnists is pretty good on this—Frank Bruni, I believe.

However, *The Times* has this other guy, Ross Douthat, who's very much on the other side. I mean, the argument that you hear a lot is that the whole idea of the religion-political distinction is a mistake and that we should pull back from this and understand that a peculiarity of the American Constitutional tradition since 1789 is that it's just wrong.

HB: But you're advocating public discourse.

DH: I am.

HB: And if you advocate public discourse, then you are welcoming views and positions and statements from people across the political divide. You welcome people of a very different persuasion to your own, but it seems difficult for me to fathom why, if this is an issue—and it certainly seems to be—there shouldn't be a wider public discussion about it.

I'm coming back full circle, in a way, to this concept of American exceptionalism. So, you almost had me convinced that America's not all that exceptional and that the standard secularist, Weberian view actually *is* manifested somehow and you just have to look more carefully at immigration and the particularities of the American Constitution and at the role played by these Ecumenical Protestant leaders and so forth, but now I'm back to being convinced that you guys are all a bit wacky.

I mean, come on.

DH: Well, it's a matter of degree. There is all this reactionary religion out there and it's deeply connected with the Sarah Palin or Rick Perry type of politics; and state universities are under all of this pressure from these boards of regents to act in terms of these conservative ideas.

A couple of years ago, the education board of the State of Texas was debating, for a while, eliminating from the curricular goals of the public schools of Texas "training and critical thinking". The reason that they thought maybe they should drop that is because they were afraid it would undercut the values of the church and the home.

Now, there you have an example of extreme provincialism, but the fact that such notions could even get discussed is an example of where you're right, as a non-American, to think that we're really pretty crazy after all.

So, my arguments about the vindication of classic secularization theory need to be understood in terms of degree...

HB: That sounds like a very eloquent academic cop-out.

DH: It might well be understood that way, yes.

Questions for Discussion:

1. What role do you think the question of ownership of the American media play in these issues?

2. To what extent do you think your average American would be interested in a public discourse about religion and politics as outlined in this chapter?

IX. Future Speculations
Pushing a historian out of his comfort zone

HB: OK, time for my last question—you've been very gracious with your time

I'm now going to ask you to speculate a little bit and tell me what you think the United States, if not the world, is going to look like, in terms of religious movements, in fifty years. You point out that, in the 1950s in America, those leading intellectuals, the lights of the Ecumenical Protestant movement, did not believe that they were on a one-way road to perdition, as it were. At the time, they held positions of great stature and great influence, and they would have been, I think, very surprised to learn what was going to happen to their world in 50 or 60 years. Which makes one wonder that, perhaps, the people who are on top today will be very surprised at what will happen 50 or 60 years hence. Or not. Based upon your experience and historical knowledge, how do you see the United States of America 50 years from now?

DH: We historians are more resistant to this thinking.

HB: Sure. That's why it was my last question.

DH: Right. So, that's harder for me to engage at all, but I'll try to wing it, with the explicit understanding that this is not the sort of stuff that I'm as invested in.

I'm pretty heavily invested in my argument about the role of Ecumenical Protestantism in American history as well as a number of the other things that we've talked about, but when it comes to predictions I don't have a lot invested in one prediction as opposed to another.

But I will venture that the education gap in the United States will continue to propel more and more educated people in secular directions and will entrap more and more impecunious people in religious cultures. That the salient consideration would then be the hardening, the sharpening, of the class distinction, of the greater and greater gap between those who are well off and those who are not, the diminution of strong, public support for education. These things, it seems to me—coupled with the way that the electoral system produces Congress and the Senate and the kinds of public policies that will eventuate from a heavily Republican, even minority-dominated national government—seem to me to make it likely that we will continue with the current bifurcation.

I see us becoming a more and more divided society. I'm not happy about that. It's conceivable that this will eventually become so frightening that there will be more people motivated to try to stop that.

And we do have, in a number of our pundits—in my colleague Bob Reich, together with people like Paul Krugman and Nicholas Kristoff—those who are rightly concerned about this, but in the absence of more capacity to control basic resources in the society and to provide better education to more people, then I would be afraid that the bifurcation will continue and that secularization will apply increasingly to the more educated classes. President Obama was right, even though he was predictably blasted for it, when he went in to the Pennsylvania Appalachian area and said, *"These people are poor and they cling to their religion."* I think that's true.

That's the best I can do, sorry.

HB: That's good. There's no reason to apologize. Anything else? Anything we left out?

DH: Nope.

HB: Well, this was great, David. Thank you very much.

DH: Appreciate it.

Questions for Discussion:

1. Do you think that David's concerns about the future of America are in keeping with his views that the United States validates Weber's secularization thesis?

2. Do you agree or disagree with David's fears that the religious-secular divide in American life will continue to grow?

Continuing the Conversation

Readers are encouraged to read David's book, *After Cloven Tongues of Fire: Protestant Liberalism in Modern American History*, which goes into considerable additional detail about many of the issues discussed here.

Religion and Culture

A Historian's Tale

A conversation with Miri Rubin

Introduction

Cultural Contact

How does an Israeli chemistry student wind up becoming one of the world's foremost authorities on religious culture in the Middle Ages? Intriguingly, the answer has much more to do with pressures of the present than you might think.

Miri Rubin's undergraduate studies were suddenly interrupted by the Yom Kippur War, so instead of continuing her scientific studies she found herself volunteering in the orthopaedic ward of a Jerusalem hospital. When it was finally time to return to university, her worldview had been irrevocably altered.

> "I remember looking at the annual catalogue containing all the courses offered at Hebrew U, which is a great university. And I just fell on history, saying to myself, Actually, with wars, suffering, loss and all that makes you think about, I really want to understand. And I really want to understand in a way that only history can give me. So I enrolled in history."

And then, as so often happens, a particularly influential teacher took over.

> "I'd never studied the Middle Ages before. And amongst all the excellent teachers I had that year, one simply soared. He's a totally amazing medievalist, still active. His name is Ron Barkai.

> "We were studying the Crusades; and in addition to his deep knowledge of the Crusades he also had the advantage of knowing Islam culture very well because his family had come from North Africa and he had excellent Arabic.

"So the whole vantage point we had on the Crusades was not as had traditionally been taught—this sort of amazing medieval phenomenon, one of the great achievements and events of its time—but actually much more like what we might call today "a cultural encounter", or perhaps even "a clash of civilizations"—something much, much more textured.

"And I remember that in the first class we looked at the attitude to war in Islam and Christianity. We read a bit of the Koran—nowadays, it's par for the course, but at the time, in the seventies, it certainly wasn't generally done. But he did it. That was my introduction to medieval history; and I was absolutely hooked."

Now an internationally renowned professor of medieval and early modern history at Queen Mary University of London with a wide range of deeply influential publications on topics ranging from the history of the Virgin Mary to the Eucharist to an analysis of anti-Jewish sentiment in the Middle Ages, Miri has consistently turned her attention to examining the unique impact that religious culture has on a wide variety of people in different times and places.

"I wanted to understand to what extent living within a religious culture makes people do or not do things, whether there is any type of structure to it and how it changes over time. I see religion as a sort of historical force that interacts with other things. It's a cultural force. It's not something that obeys other rules, as it were."

And in order to best comprehend that force, Mary insists, it's vital to develop the broadest possible perspective of our surrounding environment, regularly urging her students to twin detailed scholarly investigations with a deliberate appreciation of other cultural forces.

"When I was talking about the making of a historian, I alluded to the fact that going off to seminars, apparently not on your topic, is a good thing. I would say, even more. You have to read widely. You have to listen to music. You have to go to the theatre. You've got to talk to people. It's really, really important.

"That extra hour of reading, yet another article in the evening, rather than watching a film or reading a book or even cooking a meal—I think it's a false economy. You need to hear sounds and have thoughts that aren't from the echo chamber of your scholarship."

While Miri's route to becoming an eminent medieval scholar might seem particularly unusual and serendipitous, a closer examination reveals a common theme throughout: a steadfast determination to increase her awareness of the world around her, both past and present.

These days, some might label such an approach as "interdisciplinary". But for Miri, it's simply the only way to achieve genuine cultural understanding.

The Conversation

I. Historical Beginnings
From Jerusalem to Cambridge

HB: I would like to start with your background, trying to get a sense of the story of how you became a medievalist.

MR: I never meant to be a historian. I actually started studying chemistry at university.

HB: Oh, really?

MR: Yes. I had a brilliant chemistry teacher. I had wonderful teachers. I went to one of the best schools in, I would say, the Middle East? Maybe the world? It's in Jerusalem—a highly selective, really brilliant high school. And we had wonderful teachers in all subjects.

I grew up in Israel, and from the age of 12 I was in Jerusalem. I went to a brilliant high school and had fantastic teachers literally in all subjects. I'm not exaggerating. They were incredible.

HB: But you had a particularly good chemistry teacher.

MR: I had a really charismatic chemistry teacher. And at the time—we're talking the seventies—there weren't so many girls doing science, definitely not at university. There was a special sort of cachet to it. The sentiment was: *If you can do it, you ought to pursue it—lots of people can do other things, but since there were so few women in science you should consider that if you could do it well.*

So I went to university and I studied chemistry in the first year. And then we had a great and devastating war, the Yom Kippur War, which started at the beginning of October, just before the academic year was about to begin.

I was going to enter my second year, but that wasn't going to happen because everyone was at the front. A lot of the people I knew—young people, soldiers—were killed. So with the education not starting at university, I just went and presented myself in a hospital and worked. And I worked for about 10 months in Hadassah Hospital in Jerusalem.

HB: What sort of things did you do?

MR: I just helped out as best I could. It was in the orthopaedic ward, mostly a ward that dealt with amputees, really young men who'd lost a leg or more.

I suppose nowadays it would be called "physician's assistant" or something, I did everything and anything—you just did what you could. And that experience made me rethink everything, really.

I remember a day in the hospital where one of the top professors in another ward, who was the father of a friend of mine and used to see me regularly in the corridors, said to me, "*Look, Mary, that's enough. Things are getting back to normal* (it was now winter time), *you've done your bit. Now you have to think about your future.*"

A hospital can be a very captivating environment. It's almost like an Erving Goffman-type of total institution. You could do everything there: sleep there, eat there, shower there. You could just live there and be totally engrossed by your surroundings.

So I remember looking at the annual catalogue containing all the courses offered at Hebrew U, which is a great university. And I just fell on history, saying to myself, *Actually, with wars and suffering and loss and all that makes you think about, I really want to understand. And I really want to understand what only history can give me.* So I enrolled in history.

HB: So, if I can just interject for a moment: before the war broke out when you were studying chemistry, were you basically happy with your courses?

MR: They were a little bit on the dry side, and the people I met with were terrifically earnest and I was sort of young and silly. So I did find the social environment a bit boring, but it was basically fine.

HB: So you likely would have continued had it not been for these external circumstances.

MR: I probably think I would have done, yes.

There's a very distinctive structure to the history course in Jerusalem, whereby in your first year—because they assume that you know really very little, except for perhaps the history of Israel and some Jewish history or a very thin survey of other histories—they require that you take courses on ancient, medieval, early modern and modern history, a lecture and a seminar in each.

So by the end of the first year, at least you know something about a whole lot of different periods. I'd never studied the Middle Ages before. And amongst all the excellent teachers I had that year, one simply soared. He's a totally amazing medievalist, still active. His name is Ron Barkai.

He was then doing his own PhD, in fact, and was earning a living by teaching. We were studying the Crusades; and in addition to his deep knowledge of the Crusades he also had the advantage of knowing Islam culture very well because his family had come from North Africa and he had excellent Arabic.

So the whole vantage point we had on the Crusades was not as had traditionally been taught—this sort of amazing medieval phenomenon, one of the great achievements and events of its time—but actually much more like what we might call today "a cultural encounter", or perhaps even "a clash of civilizations"—something much, much more textured.

And I remember that in the first class we looked at the attitude to war in Islam and Christianity. We read a bit of the Koran—nowadays, it's par for the course, but at the time, in the seventies, it certainly wasn't generally done. But he did it.

That was my introduction to medieval history; and I was absolutely hooked. And then in the second year I had another totally brilliant teacher, Benjamin Kedar, who introduced me to concepts of economic history as well as the general methodology of thinking through historical arguments of any kind. And then it just continued from there: I did my MA in Jerusalem as well and encountered many very brilliant teachers.

The interesting thing about Hebrew U, and it's still true today, is that although we're tucked away in the Middle East with all our problems and challenges, culturally Israel sees itself absolutely part, if not at the forefront, of what you might call the "Western cultural sphere".

This is actually recognized by the EU: although Israel is clearly not a member of the EU and a lot of Europeans rightly have a lot of criticism on the state of Israel, the country is allowed to participate in all sorts of collaborative programs because it is recognized as having a lot to give.

HB: Perhaps it will replace the UK at some point.

MR: Ugh. Another painful point.

HB: Sorry.

MR: At any rate, while we recognized that we were geographically far from the centre of things, we wanted to be—and we felt that we merited being—part of that world, partly also because so many of the people who were living in Israel, had created the state, or were coming to it, were from European backgrounds. We have all the languages. It's common still in Israel for world literature to be translated very, very quickly into Hebrew and very, very high levels of translation, because you always have native bilinguals from a given country and Hebrew.

So that meant that all the people who taught me had been educated at the world's top universities. And there was a particular moment where the new historiography that was coming out of France, the *Annales* school, and its American offshoots like Princeton, was where my teachers had studied.

HB: So there was a direct influence.

MR: Absolutely. At the beginning of every academic year—I really remember this when I was an MA student—our teachers would have just returned from their summers of research in Europe.

And during the first gathering of the advanced seminars was all about hearing what's new, what new ideas are out there: *What is Jacques Le Goff doing now? What is Emmanuel Le Roy Ladurie thinking?* and so on.

So one can see it as a slavish following, but actually it was a real commitment to being engaged in the history that was happening. We *religiously* read the *Times Literary Supplement* to know about new books, even if they were always so expensive we couldn't dream of buying them, and perhaps not even ordering them from the library.

So although I was in Jerusalem—which in some sense, of course, is the centre of the universe to many religions—but we were in some sense provincial, but we didn't *feel* provincial.

And our aspirations, definitely those who took history seriously, were absolutely the highest in terms of our being part of some sort of global conversation about history, and in terms of what we would do when we reached the stage of deciding on our projects.

For example, during my MA in the late 70s, I did a paper on popular religion and the study of popular religion for the Middle Ages. Can it be done? Can we find sources?

This was a subject that was then extremely hot, only beginning to be explored seriously by medievalists. But to us, it came naturally. Why? Because my brilliant teacher, the late Michael Heyd, interacted with Natalie Davis, interacted with Ted Rabb, was totally part of these amazing circles of the reception of *Annales* in the top American universities. So we never felt provincial, and therefore we all went abroad for our PhDs.

HB: And of course, as you were saying, you definitely *weren't* provincial since faculty and students had direct contact with leaders of the field, you were integrated into the forefront of global scholarship.

MR: That's absolutely true. We were geographically provincial, but intellectually we felt that we belonged to the centre. And we knew it could be done because we saw all these people around us who had done it, younger teachers who had just come back from their PhDs, keen to disseminate all the latest ideas. So that was very exciting.

When I decided I wanted to do a PhD, I had to find some funding somewhere. At the time the British Council still had some very attractive bursaries or scholarships for PhDs. For personal reasons, the idea of going to America for so long wasn't a suitable choice.

But I applied for the British Council funding and I got it; and after having written to a number of really great scholars in Britain, I decided to go to Cambridge.

I didn't choose my supervisor; my supervisor was allocated to me: the quite extraordinary Christopher Brooke, who sadly died in December 2015, and who was the most welcoming and helpful supervisor imaginable for someone who had come from abroad.

He introduced me to having a glass of sherry. He showed me how to engage with extremely crusty archivists and college librarians.

HB: Those are two very salient pedagogical experiences, I'm sure.

MR: For coming to do an Oxbridge PhD, absolutely. I remember everything he taught me and try to convey it to my own PhD students now.

Meanwhile, intellectually, there was naturally a determination to maintain a commitment to a new type of social and cultural history as represented by the *Annales* school. And in a way, when I came to Britain, I had to keep a lot of that to myself. I don't mean it was dangerous knowledge, but it wasn't widely shared at all in Britain. I frequently had to actually explain to people what was exciting about that French vision of history. And that continued for decades. In some ways it still continues.

HB: Were there other aspects of cultural acclimatization that you struggled with when you first came to England from Jerusalem? So intellectually, in terms of your dispositions towards one approach or another, I appreciate that there might have been some differences, but

I imagine that, more generally, there might have been some non-trivial adjustments that you had to make as well.

MR: Well, Cambridge is both very distinctive, but also very international. There were lots of people who were finding their way—perhaps not so much in medieval history. At the time, medieval history tended to be a bit more homogenous in terms of recruiting mostly British people, which is no longer the case today.

Of course, this was before '92, which levelled out access for European students to come in, and now Cambridge is full of European students and I hope that can last. So amongst the medievalists, it was more monocultural, I would say.

And there's always kindness, and there's always shared interests, but there were definitely ways in which I had to prove myself.

So while I described Jerusalem as a place where the new thinking was available, at the same time the University of Jerusalem was founded by central European professors and the traditions of education were also very *traditional* in some ways. I had my languages, I had my paleography, I had my diplomatics. So it was a wonderful combination of having the necessary skills—although I had to adapt, I had to learn to read English hand because I worked on England for my PhD—but I also had that extra historiographical awareness that wasn't so evident here.

And I remember there was a very nice man who was doing a PhD in English political history while I did my own, which was to be on charitable activity in medieval England, particularly concentrating on East Anglia. And we'd go to the library dutifully every day.

There were seminars in the late afternoon, so after spending the day at the library I'd be on my bike going off to a 5 o'clock seminar. And I remember that he absolutely marvelled at why it was that I went to seminars, say, on the early modern, or I went to seminars in the department of anthropology occasionally, or I went to lectures in art history and so on.

He was convinced that all that was simply a waste of time, really. He thought it was some sort of disease that I had. But to me it was absolutely natural that if you're a historian, you're an intellectual: you have to know *a lot* of things, and it's a practice that's extremely interdisciplinary at its best.

HB: I appreciate that this is just one example, but how much do you think that such an attitude is attributable to the culture of specialization that tends to be fairly pervasive in this country, as opposed to something particularly endemic to Cambridge?

MR: I think it was widely shared throughout the country, but given that Cambridge is an excellent place with an abundance of very smart and committed people, maybe it was even more so there, in a strange way.

Although there were amazing resources. There was a series in art history given regularly every year, looking at cycles in art, cycles of paintings, by a remarkably brilliant expert on Italian art. It was absolutely full, but it was full of retired people and experts in the field and people from the great public.

Now, it will be different, because I think interdisciplinarity has made a tremendous way. In history, there is an increased awareness of the fact that when you talk about cultures, that pertains to areas of life that are interlocking. So I think that has changed for the better, but it was very, very different then.

HB: I'm guessing that you would say that Hebrew University had more of what we would call a "continental tradition" in terms of its general orientation.

MR: Definitely. I think it was highly continental in a number of senses when it came to the culture of academia.

For example, professors had their assistants, who were there to support them in many ways. Some people asked very little of their assistants, while others asked a lot.

I became an assistant in my third year of undergraduate studies, and I enjoyed very much working with my professor, who was a Byzantine historian, which exposed me to many fascinating aspects of Byzantine history, which was excellent. He's an elderly gentleman now, but he's a very considerable scholar. So that was very enriching.

But it did mean that the hierarchy was very, very clear: the student sought to please the master, sought to please the teacher. And that can be a great incentive. We also had the tradition of the *Hochseminar*, this really high-powered seminar of crunching texts and problems, led by the professor, which was an amazing training ground.

As you know, it's Leopold von Ranke who invented the seminar in the University of Berlin in the second quarter of the 19th century. The idea of a *seminarium* was, literally, a place where you plant the seeds that will grow into historians.

So that really dense training ground was very much something that we recognized, and it isn't so common in the British tradition.

In fact, I have a revealing anecdote about that. Shortly after I came to Cambridge and began working with the aforementioned wonderful Christopher Brooke, who was so helpful and kind, introducing me to librarians and archivists and so forth, I felt a little perplexed because after a few weeks he hadn't asked me to do anything for him.

So I assumed that he was holding back, thinking, *She's new. She doesn't know where to find anything. She doesn't know where the books are or the photocopy machines*. I imagined that he was waiting for me to "go native" and then I could be of use.

And after a few more weeks of this, at the end of one of our supervisions in the second month or so I asked him, *"Professor Brooke, is there something I can do for you?"*

He looked at me literally bemused, before asking, *"What do you mean?"*

"Well," I said, *"I can go to the library. Do you need any books or things?"* Because that's what I took for granted.

And he said, *"Oh, I may see you in the library; I'm going over there to do my own research."* It was clearly a sort of misunderstanding. We once discussed it a few weeks later and he said, *"Miri, to me, supervising you, that's a privilege, it's an honour to be training the new historians. You don't have to do anything for me other than doing your work."*

Of course I'm *not at all* suggesting that the system I came from was abusive or something like that, because we learned a lot—it's just totally different.

If you think about the history of the tutorial system at both Cambridge and Oxford, you begin to appreciate aspects of that difference. Certainly, tutors were the experts; they were the teachers and they had a certain amount of authority.

But those who they were traditionally teaching until the great democratization of education in the 20th century, were often their "social betters"—they were often "tutors to the great"—so a certain diffidence in the relationship may have crept in that became a sort of tacit tradition that no one reflected upon.

But this notion of *asking* a student to do something for you, I have literally never heard that happen in any PhD situation in this country—except, of course, in the last decade or so, where some PhDs are funded by designated research funding, where they only literally paid to be part of a project. That has introduced a totally different power relationship, and those people are very happy to have the funding and therefore accept that framework.

But on the whole, the way it's looked at here—and I certainly share that sentiment—is that supervising PhD students is one of the best things we do, in many ways it's the most enjoyable thing we do. And it was absolutely evident when I came to Cambridge that that is what my supervisor thought.

At the beginning of every meeting, he would take out his diary and put in the date for the next meeting. So I was never in a position of a supplicant: ringing—because those days one rang—or writing notes or asking to see him. He was always serving me. It was really quite extraordinary. I mean, he was an extraordinary man, but I think he was just the absolutely finest example of a tradition that was truly there.

HB: Did you ever experience any discrimination because you are a woman? Perhaps I should add by way of explanation that I had a conversation some time ago with Margaret Jacob (*Enlightened Entrepreneurialism*), and she talked about how in the early days of her research career, it was noteworthy when a male historian was *not* at least insinuating something or to some extent abusing a power relationship with a woman. What you're describing to me seems like impeccably respectful behaviour, being treated with complete equality. Was that, by and large, your experience throughout your scholarly career?

MR: It was absolutely my experience. But remember, amongst medievalists, there's always a vast number of female students. And that helps.

There are subjects where you're the only woman—even subjects in history, areas of history, where women are not so visible. There are some amazing examples of really extraordinary women, such as the great Eileen Power, and many more.

But I would say that, in terms of getting jobs and research fellowships and postdoctoral positions, I think that men were on the whole more successful than women.

And I think that was also reflected by the fact that when I arrived, there were still quite a few single-sex colleges in Cambridge. And indeed, when I began to apply for research fellowships in '84 or '85, quite a few colleges I could not apply to because they didn't have female fellows—they didn't have females at all. That, of course, is all now in the past.

But I'm sure that gendered attitudes were there in terms of implicit aspects of sociability and so on. I definitely had interactions with people who were in positions of power, but I did not feel that.

I would say if anything, the most conspicuous thing about my case was the notion that here was this Israeli person who doesn't come from the Christian tradition who wants to work on Christian religion in the Middle Ages. People just sort of marvelled at that.

I remember the great Peter Burke once saying to me, "*Miri, you are an anthropologist of medieval religion, because you come to it so much like someone who just wants to find out and has absolutely no visceral or emotional childhood memories of going to Mass, or anything of the kind.*"

There was an amazing woman called Dorothy Owen, who used to teach paleography and codicology—she was keeper of manuscripts in the Cambridge University Library. I think she taught totally out of the kindness of her hard: she used to sit there with three or four people, reading English manuscripts.

And I remember we did dating. Often the date is given as a saint's day. And I remember once that we had a dating that was Saint Barnabas Day, so I had to look up Saint Barnabas Day, because I didn't have it at my fingertips. And she turned to me and coolly informed me when it was, as if it was common knowledge. Quite frankly, nobody else in the room knew.

So there was just occasionally that sort of thing, but it really wasn't serious at all. I was fortunate in that sense, but if people tell me or you that they had other experiences, I certainly can't dismiss it. I think I was fortunate.

HB: Let me return to the remarks you just made about bringing a more, shall we say, "cultural anthropologist" persuasion than others to the subject of medieval Christianity. I would have imagined that most people who would be studying religion, culture and tradition in the medieval era would be looking at it from that sort of perspective, rather than trying to necessarily grapple with their personal experiences when they were 10 at Mass or what have you.

Were you yourself struck by a sense of uniqueness in so far as you were able to be more objective or you had more of an anthropological orientation?

MR: Well, I don't use the word objective usually. Because I think we all bring something to the situation through our own past experiences. You might well say that as someone who comes from the Jewish tradition perhaps I brought a more sceptical outlook—so we all bring something and let's not use the word "objective".

But I would say that the fact that people have this commitment to their tradition doesn't mean that they're bad at it. Christopher Brooke himself was an absolutely devout Christian. And it was made absolutely clear in everything he did that this mattered a great deal to him. And yet he was one of the most acute observers of, for instance, the possibilities of folly, competition and ugly relations within a monastery.

He wrote wonderful work about forgeries—forgeries of relics, forgeries of hagiographies—when houses had to write up a text about their alleged founder because they needed that support for their claims in order to survive.

So it's possible. And of course his great teacher was David Knowles who had been a monk for most of his life and was the great historian of monasticism whose work is still extremely important.

So I'm not suggesting that it's impossible to do it well and that people need to shed everything they know and have, but that relationship has to be somehow problematized and made explicit.

And it's much more explicit when you get an Israeli woman coming in and doing it: it makes people think about it more.

But again, with the much greater historiographical and conceptual acuity that I think we all carry around these days, even a person who is studying a cultural history that is aligned more or less with her own tradition would probably have a lot of tools to reflect on that in a creative manner.

I should also say that at the time when I was finding my way as medieval historian, there was a quite extraordinary historian of the Reformation who died far too young, R.W. Scribner, who was doing the most extraordinary work on the 16th century and was also very interested in the late medieval.

He famously used all sorts of approaches: he used visual sources, he used anthropology, he was extremely widely read in the social sciences.

So although there weren't many amongst the medievalists, there was definitely Bob Scribner, Peter Burke, and other amazing people. That's why I hung up with the early modernists so much.

HB: If I can just back up for a moment before we move forwards into more details of your work. As both an undergraduate and Masters student at Hebrew University who is impressed, or has impressed upon her, an interest and an excitement in medieval history by some particularly influential teachers.

Do you think the fact that you were living in Jerusalem played any role in interests in the Crusades, say, and gave them a particular appeal in a way that something like Asian history or even the French Revolution might not have had?

MR: Well, I should just say that all these sorts of personal reflections, are bound to be somewhat fanciful.

HB: Sure. I'm not looking for anything objective. I've learned my lesson.

MR: Right. But I would say that our bit of medieval Europe, as you rightly say, was the Crusades and their heritage. So we studied it thoroughly.

We had one of the leading historians of the Crusades in the world, Joshua Prawer, as our teacher of medieval history. We sat at his feet. We learned a great deal from him. We all wrote papers, endless papers, on the Crusades, because that is something we could do.

Also, happily, most of the chronicles of the Crusades, and a lot of the charters of the Crusades, had been published. So we had them in the library. We could study them. These were subjects we could do.

And, indeed, my MA was Crusades-related because that's something you could actually do in Jerusalem—if you wanted to do archival research, you had to go elsewhere.

But even more importantly, I was in Jerusalem. And Jerusalem, with all the pain and the sorrow and the division and the chasms, is the city where you really see that people can *also* live side by side and just about get on.

And so it is in Jerusalem that you learn about the diversity of Christianity: that Christianity isn't just Catholicism, it's also Greek Orthodox, and Armenian and Syriac and Ethiopian and so on.

And whenever we had any foreign guests, medieval scholars coming to lecture or to a conference, we would take them to *our* bit of the medieval world, which is of course the remnants from Crusader Jerusalem: The Church of the Holy Sepulchre, The Church of Saint Anne—intermingled, of course, with all the remains from the medieval Islamic city, the Mamluk city which then followed.

We really studied that thoroughly. We know our medieval Jerusalem very, very well. And that's something that you take away. It's a store of images and texts that's extremely powerful in terms of any sense of what religion can be.

HB: You spoke earlier about the international aspect of Hebrew University, feeling that you were fully integrated in the Western scholarly tradition. Most institutions directly encourage their students to go elsewhere to do their higher degrees in order to be exposed to different traditions and influences. Were you explicitly encouraged to do your doctorate elsewhere after your MA?

MR: Without any doubt. Other universities in Israel actually do it programmatically: they really go out there and find the funding for people. At Jerusalem, you had to do it yourself, but you got a lot of support, a lot of just word of mouth type of support from teachers who had to go through the whole thing ten years earlier, telling you how to go about it.

They strongly supported us as best they could—with references obviously—but generally in any way possible. Yes, absolutely. And in my year I can think of two scholars who went off to the United States at the same time. So yes, you were very much expected to do that.

HB: Was this mostly in the Anglosphere, or were there also many that were going to Paris or other places on the continent?

MR: Paris as well, most definitely, although the funding wasn't so obvious. But in America, if you go to a top university then the tradition is that the university supports your research wherever you have to go, whether it's in Europe or elsewhere.

And there was quite a difference with our colleagues in Jewish history at the time. This is quite important as well, something that has changed for the better, I think. Jerusalem was unsurprisingly a big centre for the study of Jewish history, but it was a totally different department. It was in a different building, and we never met. The sociology of the students was totally different. People doing Jewish history tended to be students who came from more traditional, and indeed religiously observant, backgrounds, as were the teachers.

And you could literally study just "history" in Jerusalem, the Department of General History—*Allgemeine Geschichte*—without ever learning anything about the history of the Jews. That's how it was organized.

Now, as it happened. I did some elective courses in Jewish history; and because I was doing so much on the Crusades, with my aforementioned wonderful teacher, I decided to do a course on the massacres of the Jews in 1096, which happened in the course of the Crusades and inspired the creation of a vast literature of poetic laments, chronicles and so on.

And you could not imagine a greater separation. I mean, when I studied the Crusades in the general history department, of course I discovered that these massacres had occurred, because they're also mentioned in the Latin sources.

And that's what encouraged me to go and do the course on the Jewish history side, but at the time there was literally nothing discussed there. Why do people go on Crusade? What do these Christians think about the Jews they were killing to produce the sources that we were studying? There was nothing there at all. That would not happen today.

There has been a real rapprochement and people who train themselves in Jewish history, well, a lot of the best ones are quite cognizant of these issues, they often know Latin and so forth. There are some amazing figures, like Israel Yuval in Jerusalem, who is as good a medievalist as I am on the Christian side as he also is on the Jewish sources. So that has changed as well.

HB: Is there still a strong correlation between those who study Jewish history and those who are observant Jews?

MR: I think it's still very noticeable.

HB: Did you meet with any confusion when you first came to Cambridge, a false conflation of identity, the belief that because you were a young Israeli woman, therefore you were necessarily a religious observant Jew?
There does tend to be a broader lack of comprehension, even today—perhaps not so much among amongst academics, but certainly amongst the general public—that one can be proudly attached to a Jewish cultural tradition without necessarily being religiously inclined at all. Did you experience any of that personally?

MR: There was, above all, a real ignorance. I mean, Israel was already much, much criticized in the world—and for very understandable reasons, of course—and then, of course, came the first Intifada, and then the second Intifada, and now Gaza, so Israel's pariah position, let's say, in certain circles only grew over the period that I've lived in this country.
And, indeed, in Israel *itself* the dissent has become sharper. So what I experienced personally was a much, much tamer version of any of that— there was a sort of timidity, a determination to "just not go there". I remember in one of the first drinks parties I went to—I had to get used to these drinks parties where everyone is standing around—

HB: Which is why your supervisor kindly introduced you to drinking sherry.

MR: Well, exactly—thanks to Christopher, I could hold my own.

So I remember one of my first drinks parties in Cambridge, I encountered a young man who was doing his PhD, and when he found out that I was from Israel, he said, *"Oh, you've done amazing things with irrigation haven't you?"*

HB: You did.

MR: Like, in 1981, the most appropriate thing to say about Israel is the irrigation! I mean, of course, it is utterly brilliant, but is that what trips off the tongue when there are all these settlements, when you have a painful issue of occupation that is distressing so many Israelis as well as everyone else, when the hopes for peace are raised and then dashed...

HB: And here you're David Ben-Gurion all of a sudden, making the desert bloom.

MR: Yes, exactly: I'm suddenly Ben-Gurion in the Negev with the tomatoes. But I could see that it was really said out of a form of embarrassment.

These days, what tends to happen is quite the opposite. A friend of mine was telling me that she was at a dinner in Cambridge a few weeks ago and when the person sitting next to her learned that she was from Israel he just announced, *"Well, I'm a supporter of Hamas."* And that was the end of the conversation.

So what I'm saying is that there used to be a lot more timidity around the issue. It's also true that, because I speak English somewhat with an American accent—because I was born in America, my parents were American and we spoke American at home—people didn't know quite what to make of me, so they just didn't go there. Because on the whole, the English don't like to embarrass others or themselves. On the whole.

HB: Or even speak frankly, most of the time.

MR: Well, that's related.

But I did have one very shocking experience, which was in the Lent of the first year I was there. There's a wonderful tradition at Kings College that there's always a performance of one of the Bach Passions, and this time it was the St. Matthew's Passion. So I put my pennies together—I was extremely penurious—and went with a colleague from my college who was training to become a teacher, a lovely Welsh person who had a beautiful singing voice, I shan't mention her name.

This was a big event. It was March, but it was a snowy March. We crossed over The Backs and into King's and we went to hear this glorious music. But St. Matthew's Passion is, well, St. Matthew's Passion.

And as we were walking back across the snow, this person—who had been a real friend of mine—turned to me and said, *"Miri, why is it that the Jews always make trouble? Jesus was just there. He didn't mean any harm to anyone—why do the Jews always reject and make trouble?"* And she honestly asked the question.

MR: And I was just speechless. I mean, how do you even *respond* to something like that?

So that was quite an education for me. She was a nice person who was going to be a teacher. She herself came from a people who have known, after all, periods of conquest and oppression.

And there was just no sense of awareness somehow, but there was also no sense about how culture mediates ideas: how Bach sat there and read biblical commentaries—we now know this, there's a wonderful book about it—that took the Bible and turned it into a particular type of interpretation. And that is what he used: we have his annotated Bible. We know what he was reading when he composed it. But there was none of that. There was none of that understanding or awareness at all.

I'm not at all suggesting that it came from some sense of Welsh chapel, not at all. These are dissident Christians on the whole, dissident traditions, it's rather just a sort of general unknowing. And I think we're far more knowing about religious traditions right now. We've had to become reeducated in religion in the last 10 or 20 years.

HB: You think so?

MR: I think we are, yes. I see it in the curriculum that my son studied at school. But we've had to, because religion is now in our midst, it's not going away.

It's not a remnant; it's with us. It takes new forms, but it's with us. So I think we're less ignorant on the whole about religions and definitely a person who is going to be a teacher would be far, far better informed nowadays, I think.

I would also say that Britain has become more diverse. People definitely know much, much more about Islam, but they also might know more about European Catholicism, say, because we have schools with lots of Polish students and Baltic students.

So the whole issue of religion is not going away. Look at the Iranian revolution, let alone American evangelicalism. It's a force in the world.

Questions for Discussion:

1. Do you think Miri would have ended up as a historian even had the Yom Kippur War not broken out after her first year at university?

2. To what extent do you think Miri's repeated references of the number of "brilliant teachers" she has had is a strong reflection of her own enthusiasm for the educational experience?

3. Are historians on the whole more broad-minded and more wide-ranging in their interests than most other academics? If so, why do you think that is?

II. Life on the Ground

Hope, human agency and hemorrhoids

MR: Gosh, this has become very autobiographical.

HB: Yes. That's a common practice in these conversations, but in your case it seems particularly relevant because I'm trying to piece together an understanding of the personal context associated with someone who is clearly so interested in religious and cultural aspects from a variety of different perspectives.

You've written on a wide array of related topics—the Virgin Mary, Christian charity, the Eucharist, William of Norwich—and you've obviously given a lot of thought to the interplay of religion and culture in different societies, both past and present. You mentioned your upbringing, or at least aspects of life in Jerusalem, where there have been both many military and cultural clashes, but also long periods of people living relatively harmoniously next to one another.

So I imagine that all of that has played a significant role in your personal orientation and outlook and, in turn, has influenced your scholarship. But maybe that's not the best way to look at things. After all, we probably wouldn't have talked much about any of this had you become a celebrated chemist.

MR: Probably the best way to put it would be that the teachers who most excited me were those who opened up the Middle Ages to me, and then a whole lot of enriching, enhancing possibilities were available in a city like Jerusalem to make that seem a sensible project to engage with. That's probably it.

But I wanted to understand to what extent living within a religious culture makes people do or not do things, whether there is any type of structure to it and how it changes over time. I see religion as a sort of historical force that interacts with other things. It's a cultural force. It's not something that obeys other rules, as it were.

Take the idea of giving to the poor. This was the subject of my first book based on my PhD thesis—I was able to look at how, within the Christian tradition, within the culture created around Christian ideas and practices, there developed a particular orientation towards charity and it was preached and it was taught and it was represented on wall paintings and people absorbed it, and so forth.

And as they built cities, or as they wrote their will—all sorts of acts that are not primarily of the religious domain—this informed what they did: what they did with their sources, what they did with their spare time; and how they wanted to be *seen* as well, as someone who is charitable or not.

But I also correlated it to what's happening in the economy, what's happening in terms of people's well-being and sense of their well-being. And I showed that there, too, there is a correlation: people are more generous, more open-handed, and more willing to engage in blue-sky thinking to create new types of institutions and communal efforts, when things are growing and prospering.

And when times are harder, even when they do help—and those who are civic leaders always have to do *something* public-minded—they tend to choose people more like themselves, they tend to choose forms of giving where you might see the results more obviously than just giving and hoping it trickles down to have an effect.

So, there was an attempt to both acknowledge the rich possibilities of a religious culture to encourage people to do "the right thing", as it were. And I worked a bit with concepts like altruism, but I didn't want to reduce everything to a position that "altruism is really a form of egoism": that they gave because they wanted to be seen—that sort of thing. I think that doing the right thing can become a habit, something very ingrained and very real. It's pretty well a Kantian-type of idea: that doing the right thing becomes a good habit.

But I also wanted to demonstrate that long-term economic and demographic processes that have to do with people's sense of their security and well-being, the well-being of the family and those immediately around them, do affect the degree to which they're willing to think of others as part of that circle.

HB: And a related implication of doing things this way, it seems to me, is to tangibly demonstrate the commonality between people today and those living in the Middle Ages. I'm speaking not so much of experts in the field, of course, but there is often this tendency of "othering" in time, where the stereotype most non-professionals have of medieval times is that these were a bunch of people acting in some sort of weird way: they were generally unthinking, religiously brainwashed people, unreflectively doing what they were told by the religious authorities.

And it seems to me that a relatively constant theme throughout your work is to be denying this outright, emphasizing how these people were influenced by the prevailing sociopolitical factors, economic factors and so forth just like we are today. Of course, the particulars were different, but the principles in play were very similar.

MR: I totally agree. I mean, I'm a fairly tolerant person, but one thing I can't abide is this whole escapism thing, approaching the Middle Ages with sentiments like, *Oh, it's weird and wonderful and we do reenactments.*

Of course, you can learn a lot from reenactments, but what I'm saying is that, while I expect to sometimes be surprised—because both people's ingenuity and cruelty can be extraordinary—so you describe it, articulate it in different cultures at different times; and it sometimes takes your breath away. But there's also their capacity to think good thoughts.

I'm not suggesting that, *It's all a big mess: we just go through the Middle Ages and we find the good and the bad.* What I suggest is that we also have to understand the processes and the structures, how one thing can lead to another, both then and now: if you put out certain types of ideologies or certain types of stereotypes, for example, you may get a certain outcome in terms of social relations. If you have certain ways of treating women, they will be treated by others. There are certain processes that we can recognize and understand, and which I believe *are* illuminating to understand our present.

Look, if we can understand atrocities committed in the 20th century, even the 21st century, understand them only in as much as we can see a cruel rationality operating, then I don't see why we can't bring that, say, to the cruelties perpetrated in the Middle Ages against some minorities sometimes, or judicial torture, or forms of execution. It's all in the world around us. There is no enormity of the Middle Ages that is not operating somewhere in the world today. The difference is that we hope and feel that in some parts of the world, we have learned from it, we've made progress, we have gotten rid of certain tendencies. But we have to *protect* those achievements extremely vigilantly. Because fundamentally, bad things can happen everywhere.

HB: Turning briefly to the scholarly community now: in terms of pigeonholing, or putting up walls around the Middle Ages and not identifying the same level of human agency and human motivations, was that ever a problem? To what extent have things changed in the last 30 of 40 years?

MR: It has changed substantially through the modern approach to history, which seeks individual people's experience more than these abstract formal categories of "law, states, parliament, rulers" and so forth. This sees every person as interesting, it sees agency in the serfs of medieval England, in the most abject women who are the subject of court cases in medieval cities, in the confused fear and resentment amongst Jews to those Christians around them.

Those experiences speak for themselves. What you need is historians who will make them speak, you need historians who will show why looking at the Middle Ages is so rewarding and that you can know things that are worth knowing.

We've had some wonderful examples amongst early modernists, such as the work of Carlo Ginzburg, when he takes a lifetime of dissent and strange self-expression by Menocchio, a miller, from

Friuli in the 16th century, the work that came out in English in the '70s as *The Cheese and the Worms*.

Here's an example where Ginzburg gets to know Menocchio, his miller, in a way that makes him every bit as interesting as someone working on, say, a 20th-century character, or government policy or what have you, where there's an abundance of material.

So, I think it's important to work to understand that sense of experience, agency, community, how people interact with each other, not because, *Well, in the Middle Ages, everybody sat around together and were terribly bonded because they were all Christian and they were all serfs*—not that at all.

It was as riven with difference, that society, as is our own—and as complex—but the historians had to come and make it happen, so that other historians of other periods who are seemingly endowed with better sources, and they can answer questions in a much more decisive manner, have to sit up and listen, because there's something to be learned.

HB: So, one thing that *does* strike me as a significant and meaningful difference between that age and our own—perhaps this is just my scientific background and orientation—is the science and technology.

Of course the Middle Ages is hardly the only historical period where such a difference occurs, but do you think it's fair to say that a tremendous distinction between people living in contemporary societies, let's say broadly defined to be within the past 150 years or so, and people living in the Middle Ages, is their scientific understanding or orientation?

And how much of a role do you think ideas of societal change brought on by scientific understanding and technology, define us as opposed to people living in that time period?

MR: I think that the experience of time may be something that has massively accelerated, what we expect to be able to achieve—but quite frankly, that's probably accelerated between now and my great-grandmother's time, or grandma's time, even. There's a very interesting German sociologist called Hartmut Rosa, who's writing a lot about "social acceleration": what that's going to do to us.

So I wouldn't say that the difference is "a scientific orientation", because they *had* a scientific orientation, they had a scientific framework: it was Aristotelian, on the whole. It believed in categories, it believed in cause and effect, it believed in a lot of what you would recognize, only it's not the system that we have; and, of course, most of what we now know they did not know.

But how many people today actually *know* the science? That's the question. I mean, when you think of it—and this is not to say, *Oh, the Middle Ages is just like any other period*, because we will get to the differences in a minute—but how many people really understand what's going on?

We have experts, of course, but they're relatively few to the number of us who are consumers. Look at our phones, look at these extraordinary cameras pointing at us, how many of us understand how these things work? When we look at the beautiful, wonderful pictures that come from CERN, say, or from space, do we really understand the science? Or do we understand them almost like performance art?

They're beautiful, they're amazing; and they also encourage us, that our money's going to the people who really know what they're doing—that is extraordinary. But do we actually understand the processes at work? I know I don't. And sometimes that seems to be a problem, but I just leave it aside because there are other things to worry about.

HB: Well, I think this is a very important point, because I think what you're touching on is this notion of trust and appeals to authority. Of course it's not just that, because those cameras and phones and so forth actually work—you turn them on and they take pictures or send text messages or whatever—but I still think that's a core element of things.

Perhaps I'm being slightly idealistic here, but one of the things that has long frustrated me is that I've always felt that the principal point of the Scientific Revolution and the Enlightenment and so forth wasn't so much that we now understand that the laws of physics are Galilean or Newtonian instead of Aristotelian, but that knowledge of the world around us was something open and accessible to everyone and didn't have to be taken on faith or relayed to us as some sort of canonical law from the high priests.

And I'm not sure that this has actually happened at any time, actually. What seems to have happened is that our definition of who is a high priest has changed, or at least a high priest worth listening to. Of course, as you say, there are serious practical issues at play— it's hardly reasonable for everyone, perhaps even anyone, to have the time and energy to become so knowledgeable about so many scientific domains, but it's almost like most people don't even bother to try at all.

MR: Yes. If you look back to the 17th and 18th centuries, say, it's a bit strong to say that *everybody* had access to this knowledge, because this is still a very hierarchical society. But it's true that something like the Philosophical Transactions from The Royal Society were not very expensive—they had a subscription system—and a doctor or even a priest who's interested, can engage, can know what's happening.

The notion of the democratization of knowledge is a very interesting one, isn't it? And there's also the issue of the relationship between experiment and law, how you deduce, and where you stop— how far do you have to go in explaining things. When do you resort to, *I don't know; and the very fact that I can't understand is only proof that God has made the world in mysterious and wonderful ways*?

So, there is a difference, but not as much of a difference as is usually posited, I think. And as you said, there is this issue of the sociology of knowledge: who is in charge of knowledge, who has access to knowledge? The whole issue of who knows what, which is, I think, only becoming more and more obscuring.

I know that everything is out there on the internet, and you can learn to build anything on the internet and so forth, but aren't breakthroughs in biochemistry, biomedicine and so on not hotly and carefully guarded secrets as well? There is secrecy, and there is mystery too around what we're producing.

What I would say though, a big difference between the modern era and many past periods concerns medicine and relief of pain. Those of us who have good medical systems in our countries are relieved from many areas of constant, nagging, chronic pain. Not that we can do everything for everyone, but I think that is a terrific relief.

And that must also affect people's relationship with each other. It may even have to do with, say, levels of violence. People are less irked, in pain, and annoyed, and therefore maybe don't lash out in the same way that they used to in the past. That may be something that could be explored: how emotions and moods and dispositions relate to levels of discomfort and pain.

There was a period when I read quite a lot of medical tracts, and I must say that I'm so happy that I don't live then. Just our ability to make people's lives more comfortable, even if they have illnesses, even if they're disabled, I think that's really important. Let alone our attitudes to them.

HB: And beyond topics such as painkillers and specific, vastly more efficacious treatments for specific diseases, there's the general issue of a much reduced life expectancy as well as various large-scale medical catastrophes like periodic outbreaks of the plague. I'm guessing that this would have some sort of significant sociological effect in terms of driving people to seek out succour and comfort from religion, as well as conceivably other cultural aspects. Do you think these things are linked in any particular way?

MR: On the issue of demography, it's very interesting. The most dangerous time of life was infancy, but if you survived infancy, life expectancy in the Middle Ages wasn't that different from a hundred years ago—it wasn't uncommon to live into your fifties, which was similar to the 19th, and early 20th century. We have lots and lots and lots of examples of extremely old people—that could happen too.

And people sought to extend life, to lengthen life—particularly those who had the money to invest, the popes, aristocrats et cetera.

There's one wonderful tract about hemorrhoid operations that my colleague Peter Murray Jones wrote about.

HB: There's a wonderful tract about hemorrhoid operations?

MR: Yes, you'll see why in a moment. It offers two ways: there's the extremely painful treatment for a shorter period, or there's the less painful one that goes on for a considerably longer time period. So there's a choice to be made, which is all to say that there is a clear awareness. The fact that people suffered, didn't mean that they did not want to do something about it—again, the question of agency.

And tracts like that—it happens to be a vernacular text, so it's in English ("Treatises of fistula in ano, hemorrhoids, and clysters" by John Arderne). It was probably a text that was in the hand of a doctor, that could have influenced the lives of people. And as hemorrhoids particularly related to riding horses, it was normally more associated with the male population than women, and we can go from there, trying to get an even clearer sense of things. But at any rate, it's quite important to remember that they shared with us the desire to make a better life, if at all possible, and to not suffer pain.

But you're absolutely right, that the cult of saints is fundamentally related to the desire to avert some of these terrible issues.

There were saints and shrines where you would bring a child, even dead, and it was said that he could revive it—that was obviously theologically a no-no, but that was also claimed.

But you know what's also really striking—and I got a handle on this when I studied the miracles that were claimed in the 12th century for this boy William of Norwich, who was considered a saint locally—that most of the people come to a shrine from really nagging, long-standing, painful, uncomfortable forms of suffering: for disabilities, for really painful pustules or growths from tumours and whatnot, trying to make life a little better.

And so, it's not just the question of dying or surviving, it's a question of also what quality of life you had. And the quality of life for a lot of people was really important.

HB: Was there an expectancy amongst many of these people when they went to these shrines of just having their burdens relieved a little bit, rather than necessarily being completely cured of everything? Was it more of a sense of searching for just a bit of relief to make it through the day, as opposed to a complete and total cure of whatever was ailing them?

MR: Well, this is where the genre is so important. We know about these types of cures because people sat down in the shrines and wrote down the miracles in order to advertise the shrine, or in order to develop a dossier to show this saint is a really strong saint.

After the 13th century, you needed to collect various types of miracles in order to support a case for canonization through the papacy. People, therefore, would naturally only put down the really successful ones: if somebody had to come back again and again, we're not so likely to have found out about it.

But there are some cases—I can think of at least one case in particular—where the petitioner is cured, and then told, "*Go away and do this, to keep the cure alive,*" and the person becomes complacent and doesn't, and then there is a recurrence.

And in one case, if I remember correctly, one of the monks of the Norwich Cathedral Priory is told to never see a doctor again, because it's always a competition between religious healing and secular healing by doctors. Often stories begin by saying something like, "*And after seen every doctor, and they had no more money left, they heard about Saint William, so they went to his shrine.*" So, there is this issue of competition between the two; and so when one of the monks of the Norwich Cathedral Priory was told that he was going to be cured as long as he doesn't go to see a secular doctor.

And then he has a recurrence and he does see a doctor and then he's told when he complains, "*Well, you did the wrong thing: you didn't fulfill your part of the deal.*"

Questions for Discussion:

1. Do you think that our modern world is more, less, or equally "faith-based" than other historical periods?

2. Do you agree with Miri's speculations that medical progress in minimizing the level of nagging, chronic pain might in general make us more tolerant and less violent on a societal level?

III. William of Norwich

Fabricating hatred

HB: Since you brought up William of Norwich, I have a couple of questions about that. First off, you published an English translation of Thomas of Monmouth's book, *The Life and Passion of William of Norwich*. I'd like to ask how that came about, but before I do, I would guess that it must have been quite a lot of work.

MR: Yes. It was 44,500 words. It's not classical Latin, it's medieval Latin. It's not so much that it's easier, it's that I'm used to reading medieval Latin. But it was certainly difficult, partly because Thomas of Monmouth was a monk with a certain version of 12th-century learned Latin, where he would show off quite a lot, by various syntactical arrangements that are very hard to render in modern English translation.

For example, after a miraculous cure, he loved saying things like, "*And they were joyfully joyful.*" Now, to us that would sound appalling, but in the Latin it has a certain something; and he does a lot of this type of alliteration, cumbersome alliteration. So I had to decide what to do with that.

So in the Introduction, I explained that he was using these various forms, and in some cases I would put in a note for the reader saying, *I've translated it this way, because this is what he said, to give you the sense of what he's trying to do*, to emphasize that it wasn't a case that I was simply being lazy with my own choice of words. So, there was that.

It was an education, though, that's true. Because I did the Virgin Mary book before (*Mother of God: A History of the Virgin Mary*), so

I had been reading a lot of devotional texts, a lot of liturgy, a lot of prayers.

And they have their own very recognizable style, and very recognizable vocabulary. So I had to re-equip myself, particularly on the issue of medicine, there was lots of describing of limbs, and diseases and all that.

But it was also just the case that my author was showing off a lot, so yes, it was an education. But a productive one, I think.

My PhD was fully based on archival research, but I remember Christopher Brooke saying to me, "*Every medievalist should at some point edit a text. Just edit a text, and bring something into circulation. It also hones those particular skills.*"

He was an amazing Latinist, and for decades was a very great editor of an extremely distinguished series, Nelson's Medieval Texts, which then became the Oxford Medieval Texts and are still going, so he did so much in terms of preparing learned texts for our use in both Latin and the translation.

I was really, really proud that he liked my translations; and if I had a question, I was able to ask him. He was very proud of what I managed to do; he was very interested and always very supportive.

HB: You could have picked a smaller text, though, I'm guessing. But presumably this was a challenge.

MR: It's interesting how it came about, which shows you how things happen in academia, and in scholarly lives. You just do not know—all sorts of serendipities arise, or at least they seem to have happened to me.

I told you earlier that we didn't have a lot of Jewish history taught us in the general history department. And I never thought I'd be doing anything to do with Jews, because I was coming to do history of medieval Europe, and its social and religious cultures.

But even when I was studying charity, the Jews were popping up in various places. So for example, if you wanted to found a hospital, you needed to put some tracts of land together, a plot to build a hospital on. And in medieval cities, Jews were allowed to lend money and take land as surety, but if somebody failed to repay a loan, they couldn't hold onto the land. They had to get rid of the land, because Jews were not allowed to hold the land.

So there was a way in which clever entrepreneurs who were developers, perhaps they wanted to endow a religious institution or indeed a college, as was the case in a number of Oxford colleges, a good thing would be to get together with some Jews who wanted to sell land and you would get an advantageous package out of it. So, I saw Jews popping up in various occasions when I was looking at hospitals. And I sort of filed that away.

Also, when I was looking at sermons, occasionally a preacher will use this as a rhetorical device to urge Christians to be charitable to other Christians, saying things like, "*Do you ever see a Jewish beggar in the street? Well, if the **Jews** take care of their own, a fortiori Christians should as well.*"

So the Jews popped up here and there in the charity project, but they *really* turned up big time when I started working on the Eucharist, that is the sacrament of the altar, the Mass, the thinking about it: *Here is a new type of sacrifice. It's not like the bloody sacrifices of yore at the altar slaughtering animals in the Temple. This is a new, spiritual sacrifice, an offering of Jesus Christ's body, et cetera, et cetera.*

It's *always* there in the theology of the Eucharist, which was the subject of my second book (*Corpus Christi: The Eucharist in Late Medieval Culture*). The Eucharist in the 13th century became the central sacrament—really, really important. And above all, as the theological requirement was that you believed that after the words of consecration, Christ is actually *present* in the consecrated bread and wine.

Well, if Christ's body is there in every parish church, in every chapel where the Mass is celebrated, its consecrated hosts are kept in vessels in churches in order to be used, to be taken to the sick and dying—it's so exposed. It's so vulnerable. It can be stolen. It can be derided.

It can be derided when a priest walks down the lanes of a village, walking to a dying person's house with the sacrament in his hands, and Jews passing by might deride it by saying something like, "*Oh, honestly, a piece of bread. They think it's their God.*"

So, the world in the centre of whose ritual activity was now this all-powerful, but seemingly also so-vulnerable God, began to be filled with miraculous stories about Eucharists that were saved from various forms of abuse.

And the Jews, then, just offer themselves as protagonists of this type of thinking, because they didn't believe it. And it's true they didn't believe it: they thought it was an extraordinary idea—although they were probably also quite fascinated by it.

So that led me to the third book (*Gentile Tales: The Narrative Assault on Late Medieval Jews*), which was generated by me thinking, "*Okay, how does a new story about Jews develop?*"

So I found myself all of a sudden working on Jews. And then when I worked on Mary (*Mother of God: A History of the Virgin Mary*; *Emotion and Devotion: The Meaning of Mary in Medieval Religious Cultures*), it was evident that Mary and Jews is a very special and difficult and extraordinary relationship. And since then, I read a lot of Jewish history; and, of course, my Hebrew helps me reading the sources.

It's just become part of the picture of this diverse medieval world, because there's no doubt at all that though the Jews were an absolutely insignificant minority numerically in most parts of Europe, their location within the culture was really quite central.

HB: So tell me more about how you became involved in translating this book by Thomas of Monmouth about William of Norwich.

MR: The serendipity was that a very dear friend of mine, Willis Johnson—an extremely well-trained medievalist who ended up working at a very high level in information technology; he's quite a brilliant person—approached me about it.

When he was still doing medieval scholarship, he thought that he might edit the text because the manuscript of *The Life and Passion of William of Norwich* was only discovered in 1891. A very distinguished medievalist and expert in manuscripts had co-edited and translated it, but there aren't many copies of this book around and the translation was extremely Victorian, both in its tone and in what was omitted: it wasn't annotated fully.

Since this was such a rich and interesting text and people were just going about downloading a few pages that were available on the internet, Willis thought that it deserved better service, because it can teach the community of scholars and students so much.

So he planned to do it. And then when his life took a different direction, he wrote to me and said, "*Gosh, I feel really bad, because this text really does need editing, but I probably won't get around to it. Can you think of someone who can do it?*"

And I was then in the throes of the Mary book, but I thought to myself, remembering Christopher Brooke's exhortation to editing texts, that it was made for me in terms of my interests. So I thought, *I'll do that.*

Later, I was having lunch with the brilliant and imaginative history editor of Penguin, Simon Winder, who is also the editor of Penguin Classics, and I mentioned what I was working on. I didn't think it would particularly interest him professionally because they do different types of books, but he said, "*But wait—would it fit the Penguin Classics?*"

I said, "*Well, it's not a classic inasmuch as it's not exactly that well known by people. But also the writing isn't exceptional.*"

But he replied, "*No, no. Nowadays we think differently of what a classic is. We think of important texts that have informed our cultures in important ways, and inasmuch as it's the first articulation of this very nasty accusation of child murder against Jews you should consider it.*"

So he encouraged me. But I must say, I felt a bit queasy somehow about putting it out there in Penguin Classics.

HB: Sure, because it does rather give a sort of stamp of authenticity of the actual content.

MR: Exactly. And I knew that most of the reading and the use of it would be in the United States, where the whole issue of cultural encounter in Jewish history is much more developed in terms of the numbers of institutions that teach it, as well as the fact that undergraduates there are far more likely to buy the texts they use in their courses. It's different.

So I wrote to ten fantastic medievalists I know in America who are great teachers and will be interested in the subject. And I asked them, *Look, what do you think? Is this something that's worth having in the classroom? Is it something that would benefit, sort of understanding that it would serve some sort of purpose?*

And they all responded very quickly saying, *Yes, absolutely. We're always recycling the few bits that are out there and this would be most useful to us. It's a very rich and interesting text.*

I also heard from people who teach Middle English literature. There is, of course, *The Prioress's Tale* by Chaucer, which is a different type of child murder, but it has an interesting affinity to this earlier story. And people there were also very interested.

But I also remember that one of these colleagues very kindly said to me, "*Miri, if you're worried about antisemitic texts out there, come on. The internet is so full of them—those who want these sort of things know where to find them. Your learned and carefully introduced text is not going to make any difference in that sense. It'll only be a good thing if you introduce it and show people how these types of narratives develop.*" So that convinced me.

HB: Before I ask any further questions about this, if I could just ask you to talk a bit more about the text and give us a brief summary of both what it says and its background, because I imagine that many people reading this might not be familiar with it.

MR: Okay. The text that I edited was copied around the year 1200, it's a copy of a text that was written between 1150 and 1173. Which is to say that it wasn't written at some point in those 23 years, it was written across that period: from 1150 to 1173.

And it's occasioned by the fact that a monk arrives as a new member of the community of the cathedral of Norwich, a lovely, beautiful cathedral. And the cathedral of Norwich is a rather new institution. It was founded in 1090, it's a creation post-Norman

Conquest. It's new; so in a sense, it's looking for a role for itself in the world, an identity. And we are told by our text that in 1144, a boy had disappeared just before Easter. And then his body was found in a wood outside the city of Norwich and it had very distinctive marks on it.

And some people claimed that those marks suggested that the Jews had killed him. That being the case, an uncle of the boy, who's a priest, goes to the Bishop of Norwich. This is Easter time, so there is a synod, there's a gathering of all sorts of ecclesiastics in the city, there's a lot of ritual activity. And the uncle says to the bishop, "*Do something about it. My nephew has been killed by the Jews.*"

So the bishop does the right thing. In everything to do with the Jews, you turn to the sheriff, because the Jews were considered serfs of the crown. They lived in England under the privilege given by the crown and protected by the representative. And the sheriff is the representative in every county—in this case in Norwich, in Norfolk.

So we are told in this text that the sheriff turns up and says, "*Absolutely nonsense. There's no evidence.*" And he protects the Jews, putting them in his castle for protection.

Now, some people in town believed the boy was special, and the bishop allowed the family to bury the boy in the cemetery outside the cathedral, which is a certain honour. And some said that miraculous signs began to occur around the tomb: a rose was said to continue to bloom throughout the winter, and so on. So that's what we are told happened in 1144 and its immediate aftermath.

So now we turn back to what I said earlier about a new monk arriving in the community. He learns about his institution. He hears these stories. And he says, "*Why, this is terrible. You've had practically a martyr in your midst. The Jews did this terrible deed and nothing's been done. They're protected. And the boy is just not remembered. He's just buried there.*"

So this is his task now, to change this. He creates a hagiography—a life, a vita—as saints need to have a vita that tells their story, often including instances from before their birth even, signs during their mother's pregnancy, a pious and virtuous childhood with additional signs, creating a narrative, which is totally confected, of how the boy came to be with the Jews in the week leading up to Easter, which also coincides with Passover—which is, in fact, the case in 1144—and they tortured the boy and physically abused him, and ultimately he died. And then they hung him from posts, between the door posts.

And he sets himself up as a sort of Cold Case investigator, because the obvious thing is to ask, "*How do you know all of this? You weren't there at 1144.*" So he says, "*Oh, I found witnesses. I went to the place of the crime,*" and so forth.

He developed this extremely articulate, very convincing, as it were, narrative. "*And then,*" he said, "*As if that's not enough, I've also heard from a convert from Judaism that this is something the Jews do every Easter—they have to do it every Easter in some community in Europe.*"

And then he says, "*And even if that were not to be believed, look at the profusion of miracles. Look at the miracles that have been happening once we brought him in and buried him in the cathedral. He had to be moved a number of times because there was such a throng of visitors and it disrupted the whole life of the cathedral, we are told. Ultimately, over a hundred miracles occur. Come on. This is the proof. What more could you want?*"

So it's inventive. It's extremely detailed in this imagining of what a killing of a boy would be. And it's *very* full of references to images and words that would suggest a recrucifixion, although it's not explicitly set up as such.

The boy has five pressure points that were pressed upon by a knotted rope in the hands of the Jews, like the five wounds of Christ, et cetera, et cetera. And above all, it's the pure lamb being taken to the slaughter. It's the purity of this boy who so didn't deserve it that demonstrates just how perverse and cruel the Jews are.

So this is the package; and this is a story that had not been told before. There were all sorts of accusations about Jews, that they had abused images of the Virgin Mary or whatever. But this story was never told before.

And after that, well, basically it's a tradition that still exists in the world today, albeit in a very minor way, but throughout the Middle Ages there were instances, tens of instances, where people accused Jews in the case of the disappearance of a child, or just because they wanted to get rid of a competitor, or whatever.

These cases did not always lead to massacres, just as they didn't in Norwich. They didn't always, because very often it just wasn't believed once it was brought to court. It just didn't convince. It didn't hold together. Sometimes, towns just didn't want the violence and intervened. And sometimes rulers protected the Jews.

But it's there in the lore. It's there in the storytelling. It's available.

HB: How much impact do you think the book had when it was written? How many people swallowed the whole story holus-bolus?

MR: Again, the book tells us that lots of people came to be cured.

So clearly it was known. But they came from a very specific surrounding, which is very much from Norfolk and particularly from villages that were on the estates of the Bishop of Norwich. So there's a sort of connection to the city. There's a coming and going of officials, so people would have heard about it and therefore try to make this pilgrimage.

It's not particularly famous. And of course it was never sponsored, say, by the papacy or anything. So it was a local tradition of sorts.

He was, of course, never canonized—not even near. But we do find that later in the 12th century, in a number of other cities that had similar institutions—that is Benedictine priories, monasteries—in Gloucester, in Bury St Edmunds and elsewhere, that there were suggestions that there were some accusations made locally, but they didn't go anywhere. So, it clearly travelled in a sort of Benedictine network to some extent, although we don't have any manuscripts to show that explicitly for that period.

And I suggest, and I was able to show a connection, that it also got copied by a number of Cistercian writers in Cistercian priories. And what's important about the Cistercians is that this is an order that was founded in the late 11th century and it was the great, great success in the 12th century. It's a big network and they're an order, they're linked up with each other very strongly through discipline, but also through regular annual meetings.

So the Cistercians travel a lot and they are inveterate storytellers as well. So there's this whole network of scholars that talk about "the Cistercian news communication network"—so the fact that I could show it being in at least two Cistercian locations also suggests that at least it got more exposure, but we can't say anymore than that, really.

HB: So there is this victimization of the Jews and the local cult of William and miracles and coming to be healed and so forth. But many people also talk about a "blood libel"—

MR: At the time, it's a child murder accusation. It's not suggested that this has anything to do with their rituals. The story gets elaborated upon, particularly in the 13th century, with stories that it has to be something that Jews do because they need it for their rituals: they need the blood for the matzah, and this sort of thing.

But this is a very early stage. This is the child murderer accusation. In fact, I don't use the words "blood libel" in the book, in my translation, but I know that other scholars do.

But because these are such weighty issues, I believe that it's extremely important to be very precise about it.

Questions for Discussion:

1. Are you surprised to hear that Miri thought that she "never thought that she'd be doing anything with Jews" given her background? How does this help better understand her scholarly interests?

2. Do you agree with Miri's original concern that publishing The Life and Passion of William of Norwich as a "classic text" might send the wrong message to some people? If so, how might that be corrected?

IV. Mother of God

An ambitious project

HB: Let's now move to your work on the history of Virgin Mary. Can you tell me a little bit about what motivated you to write *Mother of God: A History of the Virgin Mary*, as well as what surprised you during your experience, because this must have been quite a long and involved effort and I'm sure you've had all sorts of twists and turns along the way.

MR: Absolutely, yes. I came to read a lot about Mary in the course of the book about the Eucharist, actually, because when I was reading and researching stories that claimed that the Jews abuse the sacrament, I was trying to find out, is there a tradition of suggesting that Jews do this sort of thing?

So I read around in miracle stories and sermons and exempla and all the sort of various forms of nuggets of religious communication, quite apart from the theology, in order to ask, *How did people get these ideas about the Jews?*

The Marian miracles exist from the Early Middle Ages, but they really get codified and collected into a recognizable collection in Latin in the 12th century. Actually, it happens in England, it probably happened in Bury St Edmunds in the South of England, where the monks put together this collection, which then got translated into different versions in all sorts of languages all over Europe. And then in different localities people added local stories about Mary, from local shrines.

But it became a form of religious literature—very, very well known and strongly influencing visuals, the composition of religious music, and so on. So the Marian miracle is a very important part of the religious culture.

And I found that regularly in the Marian miracle, there are Jews involved—Jews who mock, or Jews who make a mistake or whatever—and then, ultimately, Mary causes them to convert.

So how interesting. In the Marian context, there's a happy ending: the Jew converts. All is well.

But in the Eucharistic context, the Jews who abuse the sacrament, there's no way back. They really have to be punished.

So I thought that was important to show that even within this religious culture, you have different pathways, as it were, in terms of understanding how appropriately to judge the Jew and what could happen with a Jewish protagonist.

So, I thought, *Actually, we need a really good book about Mary in the Middle Ages.* There were fantastic works about Mary in Anglo-Saxon England by Mary Clayton, but I thought it would be useful to inquire into this phenomenon of Mary in the Middle Ages, which, everything I'd done up to then had helped prepare me for.

And then, as I started reading background, I found that it's so peculiar that Mary, who we take to be absolutely fundamental, particularly in the Catholic tradition, the Christian tradition in the Middle Ages, is that really, there was a moment of utter emergence: you wouldn't find it in the first millennium.

In fact, if you just read word for word, Mary doesn't turn up that much even in the Gospels. Mary is in some very important locations, like in the creed that arises in the fourth century from Constantinople in these very formative councils of the church. It's actually very important in the world of apocrypha from the second century. There's a total fascination with Mary. *Where did she come from? How did this Jewish girl become the mother of God?*

And then I took a bold decision, and some people thought it wasn't a wise decision, I dare say—some have told me that they thought it was biting off rather too much.

But I decided actually to tell the story from the beginning. And it's absolutely clear that for the first few hundreds of years, if there's

Mary and the Syriac tradition or the Armenian tradition, I would obviously depend there on the research of others, and read some works in translation.

But there was this drama of how after this peculiarly nebulous presence, ultimately the European Mary developed. Because even in, let's say, the seventh, eighth, ninth century, I'm not saying that Mary wasn't known. Of course not. But it was a version of Mary that was very much created in the Eastern Mediterranean, particularly in the Byzantine end: it was very much at the level of courtly elites and so on.

But from about the 12th century, Mary is *everyone's* mother: she's Europe's mother. She is omnipresent in so many different forms and media.

So one of the things that surprised me was indeed this issue of the temporality: that there's actually a *story* to be told about Mary, that it wasn't all the same. There is dramatic change.

And it was important to reflect on it: what does it mean to have this figure of a mother at the heart of the visual, spiritual and emotional worlds of Europeans?

I actually wrote another book related to this—I was invited to give some lectures in honour of Natalie Zemon Davis, and those are published as a little book about Mary and emotion (*Emotion and Devotion: The Meaning of Mary in Medieval Religious Cultures*).

But it just led me in so many interesting directions and I tried to find a pathway through it all, but there's just so much out there; I'm delighted to see that there are people working in all sorts of areas on Mary. It's very, very rich.

HB: So that brings up two points I had wanted to ask about: the repercussions of this work within the world of historical scholarship, but also its reception outside of it.

Because I can imagine that some of your work might have stepped somewhat on the toes of those of a more religious persuasion, people who might not have been as sympathetic to historical analysis per se, and might have even taken some form of umbrage at the notion that their religious figures would be treated in such a strictly historical context.

MR: Yes, definitely. That happened. There was evidence that it made some people uncomfortable. One very distinguished reviewer said, *"Miri Rubin would have been fantastic to write a book about Mary and the Jews, but there's just so much here that needs doing in Syriac and so forth..."*

So yes, some people had concerns, but there were also those who wrote to say how much they enjoyed it, both scholars and the general public.

The thing is, as I said, so many scholars are now working on Marian themes, and I think I've provided them with the framework: ways of thinking. If I say so myself, this book is absolutely full of ideas, possibilities, roads that could be travelled where I just suggest something, giving one example, but there could be a whole PhD about it, exploring the issue.

Seriously. And, in fact, there have been. So I had the chance to think a lot about it, and I also benefited from reading a lot about other periods, later periods: I basically went up to the point when Mary "goes global", which is the 16th century when she is carried with the Hispanic empire, to Asia, to Latin America, and so forth. And then I have a little aftermath about Mary and modernity, but it's just a set of thoughts.

But the greater continuity in density in the argument is up to the end of the 16th century, because all the versions of Mary are then available. From then on, of course there were developments—there are new visions, shrines, Lourdes, whatnot. But you have everything you need to understand them by reading those earlier chapters, I think.

HB: Part of what I was referring to in my last question was related to the idea of apocrypha: the notion that people had different ideas, different thoughts, different perspectives on Mary that were later regarded as illegitimate or endorsed as part of the official canon. And while I am not personally of a religious persuasion, I can imagine some people who might be saying to themselves, *Well, hang on, this wasn't considered real or important, so we don't need to dwell on that.*

Which brings me to the question of the intended audience you imagine as you're writing. I'm guessing that most of the time when you write a book you're envisioning communicating with both fellow scholars and motivated laypeople. Is it difficult to square that circle, to write to both sectors simultaneously? Or is it not that difficult?

MR: Well, in the Mary book, I was definitely trying to do both, as opposed to *The Middle Ages: A Very Short Introduction*, which is more for beginners and students.

I thought that the scholarship and the suggestions and the footnotes would serve the scholars, but I also tried to write it in a fairly engaging manner to attract a wider audience—it's such a rich subject, so you can so easily interest people. So in that book, I consciously tried to do both. In earlier books, I didn't expect them to cross over so evidently. This is the book where I really felt that it could be for both audiences.

HB: Did that make it more difficult to write?

MR: I don't know. I mean, I really believe that if you understand something well, and you've thought through it carefully, you can share it with many people.

And then there's the issue of exemplification as well. If you seek in your materials communicable nuggets which exemplify what you're talking about, and you work hard to find the right ones, I think it can work.

But that also comes from years and years of teaching. My students are bright, my students read, but still you have to explain things to them. So I think it was the right approach for that book.

Questions for Discussion

1. Would you agree with the view that Miri's unique background and extensive academic pedigree made her an ideal person to write a book on the history of the Virgin Mary?

2. Why do you think some of Miri's colleagues advised against her taking on the project? What do you think they meant by implying, exactly, that perhaps she was "biting off too much"?

3. Is professional historical writing, on the whole, more accessible to motivated laypeople than scholarship in other academic areas?

V. Doing History
Then, now and in the future

HB: I'd like to talk a little bit about the process of doing history and archival research. A while ago I spoke with Teo Ruiz (*The Consolations of History*) and he told me an amusing story. I'm wondering if you experienced anything similar.

He talked about how, when he was a beginning scholar, he went into the archives—this was in Spain, I believe—and he was faced with this document that was something like seven or eight hundred years old. And he couldn't read it at all: he was overwhelmed with the sense that he couldn't make head or tail of it, and started to think that he'd have to go back and become a cab driver.

He told me that he later discovered that this was quite a common reaction when you're first trained: you get the sense of being overwhelmed and you can't really go forwards.

Did anything like that happen to you?

MR: At that practical level that never happened, and I think it goes back to the fact that I was fortunate to have had a very, very strong formation. As I said, when I came to Cambridge to do my PhD, people taught me paleography, people taught me diplomatics. Christopher Brooke came to the archive with me just to check that all was well and he introduced me around. I was trained for what I needed to do.

Right now, I'm facing a different sort of challenge: I'm studying Polish. I've been studying now for two years, but I wish I had a Slavic language. I know that most of the sources for my period are Latin and German, but I still feel it would be so interesting to be able to read articles written by amazing scholars, medievalists from Poland who wrote in the '60s and '70s and '80s in Polish—now they're writing much more in English. I feel that would be quite an interesting thing to do.

For me, although I haven't done archival research for a number of years—I've returned to it now, because of my current project—reading the documents hasn't been so much the problem.

If you start working on art, if you start working on liturgy, you have to train and retrain yourself, and that's also a challenge. Over the last decade, say, I've worked much more and thought much more about liturgy, about material culture, so you're acquiring all sorts of skills.

So, with Teo, it seems it was the moment of actually reading the script. Well, the stuff I've had to read, you get your eye into it very, very quickly. And in the archives, there are often other scholars there, there are archivists. There is a way around it—you can ask for help.

But for me, a real challenge occurs when you come to totally new types of sources: How do you read space? How do you understand a city through space? Or how do you look at liturgy, as an unfolding of ritual and understand what's going on? Or just equipping yourself to look at imagery, understanding that that's a form of reading too—that is also something I've had to acquire and still am acquiring. So we all have our challenges, but my current ones are perhaps not as dramatic as what Teo first encountered.

HB: You've tantalized me with bits and pieces of your latest project, so now I'm going to ask about it explicitly. What is your latest project?

MR: It's very exciting.

My original plan was to do a really interesting study of the emergence and change in this extraordinary representation of Judaism and Christianity in the form of two female figures, Ecclesia and Synagoga.

This became a way of thinking about them, of representing them side by side. It became absolutely embedded into the Gothic architectural project. There's a lot there, and something very interesting happened in the Later Middle Ages, which I shall *not* tell you. You'll have to wait until I've finished the project, but it's a really interesting project.

And I was all set up to do that. And then I was asked—it was a tremendous honour—to deliver in May 2017 the Wiles lectures in Belfast. These are a really challenging, interesting series of four lectures; and the rubric for the lectures, set down by the family who founded them, is that someone should have an importance for civilization.

Civilization was a word used a lot in the '50s—"our civilization", "their civilization", Cold War—but I know what they mean: something that is worth thinking about publicly for all sorts of people, people who aren't necessarily historians or medievalists.

It's a big event in the University of Belfast, a university in a city that has seen so much sorrow. And they got me at the moment I was on holiday in Italy, constantly hearing about all the refugees coming and Anglo-America opening the door.

So, I said to myself, *That's what I want to understand. I want to understand how cities receive immigrants, how they manage their diversity*. And given that I've always, in a way, been working on subjects that have to do with the city—from charity, to the Jews living in cities, to rituals and Corpus Christi—I do know the cities, but I've never asked this question of cities. So that's what I committed myself to doing.

And they were very happy, because they could see that it satisfied the rubric and it was interesting. It has a particular provision, this set of lectures, that you invite experts to interrogate you after the lectures. Every night after the lectures, you have dinner and then there are discussions. So I invited some really smart and wonderful people to test me, and to make it hard, to best produce the book that comes out of it (*Cities of Strangers: Making Lives in Medieval Europe*), as it must do as part of the deal.

So, I'm reading about cities now. I'm reading about cities all over Europe. That's both an engagement with the literature that is there, but I'm also going to hone in to a number of cities about particular issues.

HB: Which cities, in particular, are you looking at?

MR: I'm going to look at Siena. I'm looking at particular registers and particular documents, because obviously, you can't do everything in the time. I'm looking at the lovely little town of Gourdon in the southwest of France, which welcomed the Jewish community into its midst in 1266. I'll be looking into Paris. I'll be looking into Prague. I'll be looking into Buda, as in Budapest. I'll be looking into London.

I'm going to look at them for particular things that interest me; and, of course, I'm reading a lot of primary sources in the shape of just town statutes. Town statutes are not just documents that are set in stone, they're constantly revised and commented on. So the idea is to explore what the statutes of cities tell me about how civic leaders and lawyers thought they can create an environment that will deal with the issue of diversity and difference.

HB: I'm guessing that there is an intriguing mixture of morality, economic tactics—

MR: Definitely.

HB: —a sense of cultural ethos for the community and so forth, all that is brought to bear on these things; and that each city, each region, might have a different perspective and a different orientation—

MR: And in different times.

HB: And presumably wanting to capitalize on the geopolitics of their time. If people have been kicked out over here, then they might say, *"Oh, this might be an opportunity for us to..."*

MR: The Jews are a great example. They get kicked out of the German cities in 15th century. They go to Hungary. They go to Poland, They go further afield.

HB: Is it possible to make any sort of broad-based generalization, in terms of people in this particular city or this region tended to be more of this disposition or that disposition? Can one categorize in any way? Is that meaningful at all?

MR: Not so much in that way, but there are certain meaningful characteristics that can be identified. Take ports. Ports are constitutionally very, very diverse. They have to be. They can't not be. So, you have to face up to it and make provisions. And actually, there's a very old Roman law tradition of dealing with the port. So, that's one thing.

Then there's the question of size. Are bigger cities better at coping than smaller cities? Is it better to have people all thrown together, living side-by-side? Because the ghetto is a new thing in the 16th century: it's not the rule. And it's not the rule even after the 16th century.

Is there a difference if people have come from the immediate hinterland or from far away? How does the ethnic and the religious coincide or not coincide? So, all these issues are what I'm going to try to make some sense of; and I'm also going to look at how women are treated, because clearly women are not treated as obvious citizens of the city. They sometimes can gain a freedom of the city, the equivalent to citizenship, but on the whole, they're not imagined as the people who run the city and its fabric.

So, what are they? Are they also a form of something that has to be dealt with, in terms of where they are and what work they do and how they can contribute? So, I'm going to have one whole lecture about seeing it through the gendered thing and see how far I can go with that, which will be quite interesting, I think.

HB: Regarding the book that will be associated with this, I understand that it's a provision of giving the lectures, but presumably that's interesting to you as well. I mean, it seems a good opportunity to once again bring up these ideas that have broad, general appeal both in terms of historical and contemporary interest.

MR: I think so. It's a subject that's a very interesting subject in all places and times, so I imagine that many different types of people would be inclined to read it: maybe historical geographers, maybe people dealing with cities and other contexts and other continents altogether.

More generally, many people have thought about cities and other contexts in their own lifetimes, so you can build upon that in terms of what they expect to find, what they don't expect to find.

I've started reading about divided cities and the whole issue of cities like Belfast. Belfast is an amazing place to give these lectures.

HB: I'd like to switch gears a bit and ask how you think technology and recent technological advances have affected historical research and scholarship?

MR: It's too soon to say. On the one hand there's the remarkable ease by which I can write to a library and say, "*I want to see this document*," and they send me a scan through—it's just incredible. On the other hand, though, that means that I haven't visited that library.

HB: Right.

MR: So, there are all sorts of swings and roundabouts in that sense, that make it very hard as yet to assess.

But look at the brilliant project of Catherine Hall that's happening in UCL, this amazing project about analyzing what happened with the money that was given to ex-slave holders after the abolition of slavery—because people were compensated royally; and this also happened to many very ordinary people: there could be, say, a widow who owned quarter of a slave. It penetrated very deeply into the society. How did British society benefit from this windfall of wealth?

This sort of project could not be imagined before digital humanities, dealing with all the data—it just would have been impossible to even envision, it would have been impossible to even *think* that it could be a possibility in theory.

And this whole move that I've already mentioned: defining our sources beyond the written, to the material culture, to images, et cetera. Take my project of Ecclesia and Synagoga, just searching for those images: I'm searching catalogues, manuscripts, all sorts of data deposits that are now available. They're not just available, because catalogues were printed, but there's so much more available. But also, when you get into them, you get so much more out of it in terms of images.

I had this really strange experience. I was reading a published text, a text of a debate from the 13th century staged between Ecclesia and Synagoga: church and synagogue. So I said to myself, *Oh, gosh. I have to write that down, because I must go when I go to Paris and I'll see it.* And then I thought, *Wait. Nonsense. Most of the manuscripts of the Bibliothèque Nationale have been digitized.*

So, I google it, and I check on the deposit, and it's there. So I look at it; and the book unfolds and I see every page. So, that's extraordinary.

But what does that mean? Does that mean, then, that we have this false confidence that *we know it and we have it* and we spend less time thinking, developing our concepts, going to conferences? I don't know. Are we going to become more sedentary, so we don't go out and actually breathe the air and see and touch places and things?

HB: Well, I think that's clearly going to happen. In fact, it's clearly already happening.

MR: Yes, it's already happening, I'm sure.

HB: And the question is, *Is it manageable? Does it affect people?* My own guess would be that it would have a more pronounced effect on younger people, who haven't had the opportunity to have had those experiences.

MR: So, they won't miss it, as it were.

HB: Yes. They won't have had them at all. They won't even know what it's like to be doing that.

MR: Yes. It used to be quite normal that you'd go to a conference—particularly in Germany they're very good at it—and built into the conference, there would be a day, or a half day, of excursions. They put you on a bus. They take you. You see stuff. You go on and off the bus and I have a feeling that that's shrinking, partly because everyone's so busy, but it's also shrinking because people think, *Oh, you can google it and have a look at it later*. And that would be a shame.

HB: There's something else. So, there's googling things and digitizing things, and there are processes for doing that, but presumably, there are all sorts of ways of using technology—designing one's own search function, modelling in a particular way, interpreting data innovatively—where one is not dependent on the powers that be at Google or wherever to come up with that for you.

Is that part and parcel of modern training to have some exposure to imagining how one might best harness the technology to do interesting research? If I'm enrolled in a PhD program now, or even an undergraduate program, do I get exposed to that way of thinking at all? Or am I just in a situation where I wait and see whatever tools are thrown back at me?

MR: Well, there are some extraordinary centres where that is explicitly provided, but I think on the whole, things could certainly be improved there.

I have a colleague Eyal Poleg, who is a great Digital Humanities leader at Queen Mary. He's a medievalist; and he claims that, at the undergraduate level, although people are on their phones all the time, they don't have any understanding of digital humanities at all. Most of them really do not have any sophisticated understanding of the issues at all—or those who do, have gone to study computer science and not study history.

Eyal has been very successful, he won some funding from the European Research Council to run training sessions for PhD students so that they know how to edit their texts digitally online.

Through him, I've learned of communities of editing together: tools that allow you to successfully edit a text together, ensuring that different people do different tasks, and who does what and who checks whom as the commentary on the text progresses which is done in a very visible and transparent way, so colleagues can work together and be extremely efficient and extremely effective.

And then there's the issue of course of crowdsourcing. I see more and more people asking, "*I need help with this. I need to know that. Does anybody know?*" And it's amazing how people pop up with suggestions.

Now, the scholarship community has always been very generous in that way. People are always helping each other. Despite what people think about academics, actually people give their time. And this type of helpful sharing is occurring more and more, and it's a beautiful thing to behold.

HB: I can certainly see the positive aspects. Perhaps I'm just a negatively-oriented person, but I tend to be worried more in that direction. There's always the fear of trivialization, the idea that, *We don't actually have to worry about knowing anything, we can just google it*. I'm always worried about the prospect of people becoming less and less self-reliant.

MR: You're absolutely right. And that's where our institutions have to be rigorous and vigilant.

It can be a wonderful tool, particularly if something is out of the way that you want to find out. I'm working on cities, and I ask, "*Does anybody know a really great book about cities in China?*"

Rather than just googling something, now someone is actually recommending it to me because they read it, that makes it better: that corrects, human-wise, for the Google randomness through the mediation of a colleague.

HB: Having alluded to the negative aspects of appealing to the all-knowing Google, I'm going to ask a peculiarly related sort of question now: if I were an all-knowing being and could answer any question you would have with respect to your research and scholarship, what sort of question might you ask me? What would you be dying to know?

MR: I'd like to ask you to forecast. I'd like to ask you some of the same sorts of questions that someone like Yuval Harari, somebody I helped nurture in his Oxford years, asks. Will we or won't we retain our ability to scrutinize ethically all the wonderful possibilities that we've invented, such as intelligences that will solve problems for us? How can we retain a sense of ourselves? And what is that self? Who is that self? The 20th century has done a great deal, if you think of feminism, if you think of all sorts of changes in our attitudes to people, human rights and whatnot. But the question would be, *How do we hang on to all of that while there's this inexorable change going on all the time?*

HB: My last question is a meta question. Is there anything you'd like to add? Have we missed anything? Anything you'd like to embellish upon?

MR: Yes.

HB: Go right ahead.

MR: When I was talking about the making of a historian, I alluded to the fact that going off to seminars, apparently not on your topic, is a good thing. I would say, even more. You have to read widely. You have to listen to music. You have to go to the theatre. You've got to talk to people. It's really, really important.

That extra hour of reading, yet another article in the evening, rather than watching a film or reading a book or even cooking a meal—I think it's a false economy.

HB: And I'm guessing that you're doing your best to impress this upon your students and those around you.

MR: Yes; and they're wonderful.

HB: Well that's great, of course. But do you feel that they are receptive to this advice? Because there's a good deal of pressure in the other direction it seems to me.

MR: Yes, the pressure is on. They have to finish their PhDs in a shorter period of time and all that. But they all have other interests. A number of them are very musically active. And I encourage them by the gifts I give them, to read books, fiction.

They do resist. I'm sure they do. I'm sure they think, *It's easy for her to say*. That's natural. It's a different generation.

HB: Would you go so far as to say that not only would this make them more complete individuals, but also better scholars?

MR: Oh, absolutely. I'm not here to make them into better individuals. I'm concerned directly with their scholarship. You need to hear sounds and have thoughts that aren't from the echo chamber of your scholarship.

HB: And presumably, you yourself have drawn upon all those different sounds, in terms of launching yourself into all your different projects.

MR: I recently returned to Italo Calvino's *Le Città Invisibili*—invisible cities—which is a very strange imagination of Marco Polo telling the Kublai Khan about the cities he's seen. What is a city? And in his introduction, Italo Calvino says, *I'm writing about the Middle Ages, but in fact, I'm writing about the city today*.

HB: A great point to end on. Thank you very much, Miri. That was wonderful.

MR: My pleasure. My pleasure.

Questions for Discussion:

1. In what ways do you think today's generation of historians is superior to their predecessors? In what ways do you think that they might be inferior?

2. Is it harder to be sufficiently "well-rounded" than 30 years ago? If so, why do you think that is and to what extent can it be mitigated?

3. To what extent to you think being a great historian requires an ability to empathize?

Continuing the Conversation

Readers are encouraged to read Miri's books: *Mother of God: A History of the Virgin Mary*, *Cities of Strangers: Making Lives in Medieval Europe*, *Gentile Tales: The Narrative Assault on Late Medieval Jews*, *The Hollow Crown: A History of Britain in the Late Middle Ages* and *The Middle Ages: A Very Short Introduction*, as well as her translation of *The Life and Passion of William of Norwich*.

Exploring the Sikh Tradition

A conversation with Eleanor Nesbitt

Introduction
Isn'ts

When I had the opportunity to chat with Eleanor Nesbitt for Ideas Roadshow, I was very excited for several reasons. Not only was she an obviously thoughtful and penetrating thinker whose impressively interdisciplinary approach straddled religious studies, educational theory, ethnography and even poetry, but her specialized knowledge of both Hindu and Sikh culture would make her the perfect addition to round out our "Religions" collection that already included different perspectives on Islam, Christianity, Protestantism and Judaism. Indeed, as the author of the *Very Short Introduction to Sikhism*, Eleanor seemed the perfect guide to add Sikhism to the Ideas Roadshow mix.

Well, yes and no.

Because as I quickly discovered, in Eleanor's view, "Sikhism", as such, isn't really the right way to look at things at all. In fact, it is a word that she describes as being "really allergic to".

> "'**Isms**' really agitate me, because you're immediately into misapprehensions. India didn't have any things called '**isms**' until Europeans arrived and terms like 'Hinduism', 'Buddhism', 'Sikhism', and so on were coined by Westerners to encompass, to mean, what they perceived as religions, which they assumed in some way to be parallel to what they knew better, which was Christianity.

> "So you have this pattern that's assumed—and it's been assumed for generations now in the West, at least—a pattern of 'a founder' and 'a scripture' and 'a calendar of festivals' and 'an ethical code', and so on and so on, as if you've got these very similar bundles: one's got the name 'Christianity', one's got the name 'Buddhism', but they're

going to have comparable ingredients—they're going to have rites of passage, which of course are going to include something to do with birth, something to do with death, something to do with marriage, and something to do with initiation or coming of age.

"*So you then get a very widespread assumption when people are asking about the Sikh tradition, that when people are initiated—when, as Sikhs would say, they take Amrit—that that's somehow going to happen at about the age that somebody might be confirmed in the Anglican church or might be having their bar mitzvah.*

"*Whereas it isn't like that. A Sikh is quite likely to say for many years, and maybe all his life, that he's not in a position to observe the discipline that's required if you take Amrit, if you become a member of the core community of Sikhs who have "the outward uniform", if you like, and who follow a strict code. Even somebody who is devout and very respectful of the tradition may decide never to take Amrit, or it may be that parents say, 'Look, a child can't possibly observe what's required of them. It's better that they do this as an adult.' And then as an adult, if you break one of the rules—like, willingly or unwillingly some hair is removed from your body, you shave your beard or whatever—then it would be appropriate to take Amrit again, which isn't the way, generally speaking, people view, say, a bar mitzvah.*

"*And when it comes to the scripture—yes, okay, Sikhs have got a scripture, the Guru Granth Sahib. The word 'guru' is a giveaway—the scripture is the living guru, the living spiritual teacher. And so behaviour around the scripture is different from what's expected in many Christian contexts, for example, around the book that is the Bible. In another way, the language that's used to talk about the scripture is much more similar to the language that's used about the elements of Holy Communion in the Roman Catholic Church, for instance. For example, instead of talking about a 'page' of the scripture, Sikhs may talk about an 'Ang'—a limb—of the scripture, because this is the body of the guru. You're much closer to the "This is my body" language than you are to the words that are usually used for describing, say, the Bible or the Koran.*

> *"So having these parallel "isms" very easily leads into a way of thinking that's equating things, parallelling phenomena and experiences, and blurring the distinctiveness of them, blurring the concepts that underlie them."*

And suddenly, what I had thought would be a wonderful opportunity to simply expose myself to another culture, tradition and set of values became far more than that. By immediately bringing me up short on my knee-jerk "*ism*" orientation, Eleanor did far more than simply change the working title of her Ideas Roadshow conversation. She made me think very hard about what any religion or tradition actually *is*, convincingly demonstrating how dangerously natural it is for all of us to subconsciously interpret—if not actually downright judge—other people's unfamiliar traditions and practices in terms of what we know, rather than to simply appreciate them on their own intrinsic merits.

Because it's not just that by doing so we will miss the opportunity to deeply appreciate and understand where they're coming from—although it's certainly that as well. By unreflectively framing other people's experience through our own pre-established categories, we minimize the opportunity that a new experience presents itself to actually understand *ourselves* better.

> *"Something which has come to be more and more important to me is the key notion of reflexivity—recognizing that, certainly in research, we change what we research and we are changed by what we research. That's actually ongoing in life as a whole. And being an ethnographer it is actually just being a human being: you're using observation, and particularly listening—you're using the faculties that we use in the whole of life. And if in 'the whole of life' we become just a little bit more reflective and reflexive, I believe that's a better way forward than necessarily becoming more committed to a particular philosophy or a particular religious path."*

So, talking with Eleanor certainly increased my knowledge of the Sikh tradition, as expected. But it also gave me some particularly valuable insights into how to be a better person. And that rather took me by surprise.

The Conversation

I. Looking To Connect

Eleanor explores the world

HB: I'd like to start at the beginning and ask you to trace your trajectory that led to you becoming an expert in Sikh and Hindu studies. I imagine that is quite an interesting story.

EN: Well, one way to describe things is that I basically never left school: I carried on, doing what a theologian friend of mine once described as climbing up a tree, slithering along various branches, and then when a twig turns into a branch that will support me, moving onto that one, but not having a view at the beginning of necessarily which tree I was going to climb or where the branches were going to be or which ones I was going to go out on. So, one thing has followed another; and there's been quite a lot of intuition in it.

I started off on the south coast of England, going to school in Bournemouth, and being interested in the diversity around me. I was particularly intrigued by the fact that some friends were Jewish; some people in the locality were Roma or Romani—gypsies—others were French language students, and so on.

I also knew from very early on that I was going to study Latin and Greek. There was something about the rather academic secondary schools I went to that directed me that way, but also perhaps the knowledge that my father had been studying Greek during the months before I was born? I don't know.

There was also, increasingly when I got to university, a sense that I was going to go to India. It was never a decision that I remember taking. It was more, *Yes, the next thing I'm going to do is go to India*. One can find all sorts of reasons for going to India in 1974. There were people going out as hippies. There was a general idea that people on a spiritual search went to India. I suppose people could analyze that in different ways, but I just knew that I had an overwhelming sense of being directed towards going there, even though my tutor at Oxford, where I was doing my teaching course, strongly advised everyone against going overseas and urged them to take a job instead, because jobs were becoming more difficult to find.

And I always tell my own students when they come to me for advice, "If you haven't got any dependents who need to be considered, then follow your hunches and do not follow what your tutor says to you." That leaves them with a dilemma.

HB: Indeed. How many of them then promptly tell you, *"Therefore, I'm not going to listen to a word that you've just said"*?

EN: Well, that's right. But nobody has said that yet—I suppose I'd have to explain it to them.

HB: I'd like to back up a little bit. You said something curious about your father studying Greek right before you were born.

EN: Yes, it was New Testament Greek, because he was very embedded in the Church of England: he was a lay reader; and actually, during my time as an undergraduate at Cambridge, he was ordained as a priest. And I had never been able to understand what it was to be a member of the Church of England—I only remember feeling uncomfortable and out of place and questioning about it.

And so there was a sort of crunch that game when he was ordained and I was in this wonderful space in Cambridge where I could explore all sorts of religions and philosophies and try to find out who I was at the age of 18 or 19 or whatever. And there was my father being ordained as a priest in the Church of England; and I couldn't even say the creed.

HB: How did he feel about that?

EN: Well, I don't suppose he knew that I couldn't say the creed. I wasn't quite as open as George Eliot was. I'm based at Coventry now, and our most noted writer—certainly our most noted novelist—is George Eliot. And when I take people to Holy Trinity Church, I show them the plaque that commemorates the fact that her father, Robert Evans, was a sidesman there; and then I tell them about the letter that she wrote to her father—because she couldn't bear to tell him face to face—explaining that she could no longer with integrity worship the church with him because she no longer believed in the inerrancy of scripture. And that dilemma that she outlines in the letter is just so much the dilemma that I had, right the way through my teens and into my 20s.

HB: Had your father been involved in the Church of England throughout his entire life?

EN: Yes. His church life had been central—basic to his existence—right from his own boyhood, and certainly all the way through my childhood. I knew the importance of it. He was a telephone engineer—he was working in telecommunications—and it was only when he was able to envisage retiring from that, that he could take on the responsibilities of a more in-depth theological training and eventually ordination.

HB: I read an interview with you when you spoke about how, even when you began your undergraduate years at Cambridge in classics, you had also listed "oriental studies" as one of your interests, even though you had never been to Asia or seemingly had any real type of contact with the Asian world. That struck me as quite odd. Why did you do that?

EN: Well, that's a very difficult question to answer. Maybe at the time I had some awareness, but looking back, I have no idea why I put "oriental studies" on my form. And the fact that when I got to interview at Girton College in Cambridge I had no idea which "oriental study" I was thinking of, rather suggests that it was just one of those things that came from deep inside me somewhere but hadn't been worked out in my head.

HB: So, how did that go exactly? You're there at the interview; and the person says, "*I see you put down 'oriental studies'. What is it about oriental studies that interests you?*" And you say, "*I have no idea*"? Was it like that?

EN: The senior tutor who interviewed me actually had an interest in Egyptology, so she steered the conversation by showing me some statuette, or something, which she had in her room, and exploring a bit of that with me, because I think Egyptology must've been covered by Oriental Studies at Cambridge.

HB: So she had wanted to subsume you in her orbit, as it were?

EN: She was actually a classicist, but she was trying to find out, I think. And it was not unknown for people to arrive with their credentials in Latin and Greek and then start studying Turkish and Arabic, like one of my friends did, or some other language.

So, although I might have appeared clueless, it was also regarded as perfectly natural to start from scratch in some new language.

HB: Right. Was there also something about French?

EN: Well, it was simply that, whilst I was studying in Cambridge, I came to know that I was going to head off to India; and I knew that the only way I could support myself for a significant length of time and be reasonably useful was as a teacher. And so I did my post-graduate certificate in education in the Department of Educational Studies in Oxford. And it was with a view to the future that I thought, *Okay, I've been studying Latin and Greek and then theology, but what about my A-level French? I enjoy French. It would be good to have some training in French as well as religious education.* So that's what I did.

HB: I see. So even as a classics undergraduate at Cambridge you had begun planning to go to India, taking various tactical steps in order to do that?

EN: Yes. I was registered in classical studies because I quickly realized that it was much better to start off with languages that I'd all ready got a grounding in, rather than to be starting in something else. And I moved into theology with the feeling, *Well, this is the Middle East, and it also helps me to explain to myself perhaps how my father's spiritual and intellectual journey had gone.*

HB: And when did you decide to focus even further east and say to yourself, "*I'm going to go to India*"?

EN: It must've been my second year, possibly my third, year in Cambridge. There would have been conversations with friends who had been to India or were going to India. And I do distinctly remember that there was a program of Teape Lectures, whereby a theologian from Cambridge would go to New Delhi—I think it was always New Delhi—and a theologian from India would come to Cambridge in alternate years, and I remember Paul Sudhakar coming from South India to give the Teape Lecture in Cambridge. I don't recall exactly what he talked about now, but I remember having a *very* strong sense then that I was keen to go off to India.

HB: And what were the reactions of your parents when you did go? What, in particular, did your father have to say about it? Was he encouraging? Discouraging?

EN: I don't remember any reactions. My father would tend to go very quiet if there was something difficult; and my mother had been pretty petrified of my going to France, I remember, when I was a teenager. But the fact that there had been a great-great-grandmother who had gone to India and had returned safely was, I think, very reassuring to her—and that great-great-grandmother must have gone in the first half of the 19th century.

But I don't remember any reaction. Isn't that odd? I remember saying goodbye to them. I said, "*No. No, don't come to the airport,*" so I just said goodbye to them at home and went off to the station and caught the train. And I remember somebody on the train asking me, "*Where are you going today?*" And I replied, "*I'm going to India.*"

I taught in a school there for two academic years, from September 1974 to November 1976, and I travelled each winter. I didn't come home until March '77.

That period almost exactly coincided with what's known as "The Emergency", which was the period during which Indira Gandhi had direct rule over India and various dissidents went off to jail.

HB: So how did that work, exactly? How did you get that teaching position in India?

EN: Well, part of the story is that I griped in the hearing of a professor of divinity, that men seemed to get scholarships and bursaries to go off to Israel and women didn't seem to be quite so fortunate. And very soon after that, I had an award to go to Jerusalem to study in St. George's College—so that was the summer of 1973. I was already intending to go to India the year after, and had actually submitted an application to a school in the Himalayan foot hills.

And in Jerusalem, I met Mary and Murray Rogers, who, before living in the old city of Jerusalem, had lived in India and had a Christian ashram. Mary Rogers had been a contemporary—a very talented contemporary—of my senior tutor when they were both classics undergraduates at Girton.

And I said to them, "*I'm going to India and I'm intending to teach. Do you know anybody who might want me to go?*" And they said, "*Well, we know two schools and two head teachers; why don't you contact them?*" One was in Delhi ,and one was in Nainital, which at that time was part of Uttar Pradesh—the state of Uttar Pradesh has been subdivided since. So I wrote to the two head teachers; and only one of them wanted me—the one in Nainital. It was very simple.

HB: And that was quite serendipitous in terms of your awareness of Sikhism, because that gives you the opportunity to develop a further understanding.

EN: That's right—you see how the branches grow and the twigs come out, as I was saying earlier? I went to Cambridge because of having fallen in love with the ducks and the willow trees when I was eight, vowing to go back 10 years later. I went to Nainital because of this connection of my senior tutor's old contemporary. And in Nainital, although it was not in Punjab, it happened that probably nearly 50% of my students in the girls' school there were Sikhs; and I knew nothing about Sikhism.

And this large Sikh population was a direct result of the events of 1947, when India gained independence at the cost of partition, which meant that Sikhs and Hindus, on what was now the Pakistan side of the border, had migrated into India as far as possible.

Many of those Sikhs had been compensated with land, but it was not cultivated land. It was jungle in the foothills of the Himalayas. And by the time I went out in '74, they'd converted it into wheat farms, sugar cane farms, and so on.

And they needed their daughters to be able to marry up, to marry suitably, so what was called "a convent education" was something that they needed.

There were lots of Hindus in the school, as well: it was roughly half Hindu and half Sikh, with just a scattering of Buddhists—because of Tibetan refugees—and Christians—generally related to members of the teaching staff—and one or two Muslims.

I did know a bit about the Hindu tradition, even though at Cambridge my religious studies had only taken me into Christianity, Judaism, and Islam. What I didn't know about was the Sikh tradition.

HB: And regarding Hinduism: did you do any extra preparation on your own before you left? Did you read widely beforehand, or did you just plunge in?

EN: No, I read nothing at all. I'd read the Bhagavad Gita when I was an undergraduate on the recommendation of a student from India—I think he'd quoted from it in a speech in the Cambridge Union.

I didn't do any preparation for going to the school, as far as I remember. I asked the head teacher what I should do, and she said, "*Well, read Jim Corbett.*" And Jim Corbett was somebody who was a tiger hunter, who later on transferred to photographing animals rather than killing them; and his activities were in the area of Nainital.

So I think that just about all I knew about my new surroundings when I went out was that the finger of a girl who'd been eaten by a man-eating tiger had been thrown in the lake near the school where I was about to teach. And I had some sort of sense of the forestry because the head had asked me to look at a book on the forest.

It certainly wasn't of any concern to the people who were running a diocesan school that any teacher should know anything about Hindu or Sikh backgrounds. These were girls who were being educated in a Christian school, a Jesuit North India school. They were all singing hymns and doing all the things you do in a school like that. So their background, I think, was of very little interest to the people who employed me.

And one of the things I was doing, apart from teaching English, was teaching religious education; and I wanted to make it much wider than just straightforward Christian instruction. It was all quite challenging to me, especially the experience of being in the chapel and being amongst all these Hindus and Sikhs who were energetically singing things like "The Heathen in his Blindness".

HB: Did it prove controversial with the school authorities that you were motivated to explore religious issues more broadly?

EN: No, I don't think so because I wasn't particularly explicit about it, and I wouldn't have had the confidence to speak out. I would have introduced the girls to things like considering the nature of places of worship: why do people in different faith communities tend to build places of worship by rivers or on hilltops or whatever, trying to get them to think about these things. But I don't think I was challenging the curriculum in any way. I think I was a great concern to the padre's wife.

HB: How so?

EN: Well, she clearly saw me as extremely heretical. I did horrifying things, like wearing an orange sari, which she doubtless took to be a sign of some sort of creeping Hindu allegiance. And there was a very elderly and almost totally deaf former member of staff who would be at the dining table every evening, and she saw me come in once with a bindi or a tilak—some mark on my forehead, because I think I'd been to the temple—and was absolutely horrified, I'm sure.

But I had come out in a different generation, a different time. I'd come out to post-independent India—she'd gone deaf, probably, before independence. So, I had a completely different approach. I was wanting to discover what was going on around me and to be part of it.

HB: And how was that received by the students? You mentioned that a substantial number, 50% or thereabouts, were Sikh. Were they enthusiastic about sharing their experiences and talking about their cultural orientation with you, someone they might have sensed to be open-minded, if not a kindred spirit? Or was it not quite like that?

EN: Well, some of them have been in boarding school from about the age of four or five. So, for example, I remember once when the Sikh pupils were allowed to go down to the gurdwara—the Sikh place of worship—by the lake when it was Guru Nanak's birthday. And I offered to be one of the teachers who went down to escort them. We go down to the gurdwara. I've been to one gurdwara before—I'd been to a historic one in Delhi in my first week in India—but otherwise I'd never been in a Sikh place of worship.

And I hear a great cry go up of *Jo Bole So Nihaal Sat Sri Akal!* And I want to know what it means so I ask my pupils. And either they don't know, or they can't possibly explain—it is pretty difficult to explain and translate—and I realized that they haven't been educated in a way that enables them to articulate—probably even Punjabi or Hindi, but certainly not in English—that aspect of their lives.

They're living, as many, many students do, in a way that involves a different home language from the language of school; and that's all the more accentuated if you're in a boarding school with a different medium and a different religion wrapping around you.

HB: A small diversion: there's this word gurdwara that you just mentioned, the Sikh place of worship. I naively thought I had some sense of how to pronounce it when I just looked at the English transliteration, but listening to you pronounce it now, I'm completely at sea. You seem to put in all these other syllables, somehow.

EN: I think when I'm speaking quickly, I probably say it differently if I'm not being self-conscious.

HB: I'm certainly not trying to make you feel self-conscious. It's just that *I'm* self-conscious about it.

EN: I have had Sikhs say to me with surprise, *"Oh, you actually pronounced it the Punjabi way rather than the English way."* But if I started thinking about it, then it's more difficult.

I'm not saying that I pronounce Punjabi properly, it's just that I don't pronounce Punjabi words in a completely English way. I did have the interesting experience of being at a conference in Rome with a bunch of Indian academics on a day out, and one of them turned to me in great puzzlement and asked, *"Why do you speak Hindi with a Punjabi accent?"* Which I took as a great compliment.

HB: I also recall you mentioning that when you returned to England to teach you naturally made an effort to pronounce the children's names correctly, which was often off-putting not only to many administrators and fellow teachers, but also to the children themselves, because they had been so used to having their names pronounced in the wrong way.

Which gets back to your point about being conditioned by one's environment.

EN: Life is such a process of learning and unlearning: so, having really carefully trained myself to pronounce names more or less accurately in India, there I was in a comprehensive school in Coventry, having the Punjabi students very embarrassed whenever I called upon them, while others said things like, "*Oh, she's half-casted*," or, "*Are you going out with a Paki, Miss?*" So, that didn't work well at all.

I had one student who was presented to me in England as "Onker". And I said, "*Your name's 'Oan–kar'*," because I knew it came from "*Ik oankar*"—*there is one reality* or *one God is*—however you want to translate it. Like almost every Sikh name at that time, although this is no longer the case, there was a profound religious meaning to the name. And turning it into "Onker" just didn't work for me.

And there was another one who had the name Tirth, which clearly came from *tirath* ("tee-ruth"), which means "a place of pilgrimage". But because it was spelled "Tirth", it was pronounced as rhyming with "birth" and "mirth".

Many children probably haven't even heard their names pronounced in Punjabi, because in Indian homes it's very widespread for children to have a home name, a family name, not actually to be addressed by their registered name—so they might only hear it when they go to nursery or primary school, and then it's just up to however that first nursery-school or kindergarten teacher decides to pronounce that particular string of letters.

HB: It's a sort of English baptism, as it were.

EN: That's right. And, of course, there isn't a one-to-one phonetic connection between characters of the Roman alphabet and English pronunciation. So, often the same Punjabi name will be transliterated in different ways. In school, you'd end up having an "Amardip" and an "Amardeep", but it's the same name. One person's got it spelled with "ip" and the other "eep", so the teachers are going to pronounce them as two different names. And so it goes on.

In the end, I realized that one has to compromise in the interests of the feelings of the person concerned. And there is the interesting situation, in the UK anyway, where you now have parents who, from the point of view of the purist, mispronounce the name that they're giving their child. For example, I've got a neighbour called "*Ashok*", but his parents will call him "*Ash–okk*" because that's the way everybody around them hears it and says it.

And I've got neighbours who told me that their child was called "*Dee–an*"; and I thought, "***Dee-an***"? And then I realized what was going on. I had a pupil once called "*Gee-an*", which I realized was "*Gian*", which means knowledge. So probably "*Dee-an*" is really "*Dian*", which is a word for attention and contemplation. So, I really want to say, "*Hello, Dian,*" but I don't think I can. I think I've got to say, "*Hello, Dee-an.*"

HB: You also talk about your sense of culture shock when you returned from India. I've heard this from several people who had experienced living in a very different culture. Often people are warned of "culture shock" when they go to new places, but it seems that, for those—like yourself—who enthusiastically travel to new places, that's not an issue. Indeed, that's the whole point of going in the first place. For people of that disposition very often the culture shock really happens when they return. You describe a similar sensation when you came back to England after having spent the better part of three years in India.

EN: Yes. I think what has to be borne in mind is that I was immersed in India. Okay, I was immersed in a rather peculiar boarding school, if you like, but I was immersed: I didn't hear my parents' voices for two and a half years. Even though my father worked in a telephone exchange, it never occurred to either of us that we should actually speak by phone. So-called "trunk calls" from India were complicated; and sometimes payments were required for the call to "mature", or whatever the word was. So what you did was write letters on blue airmail forms. It didn't occur to any of us that I should come home in the holidays, like my students at Warwick University who come for the term and then shoot off back to Delhi or Bombay or wherever they live; and then they come back for term again. Well, that wasn't the way I did India at all.

So I had been well and truly saturated in India—not just the boarding school in the hills, but travelling pretty much the length and breadth of the country during my three-month winter vacations.

Coming back to the UK, I think it took me about an equivalent length of time to readapt, in the sense that for probably the first two or three years I was back, almost everything I experienced I'd be thinking, *Oh, in India it would be like this*, or, *They wouldn't say that in India*, or, *In India, it would look like that*. It took about that length of time for that to stop being my first reaction to everything.

HB: Were you discriminated against because of that? Did you face any negative sentiments voiced by various quarters?

EN: It's an interesting question. I remember the person who interviewed me for my job in Coventry, and made some remark about the fact that I was wearing a sort of long tunic top over my trousers, which I think he perceived as "the effect of being in India".

And my flatmate in my first flat was absolutely disgusted because she found I was wanting to store Indian spices and cook Indian food and have Indian friends. And that was not, to her mind, what she bargained for, having what she thought was going to be "a reasonably normal English person" sharing with her.

And I also remember a school friend's mother reacting to my accent—I'd obviously gone a bit sort of "Anglo-Indian" in something that I said—and she clearly picked up that I'd got "a different intonation" from when I went.

And then, of course, there were the sorts of comments I mentioned earlier, when pupils assumed that there must be a relationship with an Asian person or something based on the way I was trying to pronounce their names.

I always found those very interesting experiences, because it's so difficult to identify with people who face real prejudice and discrimination; and just even the slightest trace of a negative reaction like that is helpful in understanding what other people go through routinely.

I remember when my close colleague was going to get an apartment in Delhi and she was going to visit it; and her brother said to her sternly, "*Don't take Eleanor with you.*" And what he meant was that I would be perceived as a hippie, and it wouldn't be good for her when she was going to meet a new landlord or whoever was going to let the premises. That was a really useful experience, because it was the closest I was going to have to the experience that my husband and others had when they came to Britain and they'd be immediately told that a house they were interested in was already sold, because the owner had said, "*No black, no coloureds.*"

HB: Have you always been this extraordinarily broadminded? Back when this brother said, "*Don't take Eleanor with you when you visit the apartment,*" for example, did you say to yourself, in real time, "*Oh, this is a good experience. This will enable me to understand what it feels like to face persecution*"? Or were you just angry like a normal person would have been?

EN: Oh, well I suppose I was a bit upset, but I was very quickly appreciative of it as an experience. And actually, going over to my husband's experience again, he says how when that happened to him, he immediately thought of "Untouchables" in India and caste prejudice, which he'd never experienced as a person of higher caste, and how it was helpful to have that sort of experience to develop *his* understanding. So I don't think I'm unique in having that sort of a reaction.

HB: Well, perhaps I'm particularly narrow-minded or quicker to anger or something. I think I would probably have reacted differently.

EN: If I'd had really harsh experiences—if I'd had real discrimination like not being able to get a job or a house or something like that—it would have been different. These are just very, very microscopic experiences compared with what's routine for a lot of people.

More important to me were the experiences in India of people sometimes reacting to me on the basis that, "*Oh, she's white, she's Christian, she's meat-eating, she won't care about older people in her family...*"—this bundle of assumptions that were made about me, sometimes spelled out as, "*Oh, she's a hippie,*" or, "*Oh, she's a missionary,*" because that's what white people are.

HB: And how often did you find yourself subjected to those sorts of views?

EN: I was aware of that sort of perception a number of times. For example, I got the news that my mother was very ill while I was staying with close Indian friends, and somebody made some remark like, "*But we didn't think that British people cared about their relatives.*" I would sometimes encounter these sorts of assumptions: "*British people put old people in homes. They don't look after them in their family like we do.*" Those sorts of things.

Of course, we're talking about the 1970s. Now, there are far more similarities in stretches of Indian society, similarities with the pressures and experiences and strategies of lots of people in British society.

Questions for Discussion:

1. Are stereotypes about other people and cultures less prevalent, on the whole, today than they were 50 years ago? More prevalent?

2. To what extent does increased globalization threaten cultural diversity?

3. How do you think Eleanor's experiences in India would have been altered had she had the opportunity to return to England annually or even been able to phone home regularly?

4. How does travelling to a different culture enable the development of a unique view of one's own? For an added perspective, interested readers are referred to Chapter 1 of **China, Culturally Speaking** *with UCLA Chinese Studies specialist Michael Berry.*

II. Historical Overview

The first ten gurus and the Guru Granth Sahib

HB: So let's turn to examine the details of the Sikh tradition: the history, religious tenets, other people's misconceptions about it and so forth. But before I turn it over to you, I'd like to take a moment to make sure that my pronunciation is, if not perfect, at least not wildly inaccurate.

EN: Well, this is all very interesting. In English we normally say Sikh ("Seek"), but the Punjabi word, Sikh, involves a short "i", like "sick", as in ill, but ending in the sort of way that "loch", a Scottish lake, does.

What I'm really allergic to, in fact, is "Sikhism"—but if you're asked to write a book and its title's given to you, you can't do much about it.

And "isms" really agitate me more than the sorts of things we've been talking about, because you're immediately into misapprehensions. India didn't have any things called "isms" until Europeans arrived and terms like "Hinduism", "Buddhism", "Sikhism", and so on were coined by Westerners to encompass, to mean, what they perceived as religions, which they assumed in some way to be parallel to what they knew better, which was Christianity.

So you have this pattern that's assumed—and it's been assumed for generations now in the West, at least—a pattern of "a founder" and "a scripture" and "a calendar of festivals" and "an ethical code", and so on and so on, as if you've got these very similar bundles: one's got the name "Christianity", one's got the name "Buddhism", but they're going to have comparable ingredients—they're going to have rites of passage, which of course are going to include something to do with birth, something to do with death, something to do with marriage, and something to do with initiation or coming of age.

So you then get a very widespread assumption when people are asking about the Sikh tradition, that when people are initiated—when, as Sikhs would say, they take Amrit—that that's somehow going to happen at about the age that somebody might be confirmed in the Anglican church or might be having their bar mitzvah.

Whereas it isn't like that. A Sikh is quite likely to say for many years, and maybe all his life, that he's not in a position to observe the discipline that's required if you take Amrit, if you become a member of the core community of Sikhs who have "the outward uniform", if you like, and who follow a strict code.

Even somebody who is devout and very respectful of the tradition may decide never to take Amrit, or it may be that parents say, "*Look, a child can't possibly observe what's required of them. It's better that they do this as an adult.*"

And then as an adult, if you break one of the rules—like, willingly or unwillingly some hair is removed from your body, you shave your beard or whatever—then it would be appropriate to take Amrit again, which isn't the way, generally speaking, people view, say, a bar mitzvah.

And when it comes to the scripture—yes, okay, Sikhs have got a scripture, the *Guru Granth Sahib*. The word "guru" is a giveaway—the scripture is the living guru, the living spiritual teacher. And so behaviour around the scripture is different from what's expected in many Christian contexts, for example, around the book that is the Bible.

In another way, the language that's used to talk about the scripture is much more similar to the language that's used about the elements of Holy Communion in the Roman Catholic Church, for instance. For example, instead of talking about a "page" of the scripture, Sikhs may talk about an "Ang"—a limb—of the scripture, because this is the body of the guru. You're much closer to the "*This is my body*" language than you are to the words that are usually used for describing, say, the Bible or the Koran.

So having these parallel "isms" very easily leads into a way of thinking that's equating things, parallelling phenomena and experiences, and blurring the distinctiveness of them, blurring the concepts that underlie them.

So rather than "Sikhism", I would much rather be talking about "Sikhs"—as in the people. Or if I've got to have a word for what's usually called "Sikhism", I'll say "Sikh religious tradition" or maybe "the Sikh faith"—but of course faith, tradition, religion, they all have different sets of connotation. So I'd probably vary them and often be talking about "the Sikh community".

HB: Did you have a fight about it with people at Oxford University Press?

EN: Oh, no, no. Because there's no way. This is the series, these are the titles. And it's not just OUP, it's happened over and over again: writers have to fit into categories that they've not chosen.

HB: Well, here, at least, you have full reign to point out as many subtleties as possible so that we don't overly trivialize anything or imply any false categorization. And for my part, I will give you my solemn promise that no Ideas Roadshow materials with your name on it will ever have any mention of the word "Sikhism" on them.

Meanwhile, I will try to pronounce the word "Sikh" as accurately as I can—which probably isn't terribly accurate, but perhaps it's the thought that counts.

EN: But what's so interesting, of course, is that people then adopt the label that's being given by people around them.

HB: Well, I suppose they have no choice, at some level, if they want people to understand what they're referring to.

EN: It's like Hindus saying that they're "Hindu", when actually that's not the word they would have used until the 19th century.

HB: That's the wrong word too?

EN: It's even *more* the wrong word.

HB: Oh, my goodness. What's the story there?

EN: Well, the point about "Hindu" is that it's a name that arises as a geographical term: it arises from "the Sindhu", the Indus river, then being mispronounced by invaders from further West, people who are coming from further West into India.

So everything that's East of the Indus river, certainly all the ways of life, are termed "Hindu". But it's a bit like talking about "Europeism".

HB: I see. Well, at least it's better than calling Native North Americans "Indians", I suppose. I mean the Indus river *is* actually in the vicinity.

EN: Well, Hindus are now used to the word "Hindu". And speaking about talking about North America, I suppose it's worth mentioning that Sikhs were called "Hindus" for many decades in North America.

HB: Well, North Americans are just generally confused—we all know that. No need to dwell on the obvious.

Let's move on instead to someone who might say to herself, *"I'd very much like Eleanor to tell me something about the Sikh tradition and its background. I'm already certain that I'm going to run right out and buy this doubtless fascinating, albeit horribly titled, Very Short Introduction that she wrote, but in advance of that I'd like to have a few basic ideas of what we're talking about here."*

How would you help her orient herself?

EN: I very often start by talking about Punjab because almost 100% of Sikhs are of Punjabi background, and to understand the emergence of the Sikh tradition, I think one has to have that geographical fact in place somewhere.

Sikhs "arose", if you like, with the birth, or with the life, of Guru Nanak, who was born in 1469. So we're talking about a religious movement that's roughly contemporary with Protestantism in Europe. And like that, it is in some ways a protest, or at least a commentary on, the social and religious framework in which Guru Nanak lived. And that environment was one of people who are now called "Hindu" and people who we would call "Muslim".

So what Guru Nanak is doing is very much expressing the truth as it comes to him. He's believed to have had a profound experience as a young man, which is recorded in the traditions, the stories of his life. He expresses a call to a true religion, a religion of the heart, a religion that's free of the trappings of empty ritual.

And he can only use the language of Punjab, of Islamic and Indic culture. So what he does is actually not just write poems, but sing songs. And these songs, this *bani*—his utterance—is full of imagery from Hindu and Muslim and Punjabi life. And his emphasis is very, very much on the fact that life needs to be based around the *Nam*— the sort of essence, essential divinity, literally "the name of God"— and it's going to involve a balance between *seva*, which is voluntary service of others, and *simaran*, which is a spiritual mindfulness.

And it seems pretty clear from Guru Nanak's compositions that hereditary status—what we often call the caste system—is certainly irrelevant as far as spiritual progress is concerned. Sikhs have developed this into saying that the gurus overthrew caste and so on. Certainly caste, status, birthright, had no place in terms of the spiritual life.

And Guru Nanak not only went about communicating through his poetry and spreading his message, but he also settled in a place called Kartarpur and created a community, which almost certainly followed a pattern of manual work and daily devotion.

And his hymns, his *bani*, his utterance, became the basis of what was to be the *Guru Granth Sahib*, the Sikh scripture, which eventually came to consist of the words of six of the gurus: Guru Nanak himself and five of his successors, as well as the words of other inspired poets from North India.

With Guru Nanak, you not only have these insights about the nature of God or reality as fundamentally one—*Ik oankar*, the oneness of being, is often attributed to Guru Nanak—these spiritual insights, but you have the starts of the institutionalization: he appoints a successor.

So there's a place with a Sikh community, "Sikh" meaning a follower, a disciple; there's a successor in place who is *not* one of his two sons, but somebody who he appoints because of his devotion.

And so I think this is the greatness of Guru Nanak. There had been other poets who were critical of the social system and who sang about oneness with God—Kabir, for example—but somehow what came to be a distinct religious community didn't develop on the basis of their inspiration in the way that happened with Guru Nanak and then his successor gurus.

HB: And as I understand it, notwithstanding the orientation to focus on spiritual matters—to live a righteous life and so forth—there was quite a strong anti-ascetic sense to the teachings.

EN: Yes.

HB: There is a general notion that it's not a good idea to just withdraw from the world and commit oneself to studying spiritual matters, that an essential aspect of this sense of spiritual progress and developing oneself is having a complete integrated lifestyle and explicitly incorporate living very much in the world.

EN: Often people will talk about the Hindu tradition in terms of different stages: not just the classes of society from those who are doing the most menial or manual work through to those who are in the role of teacher and spiritual guide, but also stages of life, the student stage, the householder stage, and then gradually withdrawing from responsibility and becoming somebody who's spiritually completely spiritually focused.

In contrast to that, it's often explained that the Sikh way is to, as it were, encompass all of those activities and all of those stages of life together. Rather than perhaps heading towards asceticism at some later stage even, the emphasis is on being in the family and carrying family responsibilities. It's expected that people marry, it's expected that they have children. And so the emphasis is on *grihast*: on the married householder life.

And another emphasis is on earning your living through honest labour and then sharing what you earn with others. A great emphasis on giving, perhaps best expressed in the *langar*: the institution of providing free hospitality, free vegetarian food in Sikh places of worship; so that anybody who comes—provided they aren't carrying tobacco or are drunk—is welcome to partake. And Sikhs are rightly, I think, proud of this tradition of *seva*, of voluntary service.

And it's not just grounded in the gurus and going back to the beginnings of the faith, but it's constantly finding new expression, for example today, in what's seen as an age of austerity with people needing food banks, and so on. It's not at all some sort of discovery of a new way of being, but rather it's a continuation of something that's solidly there in the centre of the tradition, the involvement in the family, the involvement in society.

And it's the balance, which one of the gurus referred to as *Miri-Piri*: the temporal and the spiritual. I've said the word "balance" several times. It's not a word that particularly translates a concept in the Sikh tradition, but it's a word which one of my co-authors and friends, Gopinder Kaur, introduced me to: this fine balance, which is what the Sikh tradition is about, a balance between the spiritual and the physical, the inward-looking and the outward-looking. It's the life of the *gurmukh*, to use a central Sikh term. The *gurmukh* is the person who is facing (*mukh*), the Guru, (*gur*), as opposed to the opposite of that—which is what we mostly are—the *manmukh*, who is the person who is focused on his or her own whims and wants.

HB: Cautioning against egocentricity, to some extent.

EN: Yes. Sikhs have this word, *haumai*, which sort of means "I, me, ego"; and *haumai* is definitely to be constrained and avoided, along with anger and covetousness and a number of other human characteristics which are felt to lead people away from the Guru and away from God.

HB: How much was made of this idea that, as you've mentioned, Guru Nanak did not appoint one of his sons as his successor but deliberately chose someone else. It seems to me that's a very strong statement, especially when you're starting a tradition.

There are of course, obvious historical precedents for good government that involve looking beyond one's own kin; as a classicist, I certainly don't have to tell you that perhaps one of the more flagrant examples of this sort of thing is the run of particularly successful Roman emperors in the 2nd century who adopted that policy.

Is this something that in the Sikh tradition is underscored? Do people draw attention to the significance of deliberately looking for those who are the best qualified for the job, particularly in a cultural tradition that encourages family life and family orientation?

EN: It's very much mentioned by Sikhs and in writing about the Sikh tradition, not least because one of Guru Nanak's sons, Sri Chand, was extremely pious—in fact he was an ascetic—and there are still people who follow his tradition.

So it seems to be very clear, that Guru Nanak is saying, "*No, I don't intend my followers to be ascetics; don't follow in the way of this son of mine, go in the way of Guru Angad, Lehna,*" whom he appointed as his successor.

But later on, it is the case that the later gurus were all of one family, the Sodhi family. The succession wasn't straightforwardly father-son, but they were all members of that family. And certainly Sikhs would say, "*Well, there isn't a problem with that. The most suitable person **may** be a blood relative, but being a blood relative is not the chief criterion.*"

But historically, not surprisingly, there has recurrently been competition and disagreement over who the next guru should be.

HB: And as I understand it, there were ten gurus, leading to the last one in the early part of the 18th century.

EN: It was 1708 was when Guru Gobind Singh died. Sikhs don't like to use such a final word as "died", but it's difficult in English to use idioms like "light merging with light", to actually use the respectful language that's required. But certainly the 10th guru's earthly life ended in 1708.

It could also be questioned whether he was the last of the gurus, because Guru Gobind Singh established the fact that following him, there wouldn't be a human guru, but there would be the Guru Panth and the Guru Granth, the Sikh community and the Sikh scripture; and in practice it's the *Guru Granth Sahib*, the scripture, which is especially regarded as the continuing living guru.

In English we have the word "guide", which can either be a person or a book; and similarly we can think of "guru" in that way, but in this case with the "guru book" being in many ways treated as the living guru, often having a separate room to be put to bed in at night, for example, to repose in the gurdwara, rather than staying, as it were, on display in the big hall in which devotees gather in the daytime.

And there will be various other details of care for the *Guru Granth Sahib* which mirror the way in which a guru would have been treated—and that, in turn, mirrored the way in which a Mughal emperor or a local King would have been treated: the *Guru Granth Sahib* is to be beneath a canopy, to be fanned with a particular *chauri*, which has come to be a symbol of respect for the authority of the *Guru Granth Sahib*. It is a reminder of how, in the days before electric fans and air conditioning and so on, an emperor, and then a Sikh guru, a spiritual personality of great eminence, would have an attendant fanning them. So we have this continuity from the first guru, right the way through the nine successor human gurus and into the *Guru Granth Sahib*.

HB: You give this anecdote of a request for flying something like 150 copies of the *Guru Granth Sahib* to Vancouver, and they each had to have their own seat on the plane—a particularly vivid example, I think, of regarding this as equivalent to a living guru.

EN: Yes. And something which has developed quite strongly in recent years, which has been documented by my colleague in Sweden, Kristina Myrvold, is the way in which when a *Guru Granth Sahib* can no longer be enthroned in worship because the pages have become too worn, it's no longer a physically perfect volume, it will actually have a formal cremation ceremony in a particular place in Punjab, as a human would be.

That's also a reason why most devout Sikhs when I was doing my research, say in the '80s and '90s, wouldn't have the *Guru Granth Sahib* at home. Not having the scripture at home didn't mean that they weren't devout, it meant that they didn't have a room in their house which they could devote to such an important guest.

Nowadays, of course, where everybody has got the *Guru Granth Sahib* on their mobile phone and on their laptop; and I wonder what the implications are of that.

Questions for Discussion:

1. To what extent are our current names of other people and cultures a reflection of our own cultural and historical biases?

2. What impact, if any, do you think modern technology will have on the way Sikhs approach the Guru Granth Sahib?

III. Identity

Turbans, Five Ks and evolving perspectives

HB: For most people who don't know very much about the Sikh tradition, one thing they might be familiar with is the turban or the sword, and they might well be wondering how those attributes fit into this picture that you've just been describing.

EN: Yes, many people recognize Sikhs primarily by the turban. The turban is a headdress, a head covering, which is actually much more widely worn than by Sikhs—and I'm not just talking about India.

But when Guru Gobind Singh required that one of the five outward signs of initiated Sikhs would be uncut hair, it was natural that men, at least, would cover their uncut hair with a turban.

Sikhs often talk about the turban as their "crown", and the attachment to it is a profoundly emotional one. So that if, for instance, let's say in a school playground, somebody messes with a Sikh lad's turban, that isn't like just knocking somebody's hat off. It's felt much more keenly as an insult to the community and to the faith.

The turban itself has quite a history. Very many Sikh men who are not initiated in the Amrit Ceremony—the ceremony involving blessed, sweetened water in a particular ritual—nonetheless wear the turban as a way of identifying with their community. The wearing of it doesn't mean that they are observing the full discipline.

And something which has happened increasingly towards the end of the 20th century and into the 21st century, certainly in the UK, is that women who have taken the step of being initiated into the Khalsa, into the committed community of Sikhs, are also adopting the turban.

And they will explain this in a number of different ways.

One is that the emphasis of the Sikh tradition is on equality and that includes gender equality. So if Sikh men are required to wear the turban, then obviously Sikh women should also wear it.

Another thing is that history itself is to some extent being revisited, and I would say reinvented. And with the help of the internet, there's more and more portrayal of historic Sikh women as turban-wearing, when there is actually no historical evidence that they did. But people increasingly feel sentiments like, *I'm doing what my Sikh foremothers did: they went to battle wearing a turban.*

One can also look at it in a more sociological way and say, "*As Muslim women in countries like the UK are increasingly deliberately adopting a conspicuously Islamic form of dress which their mothers and grandmothers may not have worn, similarly, young Sikh women who have a similarly strong identification with their faith, feel it appropriate to be wearing the turban.*"

I remember perhaps 20 or 30 years ago, writing about women wearing the turban, and one of my colleagues in religious education saying, "*No, they don't. It's only men who do.*" But I think now, many, many more people—certainly in the UK, if not in India—have seen Sikh women who wear the turban.

Often the turban was explained as being a way of being distinct, and that presumably meant distinct from Hindu and Muslim society. But since 9/11, many Sikhs have had to cope with insults and sometimes physical abuse. And I believe that the first fatality as a reprisal for 9/11 in the United States was actually a Sikh, because of the way in which the turban, in swathes of the popular imagination, has been equated in recent decades with the Taliban and Al-Qaeda. So the turban's history carries on; and wearing the turban can involve a considerable determination and courage.

In the UK, a large number of Sikh men are not turbaned and do not have long hair, and may not even have the *kara*, the steel bangel or wristband.

So you've got movement in different directions simultaneously: people becoming more and more overtly religious and loyal, so that women as well as men are conspicuously Sikh; and at the same time, in parallel, many young Sikhs in India and elsewhere exhibiting no outward evidence of their Sikh heritage or of a Sikh commitment.

Some would say, *"Well, what's important is that I respect the teaching of the Gurus, the emphasis on service of humanity and so on, rather than what I wear."* Whereas for others it's, *"Well, you can't. You can't pick and choose. The 10th Guru has given us our outward form and our discipline, and you have to take the whole package."*

HB: Of course many religious movements, to use a broad term, have a wide range of different levels of commitment and adherence. There are clearly many different strains of Christianity, even within larger classes such as Protestantism and Catholicism and Eastern Orthodox. In Judaism, there are fairly well-established distinctions, at least in many parts of the world, between Orthodox and Conservative and Reform.

For somebody looking at things from the outside, would they say, *"Oh, well, these individuals who shave regularly and who don't have outward signs of being an obvious member of the Sikh community, they would be equivalent to a reform or secularized version of Sikhism."* Does that parallel work at all, or does it not work?

EN: I don't think it works, because in my experience of working with Sikhs, the widespread perception is that, to be "a proper Sikh" means to have uncut hair; and at least in the case of men, to be turbaned. And that, in my experience is the perception of Sikhs, regardless of how religious or not they individually are.

So you might hear somebody saying something like, *"Oh, I can't be interviewed to talk about Sikhism, even on the radio, because I'm not a turbaned Sikh. I'm not a proper Sikh."*

It's not that there's a separate movement, a reform movement, in which people are short haired, and that's okay. There are lots of gradations; so to be a really proper Sikh means that you can't trim your beard, for example; or as a woman, you can't remove any facial hair.

This often gives rise to personal dilemmas for individuals. For example, I had a dentist who was an Amritdhari, an initiated Sikh;

and she explained to me, "*Look, I've had to compromise the discipline because as Amritdhari Sikh, I couldn't pluck my eyebrows and that sort of thing. But as a dentist, I've got to present in a certain way.*" So there are those personal dilemmas, and different people will resolve them in different ways.

There is often a sort of fear amongst very committed Sikhs that somehow their tradition will disappear if it's not somehow visually distinct. In the past, there was a fear that it would somehow merge into Hindu society or that it will somehow merge in a more secular Western society.

All Sikh reformers and all Sikh spiritual leaders that I can think of are turbaned, bearded, maintain the outward signs of the Sikh tradition. There are communities that overlap with Sikh tradition, in terms of their history and their devotion and all the rest of it, where that's not the case, but that's different.

HB: To what extent does the reliance on a sacred text written hundreds of years ago pose problems for the evolution of the tradition? I appreciate that, by religious standards, this is a strikingly modern text, but in many ways the same concerns about interpretation and potential rigidification that other religious traditions face presumably apply, at least in principle. And then there's the fact, of course, that there's no one authority figure—a Pope, say—who is universally regarded as being the ultimate living authority regarding the interpretation of the sacred text.

EN: Well, there's certainly been an evolution of the Sikh community and the Sikh tradition. Of course, a sacred text—particularly one that's in an archaic language and almost completely in poetry—can be interpreted in a number of different ways.

Subsequent to the completion of the *Guru Granth Sahib*, codes of discipline have been formulated, and they have definitely changed over the years.

Even the one which is currently most widely observed, or at least referred to—the Rahit Maryada, which was published in Amritsar in Punjab in the middle of the 20th century—is not universally followed.

That is to say, I'm not talking about people who don't keep the rules, but rather pointing out that there are also communities that have an alternative *rahit*, another slightly different code of discipline.

The nature of institutions, and the character of human beings, is that nothing stays completely still. We certainly see that in the Sikh tradition at the moment; and interestingly, I think the diaspora—Sikhs outside India—are playing and will play quite crucial roles in the future direction of the Sikh community.

I don't mean it to be a direction away from the *Guru Granth Sahib*, but in terms of practice.

An example at the moment is the situation with regard to mixed marriages, where to my knowledge there isn't the same level of controversy in North America and in India as there is in the UK. In the UK, those who are strongly resisting the conducting of the Anand Karaj, the Sikh marriage in the gurdwara in the presence of the scriptures, are looking to a ruling that came from Amritsar in 2007, in line with an interpretation of the Rahit Maryada, the code of discipline.

There's this interesting interaction between concerns in, for example, England, and rulings coming from Punjab. The fact that an increasing number of marriages in the UK are between a Sikh and a person of a different religious and cultural background, would appear to be one of the reasons why this has, as it were, come to a head and why we're seeing what, in terms of some Sikh organizations and gurdwaras, is an insistence on tradition.

Whereas others, including Sikhs are saying, *"But it's never been our tradition to refuse a couple permission to marry in the Sikh way, in the presence of the scriptures."*

So we've got to wait and see what happens.

Another thing that's happening very much in the diaspora is the emergence of the Ravidassias as possibly a separate religion, at least in terms of how people enter themselves on the census return and in terms of worship in their religious meeting place and so on.

In Vienna, in 2009, a Ravidassia—a person of what is considered a lower Punjabi hereditary community—was killed. And following that event in Vienna, there has been, I think, a deepening of the division between the Ravidassia community and Sikhs in the Punjab.

Again, you've got this interaction between Punjabis overseas and what happens in the Indian homeland; and you've got very fast communications now because of the internet and so forth.

So there's change going on. I don't think you need to have a Pope, or even a priesthood, for evolution to happen. And it's worth noting that, although Sikhs themselves use the word "priest", there is no priesthood in the Sikh tradition in the sense that "priest" is normally used—either by Christians for a professional who's been ordained, or for a person of Brahmin birth in the Hindu tradition.

The Sikh tradition is lay. Not only is there no Pope, there's also no clergy in the Christian sense.

HB: OK, but once again let's put ourselves in the position of the objective/ignorant observer—which is, as it happens, a most appropriate label for someone like myself.

And from my objective/ignorant perspective, there is simply a desire to get a basic picture of what this all means, what it means to be a Sikh. I might have heard of the so-called "Five Ks"—two of which, I believe, the uncut hair and the bangle, you've already mentioned—with the others being a sword, a comb, and the wearing of cotton breeches. All of these things, and many more—like vegetarianism, like wearing a turban, like adopting specific codes of disciplines—I can learn about in more detail from reading, say, your Very Short Introduction with the Very Inappropriate Name. And I would certainly heartily recommend that anyone who is interested should do so.

But my question is really about identification, both within and beyond a community, or several communities. Because it seems it's not just as straightforward as one might think. In particular, if in some way I can still be a Sikh without wearing a turban or not carrying my sword or sometimes shaving or whatever, then I am forced to wonder what, exactly, does it mean to be a Sikh?

EN: Well, at this point it's important to stress that I'm not a Sikh, and I am an ethnographer; and ethnography takes seriously the way people self-define.

So a Sikh might say to me, "*That person is not a Sikh. He's done this, this, this.*" But for me, having a more anthropological approach, if this person says, "*I am a Sikh,*" it's not for me to say, "*No, you are not.*"

But what that person will say—almost certainly, as I've already mentioned—is, "*I'm a Sikh, but I'm not a **proper** Sikh.*" And that, over and over again, is a distinction that people have made in my hearing.

Of course, there are going to be Sikhs initiated into the Khalsa—who follow, as they see it, these strict routines and disciplines—who will say, "*So-and-so is not a Sikh.*"

One Sikh who was a pioneer, in terms of helping with the production of materials on the Sikh religion for textbooks in British schools, actually once said to me, "*The way I'm presenting it in these books is that I want anybody reading this who is not matching up to feel, **Well, I'm not a Sikh. This book tells me what a Sikh is and I'm not one. I ought to be doing such and such**.*"

Whereas, I couldn't do that. I have to take seriously somebody's self-definition as well as the definition of others, because people will know that those who are celebrating the Vaisakhi festival, who are going to the gurdwara, are Sikhs—they won't necessarily make an assessment in terms of whether every day somebody recites the daily prayers and so on.

And in any case, as I said earlier, there isn't an age at which everyone's expected to take that step of commitment. It's something which many Sikhs will aspire to at some point later in their life—or perhaps know that realistically they can't handle it—because they're in an environment where it's not possible to maintain the discipline in some way.

As far as vegetarianism goes, that's slightly different, because as far as we know, what was ruled out was eating halal meat—meat of a sacrificed animal. What has come to be understood by many Sikhs who undertake Khalsa initiation, is that they must be strictly vegetarian. And in fact, what they're doing is interpreting vegetarian in the Hindu religious way of abstaining from meat and fish, but it's lacto-vegetarianism. In practice, many, many Sikhs are vegetarian, whether or not they have taken Amrit.

The *langar*, the institution of shared hospitality, is vegetarian, almost without exception. Sikhs will explain, for example, that it means that everyone's included: whether you're vegetarian or non-vegetarian, vegetarian food is likely to be acceptable.

There is a strong cultural sense that it's not appropriate to be eating animals that were slaughtered in a holy place, but that is not a Sikh insight. That is something from the wider Punjabi society that was deeply infused with Hindu thought.

So many Sikh reformers and many Sikh teachers emphasize, *Yes, you have got to be vegetarian*, but it is a moot point: it's open to discussion—I've written on Sikhs and vegetarianism—in a way that, say, having the *kirpan* (sword) or having the *kara* (bangle), or having the uncut hair, or wearing the *kachera*—the stitched breeches, if you like, rather than the wraparound garment that many people in India wore. Those are not up for discussion in the same way, I would argue, as diet is.

Questions for Discussion:

1. Is there an equivalent to "not being a proper Sikh" in other religious and cultural traditions?

2. To what extent is it reasonable that an external evaluation of cultural identity can ever take precedence over an internal act of self-identification? For a more detailed discussion of this issue within a Jewish perspective, see Chapters 3–4 of **Rabbi With A Cause: Israel and Identity** *with David J. Goldberg.*

IV. Towards Deeper Understanding
On all sides

HB: Right. Let me return to your story and talk a little bit about your work as a religious ethnographer informed by your experience of teaching people of a wide variety of different faiths and also conducting longitudinal studies of to what extent these people were able to integrate in British society and their evolving sense of identity.

In your experience, have attitudes towards Sikhs and Hindus, as well as other individuals from the Indian sub-continent and beyond, changed a great deal? Do you have a sense that people with those backgrounds are, on the whole, feeling more comfortable and more confident in the United Kingdom today, than they were when you first started doing these sorts of studies?

EN: Well, I haven't carried out any explicit studies to precisely determine that.

HB: I understand. I'm not looking for a rigorous scientific evaluation. I'm just wondering how it seems to you given your wealth of experience on the ground, as it were.

EN: Certainly, there is a confidence in many, many ways: the fact that people of Indian origin are represented above the national average in the professions of law and medicine and so on—more generally, in terms of wealth, they are doing pretty well.

And their faiths have got a type of status now associated with landmarks: in the cityscape you can see gurdwaras, you can see temples—they're not just converted houses as they were in the '70s and '80s. They're not even adaptations of houses with a few extra bits to show that they're Sikh or Hindu, but are instead purpose-built, often very big, buildings—sometimes mirroring architecture in historic Sikh places of worship, in the case of the Sikh community.

So that, I think, gives a sort of feeling of belonging, but there is also, in some ways, an increase in racism. Islamophobia has had an impact on Sikhs because of Sikhs being assumed to be Muslims. And post-Brexit in the UK, although members of Sikh and Hindu communities voted for leaving the European Union, individuals are experiencing verbal abuse.

For example, I spoke to somebody recently who'd lived almost her whole life in the UK—I'm talking about somebody in her '60s. And for the first time ever she was verbally abused—told to "go home"—in her city. So that's an insecurity which is coming, along with the security.

HB: Well, I appreciate that these are anecdotal bits and pieces; that, as you say, you haven't done any rigorous studies on this. But it's obviously a real worry. One has—well, maybe I should just say, "*I have*"—a real concern that many Western societies are drifting towards greater intolerance: an increased willingness—indeed, in some cases, palpable desire—to blame immigrants for perceived societal ills, hurl racial epithets, and all sorts of despicable and highly immoral behaviour.

So I have a real sense of concern, but I'm trying to ascertain to what extent this is simply because I'm becoming an older person and thus more prone to say such things like, "*The world is going to the dogs*", or to what extent it actually is a real and pressing phenomenon. Things like Brexit and the rise of dangerous, nakedly populist movements in places where one wouldn't have assumed they would be successful, like the US and the UK, seem to represent an objective sort of data point.

So, notwithstanding the fact that you haven't done any rigorous studies on this recently, it's perhaps worth pointing out that you *did* do some longitudinal studies several years back, where you had the opportunity to speak to people of various different faiths, and various different persuasions, and various different skin colours.

EN: Well, that strictly longitudinal study was amongst Hindus, young Hindus in the West Midlands I first interviewed when they were between the ages of 8 and 12, and then again when they were about the age of heading to college, or actually at university.

And both times I had a sense that they felt pretty confident. I wasn't focusing on that particular question—I think partly, perhaps, because we were talking in a city, where they were not a small minority and they hadn't had the experience of feeling isolated.

They were very comfortable with the English language—they'd grown up and been educated in Britain—so in some ways they felt more established than older members of their family might. It would be interesting to carry out similar research now. In fact, some of my interviewees have children who are older than they were when I first interviewed them.

It's been interesting—this is simply observation, not based on any sort of formal research—seeing the continuities in, for example, how their parents are sending them for supplementary classes to learn a musical instrument that can be played in worship—I'm talking about Hindus and Sikhs here. Or to study Punjabi or, in the case of some Hindus, studying Gujarati. So, there's a sense of young people who are growing up confident in the UK, while feeling that they've also got something extra.

And that actually came out in a study that I conducted more recently in so-called mixed faith families, where one parent was a Sikh or a Hindu or a Muslim or Christian and the other was from a different one of those faith backgrounds. And very much the feeling came across that these are young people who feel their life is perfectly normal, but they've got something extra: somewhere that you can go on holiday that maybe other people don't, or maybe some knowledge of a language, or of knowing that there are different ways of eating food or different foods that you can eat in different places or different festivals as well as Christmas—that sort of sense.

And I feel that that's actually true of a lot of the Hindu and Sikh families. And, of course, increasingly there is out-marriage: increasingly families are mixed families, which brings with it a different sense of rootedness from a situation when people are exclusively marrying within a particular community and that's being reinforced all the time.

HB: To my mind, at any rate, this brings to mind the standard Weberian secularization view—that as a society gets more and more technologically sophisticated and more cosmopolitan in terms of cultural diversity, the importance of "enchantment" or "religious orthodoxy" or "superstition"—depending on one's persuasion and inclinations—will naturally decrease over time. Do you agree or disagree with that view? Do you see any evidence, or lack of evidence, for it throughout your research?

EN: Well, I often say that there are different trajectories that carry on almost in parallel with each other within an individual's life or within a family or within a community. It can be that simultaneously there's evidence of increasing secularization—lack of interest in religion, lack of knowledge of a faith tradition and so on—whilst at the same time it may be that a member of the same family is discovering what they think their tradition is all about, identifying primarily in a religious way, rather than say a national or other way.

So I think we're talking about a "superdiverse" society, to use Steven Vertovec's word, and that superdiversity includes these different trajectories.

And Karen Armstrong is one of the writers who suggested that actually secularization and fundamentalism, or maybe even radicalization, are very, very closely connected with each other: they have roots in the same society and they also—I'm not sure that she went on to say this—they interact with each other.

So while some people in society regard religion as irrelevant and their cultural heritage as a nuisance and just a detail of their lives, that can have an effect on others which drives them closer to what they see as their heritage, but in the process what they come up with is different from what older members of their family ever experienced.

It has to be because it's a different time, it's a different place, and they're making comparisons with maybe Christianity, maybe a secular worldview, which older generations couldn't because they weren't growing up in that way.

Often I've come across young Sikhs, perhaps they've been talking to a group of visitors in a gurdwara, who say, "*Look, I went to university. I did all the things that one does: I cut my hair and I drank, and I did this and I did that. And then I realized that my life lacked meaning, and that I should find out more about the guru's path.*"

Or I meet someone who says, "*I didn't really know very much about any of that but then my child came along, and at school she was asked, 'What does it mean to be a Sikh?' or 'What does it mean to be a Hindu?' so I started thinking about it. I got books from the library. I went on the internet...*"

So in different ways there are these different impetuses which go against the steady secularization view of what's happening.

HB: And you consistently draw attention to the potentially false barriers between religion and culture, that it's often very inappropriate to put people into various boxes and say, "*Here is where religion ends and there is where culture begins.*" There is a continuum there.

EN: In any case, whenever we use those words, even native English speakers, we use them in ways that overlap: it's quite difficult to define religion without including something of culture or define culture without mentioning something about religion.

What is "British culture"? People will say "it's Christmas". What's "Christmas"? Well, some people are going to talk about it in terms of the Christian narrative, others are going to point out about pagan midwinter festivals or contemporary commercialism, but it's very, very difficult to talk about society and culture without at some point mentioning religious tradition. And in this case, when we're talking about British society and British culture, the Christian one. And the same is true for whatever group of people we're talking about.

It's very easy for young people growing up in Britain who come from a South Asian background to perceive their religion as distinct from culture in a way that their parents couldn't. So, a young person might say something like, *"Look, I'm not wearing salvar kamiz like Punjabi people generally did. I'm wearing **this** form of dress because it's Islamic. My parents and grandparents regarded their form of dress, their way of veiling, as being Islamic, but actually it was subcontinental, it was South Asian, and they didn't see the difference. Whereas, **we** can see the difference growing up in the West. We can see that difference between our parents' culture and their religion."*

HB: OK, I think it's time to push you a bit. You've been very generous with your time, and you are clearly a lovely person, so it's not an easy thing for me to be doing, but I have this question I ask people who specialize in religious studies so it only seems appropriate to ask you too. So here goes.

Imagine, for a moment, I'm Richard Dawkins—which I'm quite assuredly not, as it happens—and I'm sitting here across from you saying things like, *"It's time, as enlightened human beings, to put all of this silly superstition behind us and move on, it's time to embrace science and embrace the modern world and forget about all of these silly old folk tales that have resulted in so much division and are so clearly holding us back."*

How would you respond to that sort of comment?

EN: Well, I'd respond by saying, *"You're a biologist. If I made a statement about biology on the basis of not having studied biology, but simply by being a human being and knowing a little bit about other animals, you'd say, quite rightly, 'What business have you got to be pontificating about biology?' So my view is, 'Hang on. What study of religion, either as a theologian or as an anthropologist, have you carried out? How is it that when you've got such a reductionist view of something which isn't your area of primary expertise, you feel that somehow you can present yourself as an expert?'"*

HB: That's a good answer. I'm quite glad I asked you after all.

I'd like to return to a more personal level again, if I may. You're someone who has travelled widely, you've taught a great deal, you've done professional research, you've written a considerable amount of poetry and you've done many other things besides, I'm sure.

In terms of your personal religious orientation, how would you describe yourself?

EN: As of this minute in this room?

HB: Why not? Or yesterday, if you prefer.

EN: I'm less unhappy with the label Quaker than most labels.

HB: And on a professional level, would you regard yourself as a cultural anthropologist? Because when I read your writings or hear you speak, that's the sort of tag that springs to my mind: someone who looks into different cultures and different worlds and who makes comparisons and perhaps links, but certainly doesn't advocate in favour of, or against, any one particular worldview or interpretation. But perhaps you regard yourself quite differently.

EN: Well, that makes me feel like an impostor, because I'm not somebody who came up the route of studying classical anthropology and so on. I've definitely benefited from the insights of anthropologists, but I don't think I'd better claim that I *am* an anthropologist. I've benefited from the insights of a number of disciplines.

But yes, I do see myself rather as you've described. And that seems to me just part of the excitement of living in this wonderfully diverse and evolving, changing world. And it's helpful, I think, to be able to put one's own experiences—discoveries, painful experience, whatever—in a wider context, to look at them in a wider perspective than if I had only allowed myself to be contained within one tradition.

It would be much greater still if I spoke more languages or I'd met more people or lived in more places, but at least I've got the benefit of being able to see some of the patterns and to reflect on them.

HB: You mentioned just now that being a Quaker was the label that you were least unhappy with...

EN: Yes. I am a member of the Religious Society of Friends (Quakers) in the UK, and I am currently co-clerk of Coventry Quaker Meeting. So I guess I'd better not be so coy about it.

HB: Well, that's entirely up to you, of course. I'm just wondering to what extent your professional experience with other religions and cultures has informed your own, in terms of the evolution of your own beliefs. That's really what I'm aiming for.

EN: Well, that would be better for somebody else to describe really.

HB: Really?

EN: Looking at things from the outside, you see, just like I try to describe other peoples.

HB: Well, that makes you an anthropologist in my eyes—I don't care who I offend by doing that. Any lingering doubt has now been officially erased.

EN: Well, I think some of my gut feelings have remained regardless of what my observation or my intellectual journey might be telling me. And I have to bear that in mind: some of my instant reactions are not going to be in accordance with what I spell out as being my philosophy, but may actually go way back to prejudices I've inherited or experiences I've had long before. It's not that one just goes on and on changing or improving in some way. There's a tremendous amount that carries on being there in the sediment.

HB: Well, there's the well-recognized importance of thinking critically and rigorously assessing one's biases as you've just described, not falling into the trap of assuming that one is more objective or unprejudiced than might actually be the case, but then there's the other side of the coin, as it were, that you explore in your poem, "Examination question" where you highlight the importance of the subjective, of not looking at things too critically or, I might say, "anthropologically".

EN: Yes, I suppose I'm getting into awe and wonder and a different sort of response. The thought that comes to me more often than any other is, *Life is a mystery.*

HB: Indeed. Anything you'd like to add? Anything we haven't had sufficient opportunity to talk about?

EN: Well, I suppose one of the things that has been important to me has been realizing the significance of method, methodology—particular methods in the creation of knowledge—and in my case in ethnographic research.

I feel that one of the most important things for all of us, is to be sympathetically critical of just about anything we're told or find and to be always asking ourselves: *What is the agenda? What is the motivation? What's the agenda of whoever it is who's created a webpage or written a book or declared that such and such is the case?*

And there's also the key notion of reflexivity—that's something which has come to be more and more important to me—recognizing that, certainly in research, we change what we research and we are changed by what we research.

That's actually ongoing in life as a whole. And being an ethnographer it is actually just being a human being: you're using observation, and particularly listening—you're using the faculties that we use in the whole of life. And if in "the whole of life" we become just a little bit more reflective and reflexive, I believe that's a better way forward than necessarily becoming more committed to a particular philosophy or a particular religious path.

HB: So perhaps it's just me, but listening to you say these words what comes to my mind is an oblique, albeit extremely polite, commentary on aspects of contemporary society. I sense a concern about an increased level of dogmatism, opinion and often deliberately-stoked controversy.

When I hear you talk about being responsible from an ethnographic perspective, questioning people's motivations, being sensitive to how listening to others and exploring different situations and different worldviews will impact our own, I think to myself, *That's not something which resonates very strongly with the zeitgeist right now when everyone seems to be pushing a twitter feed telling everyone else what they should be thinking and "multiculturalism" has somehow become a highly politically polarizing word fed by an ever-strident and equally polarizing media.*

EN: Wow, are we doing another two and a half hours? You want me to comment on multiculturalism or the media?

HB: Well, I don't want you to comment on anything in particular. I'm just giving you a sense of how I interpreted your words. Quite possibly I am far too media-focused. If you think I'm way off-base, feel free to tell me so. But I'm not sure either one of us is up for another two and a half hours...

So instead, let me ask you something different, something more specific. What advice would you have for a young person, say a 13-year-old girl in Coventry, who isn't Sikh, say, or a member of any particularly well-defined cultural group, but is going into a class filled with people of various different ethnicities and orientations and cultures. Is there any specific advice or recommendation that you would give her in advance in order to give her a deeper and more appropriate understanding of the individuals and the traditions around her?

EN: What I did with one young person of about that age who'd actually expressed the wish to visit a gurdwara was to simply take her to one. She sat there and she received food. She looked around and enjoyed the experience.

A lot of the time, people of all ages would actually really like to go and see where Jews hang out, or what Muslims do in the mosque, or whatever and they haven't got the opportunity; and there are opportunities, but you have to really look for them: schools may organize visits, maybe multi-faith walks or what have you.

But usually somebody from a different community, a community that's different from your own, is very happy to show pictures of weddings and talk about them, or take you along to some community centre or some events that they're involved in.

But especially if you're 13, you may hang back and you don't like to ask. It might be embarrassing, but actually, the other person is usually very, very pleased. An older person will often say, "*Our 13-year-olds aren't interested. It's great that you're interested.*"

Most people are not out to immediately convert you to whatever, but because a lot of people in Britain come from Christian backgrounds, or know something about Christianity, there is a fear that if you make an approach to somebody from a different religious group, they are going to immediately want to snap you up and convert you.

So I think the young person has to have confidence that she can approach someone—perhaps somebody in her class or the parent of someone in her class or a neighbour—and just ask them a little bit. Often it's something that's happened in school that provides the opportunity: "*We've got this project. Could you tell me such and such?*"

And equally, young people and older people need to be comfortable with sharing and explaining without trying to win over. And that's not difficult for Sikhs generally, because Sikhs and Hindus tend to grow up respecting different faiths. It's more difficult for young people from some other traditions: they can feel guilty about asking about another tradition. My hope is that nobody feels guilty of disloyalty if they're simply trying to find out a bit more about their neighbours.

HB: And what about a teacher who feels intimidated or uncertain by such a situation? I know you've done a great deal of work in education, what advice would you give to a teacher who finds that she has, say, a Sikh child in her class and is uncertain about what to do, wanting to engage with the child but somewhat fearful that she might take the wrong approach?

EN: Some children really enjoy the opportunity to share with the class. But my advice to the teacher is, *Don't assume that's the case.* The young person may feel, *"I'm not a proper Sikh."* They may hate having attention drawn to them and their tradition.

As a teacher what you need to do is to talk to that young person separately, and maybe talk to that family as well, and try to get some sort of sense of where they fit on the map: Is the family very, very strongly committed to worshipping in a particular place and strongly connected to India? Or are these people really not very comfortable about being singled out as specimens of a particular faith?

And as background to that, the teacher needs to do a bit of reading and researching if at all possible. The trouble is that teachers don't have much time, but if they can get any sort of sense of the diversity within a tradition—like getting the sense that there are Catholics and there are Protestants, and there are Orthodox—and then having a bit of a map on which to locate what you find out about, say, a child from a Christian background. If the teacher can do something like that, I think that's really helpful to avoid either ignoring somebody or embarrassing them.

And most of the time, whatever their degree of observance or not, a family is going to be appreciative of the fact that the teacher is showing interest and that the teacher is not wanting to embarrass the young person.

HB: Are there some teachers who would be fearful of engaging, even in private, in this sort of discussion? A fear of even mentioning religious issues within our avowedly secular culture?

EN: Definitely. But the fact that religious education, as a non-confessional subject, is statutory in the UK, does mean that there is less embarrassment about that, because there is a requirement on schools to be engaging with religious diversity in the curriculum.

HB: Is this a good thing? Should there be more of that in other places where it's not a requirement?

EN: I like to think that if French education, for example, had included more religious education, and less of an emphasis on *laïcité*, there might, just possibly, be more understanding by some people of, let's say, what it means to be a Muslim in France. But who knows? It's not for me to judge another society, but I often feel that we are fortunate in the UK to have this non-confessional subject, which is nonetheless a requirement.

And even in faith schools, the religious education will often be influenced by that dominant model of religious education and will often be multi-faith, rather than, *You're in a Catholic school, you only learn about Catholicism* or, *You're in a Sikh school, you only learn about Sikhism.*

Ideally in just about every subject, teachers should be aware and alert to what we talk about as the spiritual and social development of children and the religious background of pupils. But the reality is that it's useful to have a slot or two in the curriculum where there can be a primary focus on religion.

One problem is that so much of the teaching is by non-specialists; and even a specialist religious education teacher can't be a specialist in *all* the shades of *all* the religions and non-religious philosophies that there are in the world.

So I think what's really important is for the teacher, whatever the teacher's stance or commitment, to be modelling to children that, *We're all inquirers, we all get things wrong and that there's something that we can all learn from each other; and as teachers, that's what we're doing.*

It's not that the teacher "knows a lot" and is "imparting" that to the student. The tendency to involve a child from, say, a Sikh or Hindu or Muslim background in the class as almost a spokesperson is commendable—but as I said, it can be a little unkind to a child who's not feeling confident or willing to be in that position. But it does illustrate the fact that we're all learning from each other.

HB: That's a great point to end on. Thank you so much for your time, Eleanor. It was a great pleasure talking to you.

EN: Thank you, Howard.

Questions for Discussion:

1. Should non-confessional religious education be mandatory everywhere? What would be the advantages and disadvantages of such an approach?

2. Do you agree with the "Weberian secularization thesis" that Howard refers to in this chapter? For an additional perspective on this issue, see Chapter 4 of **Religious Entrepreneurs?** *with UCLA historian Nile Green and Chapter 2 of* **Battling Protestants** *with UC Berkeley historian David Hollinger.*

3. To what extent are those with an inadequate understanding of their culture's religious traditions unable to fully appreciate their own history?

4. How has this book informed your understanding of the Sikh tradition or religion more generally?

Continuing the Conversation

Those interested in more details about Sikhism are referred to Eleanor's books *Sikhism: A Very Short Introduction* and *Sikh: Two Centuries of Western Women's Art and Writing*. Those with more general religious interests may be interested in *Making Nothing Happen: Five Poets Explore Faith and Spirituality*, featuring Eleanor and five other poets.

Ideas Roadshow Collections

Each Ideas Roadshow collection offers 5 separate expert conversations presented in an accessible and engaging format.

- *Conversations About Anthropology & Sociology*
- *Conversations About Astrophysics & Cosmology*
- *Conversations About Biology*
- *Conversations About History, Volume 1*
- *Conversations About History, Volume 2*
- *Conversations About History, Volume 3*
- *Conversations About Language & Culture*
- *Conversations About Law*
- *Conversations About Neuroscience*
- *Conversations About Philosophy, Volume 1*
- *Conversations About Philosophy, Volume 2*
- *Conversations About Physics, Volume 1*
- *Conversations About Physics, Volume 2*
- *Conversations About Politics*
- *Conversations About Psychology, Volume 1*
- *Conversations About Psychology, Volume 2*
- *Conversations About Religion*
- *Conversations About Social Psychology*
- *Conversations About The Environment*
- *Conversations About The History of Ideas*

All collections are available as both eBook and paperback.

www.ingramcontent.com/pod-product-compliance
Lightning Source LLC
Chambersburg PA
CBHW030903080526
44589CB00010B/117